SPIRIT, NATURE, AND COMMUNITY

SUNY Series, Simone Weil Studies
Eric O. Springsted, Editor

Spirit, Nature, and Community

Issues in the Thought of Simone Weil

DIOGENES ALLEN
ERIC O. SPRINGSTED

STATE UNIVERSITY OF NEW YORK PRESS

Published by
State University of New York Press, Albany

© 1994   State University of New York

Printed in the United States of America

For information, address State University of New York
Press, State University Plaza, Albany, N.Y.,   12246

Production by E. Moore
Marketing by Theresa A. Swierzowski

Library of Congress Cataloging-in-Publication Data

Allen, Diogenes.
    Spirit, nature, and community : issues in the thought of Simone
Weil / Diogenes Allen, Eric O. Springsted.
        p.   cm. — (SUNY series. Simone Weil studies)
    Includes bibliographical references and index.
    ISBN 0-7914-2017-5 (CH : alk. paper). — ISBN 0-7914-2018-3 (PB :
alk. paper)
    1. Weil, Simone, 1909-1943.   2. Weil, Simone, 1909-1943—Religion.
3. Spirituality—History—20th century.   I. Springsted, Eric O.
II. Title.   III. Series.
B2430.W47A66   1994
194—dc20   93-36973
                                                                            CIP

10 9 8 7 6 5 4 3 2 1

This book is dedicated to our many friends and colleagues of the American Weil Society with gratitude for their many helpful insights and wonderful conversations.

CONTENTS

Part IV: Persons and Communities

Part V: Epilogue

PREFACE

From the appearance in 1946 of the aphorisms taken from her notebooks and published as *Gravity and Grace* to the present, Simone Weil has remained in the public eye in various guises. While *Gravity and Grace* showed profound moral and spiritual understanding thus making her a newfound spiritual guide, Weil has also been known as a political activist. Her biography has also excited much debate about her own person, as judgments have run the gamut from saint to insane. More recently she has come to be appreciated as a philosopher of some considerable depth. For example, George Steiner has claimed "there has been in Western tradition one woman philosopher of rank: Simone Weil."[1] But even judgments of that sort have hardly settled matters about Weil, even for those who make them. Steiner himself, after admitting Weil to the rank of world class philosophers, quickly marginalizes her by adding: "She was also a transcendent *schlemiel*."[2]

While it is possible that all these various assessments and presentations of Weil bespeak a deep confusion somewhere, the fact that Weil has been paid so much attention, in so many ways and over a fifty-year period, may well suggest that her writings have the marks of becoming classics. She is an author who can be read in many ways and over long periods, all with profit.

Not that Weil is in danger of founding a school posthumously. While indeed her thought is the headwaters for a rather constant stream of secondary literature, just as often as not, her name appears not in studies undertaken through careful collegial sorts of research, but in brief quotations in books by people who have simply been struck by her. And just as often books on her simply seem to appear out of nowhere. Clearly any number of people, in dealing with the problems that we face in the evening years of the twentieth century, believe they have to deal with her somehow, either as part of the solution or part of the problem.

Perhaps that episodic, hit or miss, approach is just as well. Too many original and profound thinkers become prisoners of the "isms" appended to their names. But there is also a problem here as well. Far too often it seems that works on Weil have sought to reinvent the wheel, covering ground that has been well covered elsewhere. Or they simply make mistakes in reading her, repeating errors that have been adequately cleared up elsewhere. Thus, far from taking up where scholarship on Weil has left off, they spin in the same circles. Too often, then, we simply do not get anywhere in understanding Weil.

It was this sort of problem that provided the original impetus for this book, as we hoped to set the record straight on a few issues in the thought of Simone Weil. To a degree this book still does intend to do exactly that. For example, in chapter 1 we point out the public and private—but rarely discussed—evidence for claiming that Weil was baptized before her death. Any number of books need revision on this fact, which in many cases, such as Thomas Nevin's *Simone Weil: Portrait of a Self-Exiled Jew*, completely undoes the picture of Weil they would paint. Not that more orthodox hagiographers can take a great deal of comfort in that either, we note.

In several other chapters we also try to provide clarification on certain important conceptual issues in Weil. For example, chapter 3 deals with one of the most textually complex issues in Weil, the nature of necessity, and we intend here at least a map by which to travel its highwways and byways. Similarly, chapter 4 attempts to unravel the issue of reading, chapter 6 the phenomenon that Weil called "affliction," and chapter 7 Weil's stance on particular loves. All these issues are crucial to even using Weilian concepts accurately, and too often they simply are not understood well at all. Chapter 5 while going beyond what could be called "setting the record straight," does among other things hope to give the reader some direction in reading Peter Winch's excellent *Simone Weil: The Just Balance*.

But simply to provide a conceptual map is no longer enough in discussing Weil, as long as other works, such as Miklos Veto's *The Religious Metaphysics of Simone Weil* (1970; English translation 1994) and Springsted's *Christus Mediator* (1983) remain in print. These works, which concentrate on the philosophical, theological, and conceptual, have been joined by more recent works that combine biography and a presentation of Weil's thought, such as David McClellan's *Simone Weil: Utopian Pessimist*. Therefore in order to say anything worthwhile it is also necessary to engage in interpretive issues, and issues of direction, for even when one is straight on some of these conceptual issues, how exactly one is to take them, and hence how one is to evaluate Weil as a thinker, still remains to be settled. Hence each section tries to do something other than pontificate, as within each we above all try to give a direction to the reading of Weil's thought by discussing her work vis-à-vis other contemporary philosophers and contemporary philosophical options. Here our engagement with Winch is particularly evident. That work, in both our judgments, has done more than any other recent work on Weil to stimulate new thought about her project. We have been discussing Weil together since 1975; since 1989 that discussion has nearly always included Winch's work as a partner. But it is not simply Winch himself; it is the options and directions that he suggests, and with which his position is associated, that are important and helpful. We hope to have mined some of them. Here we might briefly mention another work that is likewise helpful, Blum and Seidler's *A Truer Liberty*. We have not dealt with it directly, but find it along with Winch a friendly traveling companion.

Many of the essays in this book have appeared elsewhere, although several of them have been published only in French. Yet as we compiled them along with the new material prepared especially for this volume, we found that they are not simply separate pieces, but ones that involve a progression or perhaps evolution in understanding on our parts of Weil. For what were in the late 1970s and early 1980s matters of setting the record straight, have become for us the groundwork for a cohesive interpretation of Weil. While it may be best to let a reading of the entire book speak to this interpretation, we should note one important feature of it. Central to this interpretation is the claim made in chapter 5, and used elsewhere, that not only is Weil's notion of the supernatural tied to our natural history, which Winch claims and with which we agree, but that the natural in Weil must at the same time be understood in the light of a supernatural history. This we feel ties many of Weil's concerns about necessity, spirituality, and community together, for they become part of a single history. We note this in advance for the reader, for it is an interpretation that puts many of the seemingly "metaphysical" issues of earlier chapters, such as Chapter 3 on "Divine Necessity," which might otherwise seem maddeningly archaic, into a much different light than they would otherwise be seen. It would do the reader no harm to read this chapter first, should he or she wish to do so, although each section is designed to move from more straightforward individual issues to integrative, interpretive ones.

As a matter of information to the curious, let it be noted that Allen is the author of chapters 2,4,7, and 8; Springsted is the author of chapters 1,3, and 9–11; chapters 5 and 6 are jointly done, although there is certainly a sense in which the work of either author owes a great deal to the other even in individually prepared chapters. We have been talking about these things too long together to be able to separate them neatly into private property, and hence it is appropriate that we present them here together and take blame together, no matter what our own individual shortcomings or virtues. To this end, with the exception of chapter 1, where the authorial "I" really is an individual, we have consistently reworked earlier material to always use "we."

We would like to extend special thanks to Simone Deitz for her contributions, and her sincere and delightful help. Chapter 1 really is her story; we have simply tried to get others to listen. We would also like to thank Peter Winch for conversations and comments about the issues discussed in chapter 5. Helpful comments by Martin Andic and David Wisdo were immensely useful in giving the manuscript final shape. Finally, our appreciation goes to Mr. Quinn Broverman, a philosophy student at Illinois College, for his labors at taking a great deal of diverse material, some of it half in French, and putting it into manageable form in the computer.

ACKNOWLEDGMENTS

"Divine Necessity: Weilian and Platonic Conceptions" originally was published as "Théorie weilienne et théorie platonicienne de la nécessité" *Cahiers Simone Weil*, septembre 1981.

"The Concept of Reading" and "Rootedness: Culture and Value" originally were published in *Simone Weil's Philosophy of Culture*, ed. R. Bell (Cambridge, 1993: Cambridge University Press) Copyright Cambridge University Press.

"The Enigma of Affliction" was originally published as "Le Malheur: Une énigme (Simone Weil et Epictete)" in *Cahiers Simone Weil*, décembre 1979.

"George Herbert and Simone Weil" was originally published in *Religion and Literature*, Summer 1985.

"Of Tennis, Politics, and Persons" originally was published in *Philosophical Investigations*, July 1993 (reprinted by permission of Basil Blackwell Ltd.).

"From Words to the Word" originally was published as "Des paroles à la parole" in *Recherches sur la philosophie et le langage*, no. 13, 1991.

A much shorter version of "Winch on Weil's Supernaturalism" appeared as a review in *Journal of the American Academy of Religion*, Winter 1991.

Chapters 1, 2, and 7, and most of 5 appear here for the first time.

ABBREVIATIONS

CSW   *Cahiers Simone Weil* (quarterly journal of l'Association pour l'étude de la pensée de Simone Weil)

EL   *Ecrits de Londres et dernières lettres*, Paris, 1957: Gallimard

ER   "Essay on the Notion of Reading," trans. Rebecca Fine Rose and Timothy Tessin, *Philosophical Investigations*, vol. 13.4 (October 1990)

FLN   *First and Last Notebooks*, trans. Richard Rees, London,1970: Oxford University Press

GG   *Gravity and Grace*, trans. Emma Crauford, London, 1972: Routledge and Kegan Paul

GTG   *Gateway to God*, Glasgow, 1974: Collins

IC   *Intimations of Christianity Among the Ancient Greeks*, trans. E.C. Geissbuhler, London, 1957: Routledge and Kegan Paul

LP   *Lectures on Philosophy*, trans. H. Price with an introduction by Peter Winch, Cambridge, 1978: Cambridge University Press

NB   *The Notebooks of Simone Weil*, 2 vols., trans. Arthur Wills, London, 1956: Routledge and Kegan Paul

NR   *The Need for Roots*, trans. Arthur Wills, with a preface by T.S. Eliot, New York, 1971: Harper and Row

OL   *Oppression and Liberty*, trans. Arthur Wills and John Petrie, Amherst, 1973: University of Massachusetts Press

SE   *Selected Essays: 1934–43*, trans. Richard Rees, Oxford, 1962: Oxford University Press

SL   *Seventy Letters*, trans. Richard Rees, Oxford, 1970: Oxford University Press

SNL   *On Science, Necessity and the Love of God*, trans. Richard Rees, London, 1968: Oxford University Press

WG   *Waiting for God*, trans. Emma Crauford, New York, 1951: Harper and Row

PART I
No Longer on the Margins?

1. THE BAPTISM
   OF SIMONE WEIL

SIMONE WEIL both in her writings and her person, appears to be a woman of the deepest spirituality. Although often heterodox in particulars, her basic vision is profoundly Christian. She herself claimed that she was Catholic. But there is something puzzling about that claim, for it has always been assumed that she never was baptized. We know that she discussed the issue at length with Fathers Perrin, Coutourier, and Oesterreicher, as well as other priests. Nevertheless, it has always been thought that her relationship to the Church depended strictly on intellectual, spiritual, and cultural sympathies, and not on ritual factors.

Some writers have made a great deal of this fact, although not all have come to the same conclusion. For some, Simone Weil has become as it were, a secular saint, able to draw upon the spirituality of Christianity without being officially a part of it. For others, such as Thomas Nevin in his *Simone Weil: Portrait of a Self-Exiled Jew*,[1] Weil is seen as one who was simply trying to "pass" as a Christian, remaining permanently and unalterably outside Christianity.

There is reason, however, to reassess the assumption that Weil was never baptized. Beginning in the 1960s evidence to the contrary has trickled in. Jacques Cabaud in his second book on Weil in 1967 offered hints, based on still unpublished testimonies, of a baptism *in extremis* by a nonordained hand.[2] Cabaud, however, was not any more specific than this and did not identify his source. Thus tantalizing as the suggestion was, it offered little to go on.

In 1971, however, Wladimir Rabi, editor of the Jewish journal *Les Nouveaux Cahiers*, published an astounding article in which he told the story of such a baptism.[3] Rabi had originally heard the story from a Michele Leleu, who had heard it from a person identified in the article only as X. This occurred while both she and X were attending a congress of the International Association for French Studies in Paris in 1965. X was the person who performed the baptism. Rabi in his article not only retold Leleu's story but also printed the results of an extensive search for information on the subject. Rabi, who died a few years ago in an auto accident, believed the story but doubted the baptism had any significance.

Simone Pétrement in her biography of Weil in 1974 brought the story to public attention again. She dismissed it as unlikely. Since then it has received little attention.[4]

I bring it up once again for a very simple reason. Like most Weil scholars, I knew the story primarily from Pétrement. But in May, 1981, after the first annual meeting of the American Weil Society, I received a telephone call from Simone Deitz, who, as all familiar with Cabaud's biography are well aware, was Weil's close friend first in New York and then again in London when both were with the Free French. Deitz had just that day learned of the meeting from its announcement in *Cahiers Simone Weil*. In the course of our conversation about all sorts of matters, Deitz told me that she had baptized Weil. We talked at some length about it.

Later that summer, I was fortunate to be able to spend an afternoon with Deitz. It was at that time that she lent me her copy of Rabi's article (which had on it an inscription to her by Rabi and an identification of herself with X noted in the margin in her handwriting). I had not seen the article before and was therefore able to acquaint myself with numerous details of the story that were not in Pétrement's account. What was even more important than seeing Rabi's article, though, was the time Deitz and I spent going through Pétrement's account while I held the English text in hand and she commented on it.

Three years later I presented her account at a meeting of the American Weil Society at the University of Notre Dame in 1984. Since then even Deitz herself has told the story at a meeting of the American Weil Society held at Harvard University in 1988, which presentation was videotaped. The following is Deitz's story with an assessment of the evidence.[5] Added to the story are my comments on how this story is significant for our understanding of Simone Weil.

THE STORY

The story of Weil's last days and her baptism *in extremis*, at the center of debate, is this:

On April 15, 1943, Deitz, who was Weil's good friend in both New York and London, noticed Weil had not appeared at work and went to her apartment, only to find her unconscious on the floor. Deitz had Weil taken to Middlesex Hospital in London, where she was diagnosed as having tuberculosis, a condition Deitz claims Weil was well aware she had, even at the time she left New York.

It was while at Middlesex that Weil asked to speak to a priest. Deitz asked Abbé de Naurois, chaplain of the Free French Forces in London, to visit her, which he did three times in the spring of 1943. The visits did not bear much fruit. According to Deitz, Weil said of the meetings: "I said to him I want to receive baptism but I want to do it only under certain conditions. I don't admit that unbaptized infants are excluded from Paradise and it is necessary that my attitude in that not be in contradiction with Catholic dogma." The abbé responded: "That will never do. You are a proud one!"[6] Furthermore, Deitz reports that Naurois said Weil appeared "too feminine," "too khâgneuse," and "too Jewish."[7] Thus the question of baptism went by the boards, at least insofar as it involved any ordained person. (It should be noted that Naurois denies having made these statements, although he does admit to having been irritated by his discussions with Weil.)

It was after these visits that Deitz herself asked Weil: "And now, are you ready to accept baptism?," to which Weil replied, "with much warmth" 'Yes.'" Deitz then took some water from the tap and pronounced the formula, "I baptize you in the name of the Father and the Son and the Holy Spirit." Although Deitz is not exactly sure what the date of the baptism was, she is confident that it did take place at Middlesex.

On August 18, Weil was transferred to Grosvenor Sanitarium in Ashford, Kent. On August 24 Simone Weil died in her sleep. She was buried on August 30 in Ashford in the section reserved for Catholics. Seven or eight persons were in attendance, including Deitz. The priest missed his train and Maurice Schumann therefore read the prayers (being, Deitz claims, conveniently ready with Catholic prayers for the occasion). Deitz claims the priest was supposed to be Naurois and she believes he missed deliberately.

THE EVIDENCE

What are we to make of this story and how are we to judge its veracity? Of course in the end it comes down to whether one accepts what Deitz has to say or not, as well as accepting whether people—even strong willed people such as Weil—can make religious decisions that are unexpected. Yet if this is where we must come to in the end, there are nevertheless a number of points that bear investigation before we do so.

Rabi has done the majority of the work in ferreting out the accounts. He brings at least four people into play—Michele Leleu, who was the first to hear the story and repeat it; Maurice Schumann; a Dr. Kac, who was a doctor with the Free French and who knew both Deitz and Weil; and finally Deitz herself, with whom Rabi communicated at least twice by letter. The rest of the evidence offered here is what has been told me by Deitz. Finally, there are some conclusions offered by Pétrement that may be relevant although she offers no new evidence one way or another. (Deitz, although invited to do so, declined to assist Pétrement in her biography, which also explains why she is not named at numerous crucial places in it.)

Before looking at the evidence itself, a word about what is evidence in a case like this is appropriate. Richard Swinburne has argued that we ought normally to believe personal testimony with only the following exceptions: (1.) when the person habitually lies, particularly in the type of case being considered; (2.) when the event could not possibly have occurred on independent logical grounds; (3.) when the description of the event and the event itself can be explained as actually having been something else, but which under certain conditions could have been mistaken by the observer, and thus reported in error.[8] Since there is little chance that Deitz could have mistaken what she was doing, if she did anything, we will confine ourselves to asking whether it could have happened, and whether Deitz is normally the sort of person we ought to believe. I note at the outset, however, that I see no reason to doubt her veracity on this sort of event, which does not depend much on personal interpretation.

The Evidence Against

The evidence against the story is counted on one hand.

1. Naurois denies the allegations that he called her "too proud as all Jews are."⁹ This gives us a weakness in consistency, as he gives a different version of his visit. He does, though, admit to the visit and to having been irritated by his discussions with Weil.

2. A much larger problem is that such a baptism would seem to be out of character for Weil. This is the most oft voiced objection to the story. A number of texts are important here. There are, of course, her letters to Father Perrin in *Waiting for God* in which she voices her objections to being baptized. Her reasons there are various: there is first what she saw as the dangerous social nature of the church; second, her own unique vocation to remain outside the church; and third, her objections to the intellectual constraints put on believers. This last objection is dealt with expansively in her "Letter to a Priest," where she asks Father Couturier whether one can be baptized if one holds certain beliefs. It is there that she then lists a number of beliefs, many of doubtful orthodoxy, to which she has had varying degrees of attraction. This objection is then brought forth one more time in the so-called "Last Text" where she refuses to "recognize that the Church has any right to limit the operations of intelligence or the illuminations of love in the domain of thought"(GTG 72). She further claims that because of the dogmatism and her belief that such dogmatism illicitly confines the intellect, were she to be granted baptism, "a break [would be] made with a tradition which has lasted at least seventeen centuries"(GTG 73). She then adds: "For this reason and others of a similar nature, I have never up to now made a formal request to a priest for baptism. And I am not doing so now"(GTG 74).

3. Maurice Schumann, in writing to Rabi, said that Deitz's story is not impossible. Yet, he added, his own personal memories and the texts of which he was the owner as well as published texts "don't accredit the thesis."¹⁰ Thus Schumann regards this as out of character.

4. Pétrement adds the same sort of argument in her discussion of the story. She argues, based on the "Last Text," that even if a priest consented to baptize her, it would not have been what Weil wanted, since it would not have involved the whole church—that is, a change in its dogmatism. Pétrement then goes on to argue that one of the major reasons Weil would have wanted to be baptized would be so that she could partake of the eucharist, and this she

never asked for. Pétrement says: "This proves that, in my opinion, she did not consider the baptism a valid one."[11] Furthermore, Pétrement indicates that Weil did not sign herself into the sanitarium with any religious preference which, Pétrement argues, she surely would have done if she had considered the baptism valid.

5. Finally, there is the problem of Deitz's own silence. Why did she wait twenty-two years to tell anybody the story? (It was not told to Leleu until 1965.) Furthermore, why even after that did she remain so reticent about saying anything more for so long?

The Evidence For

1. Deitz's silence can be easily explained by a matter she mentioned to Michele Leleu when she first told her the story in 1965. The reason for the silence, she said, was because of Madame Weil, Simone's mother, who told Deitz "I don't want anybody to speak of that while I'm living"[12] (Madame Weil died in 1965). Although the family was not religiously Jewish, apparently it was not particularly keen on any members actually converting to Christianity, a not particularly unusual attitude in families such as the Weil family. It is significant that when the grave marker for Weil's grave was placed in 1958, although she had been buried in the Catholic section of the cemetery and her writings on Christian subjects were well known, the marker had no Christian symbolism on it. The family, of course, was ultimately responsible for its choice.

This may explain why the story was not told until 1965. But why the reticence to say much publicly since then? Here things are less clear, since they are Deitz's own personal reasons for not coming forward. Essentially, they are, as related to me, because she has felt that there is an image—nay, an icon—of Weil that has hardened in many people's minds that such a story challenges. The reaction to the story, particularly in France, has not always been amiable. Deitz simply felt that she had been personally hurt by having her credibility called into question. She has also felt that everybody wants all sorts of information from her for their own opportunistic reasons. Here there is good reason to believe her on the point that it is an image that is being challenged, since most of the arguments against the story have been based on its being out of character. Deitz is challenging the perception of the character. It is, of course, possible that a person can appear in two very different lights (and Deitz thought Weil was very capable of this); but to admit this is also to be forced to admit that neither light is privileged and incapable of modification.

2. Pétrement has suggested, beyond the "out of character argument," two lines of argument against the baptism—that Weil never asked for the eucharist and that she had not signed herself into Grosvenor Sanitarium as a Catholic. Deitz, in a letter to me in 1984, sheds light on these problems, showing that they are not at all insuperable anomalies in the account, even if most other people do not encounter them in their religious lives. She noted that she herself was baptized in a similar fashion (she was of Jewish heritage, too)—that is, by a nonordained friend, and then later when in a *clinique* in Paris in 1941 did not register as a Catholic. She also pointedly noted, "Do you think Simone would have asked for the host if she didn't want to bring the baptism in [*sic*] the open?" Also, "Don't forget before dying *it may have been a sacrifice on her part to deprive herself of what she wanted most.*"

3. Rabi introduces the testimony of a Dr. Kac, a Free French doctor in London, who had examined Weil in January 1943, and who also knew X, who was in the Free French. He wrote to Rabi: "Knowing the state of permanent exaltation of Simone Weil and the zeal that X . . . could display in order to gain a soul, the fact of Simone Weil being baptized with tap water appears to me more than possible . . . more than probable."[13] I note here, however, that Deitz in response has said, "*I have never been a zealous person (religiously speaking). I've never thought to bring a soul to God without her or his consent. I am not that dumb!* It is not my type." Thus, although zealousness and manipulation would support the story, they seem not to have played a role. Given Deitz's own experience, it seems far more likely that she and Weil were able to reach a common understanding due to their own very similar circumstances, an understanding that Deitz for many years in fact tried to keep a strictly private matter. And to wish that it remain a private matter *does* seem to be in line with Weil's character.

4. Finally, there is Weil. As we have seen in numerous places such as her letters to Father Perrin and in "The Last Text," she does not want anyone to be sanguine about the possibility of her baptism. Why she was reticent about baptism is quite clear—namely, she believed that to join the Church was to submit illegitimately to a blockage of the free flow of her own thought. It is important that this issue be kept in front of us as the reason why she did not enter. Her other criticisms of the Church are exactly that— criticisms—and are only brought up by her as reasons to avoid entrance in connection with the free thought issue. The only possible exception is that she also thought it a vocation, and thus a matter

of obedience to remain outside. Yet she clearly conceived her vocation as having large intellectual dimensions.

Nevertheless, despite this attitude Weil allowed herself a reservation on the matter. In Letter IV to Father Perrin, she says she believes it to be God's will that she stay outside the Church in the future "except perhaps at the moment of death"(WG 75). In other places she allows that if her being outside the church is a vocation and a matter of obedience to God's will, that, should God's will change, she would join the church. She says in the fifth letter in *Waiting for God*: "It is for the service of Christ as the Truth that I deprive myself of sharing in his flesh in the way he has instituted. . . . I am as certain as a human being has the right to be that I am deprived in this way for my whole life; except perhaps—only perhaps—if circumstances make intellectual work definitively and totally impossible for me"(WG 86).

I, with Deitz, note this latter reservation, but also note that at the time that the baptism did take place, Weil probably had *not* given up on the possibility of future intellectual work or on living longer than she in fact did. Not everything rests on it, however, for there is also the fact that Weil apparently thought often about baptism. Once raised as a possibility, it never seemed to be far from her mind. For example, she asked, in a conversation with Father Perrin, "And if a child baptized me, would it be valid?"[14] Later on she pointed to the Mediterranean on which she was to embark on the risky voyage to New York from Marseille, and said to Perrin: "Don't you think that would be a beautiful baptistery?"[15] (Namely, if the boat were to sink). We also know at least five occasions when she discussed the question of "if one believed so-and-so could one be baptized?" with priests. (Perhaps significantly a number of them were Jewish converts.) Finally, in writing to her brother when his first child was born, she advised him to have her baptized, saying: "I would not hesitate for a second if I had a child to have it baptized by a priest."[16] The evidence here is that although Weil might not have been seeking baptism, nevertheless, she did not refuse it categorically. Indeed, apparently she entertained the idea of baptism regularly. Thus it would not seem to be completely out of character at all for her to consent to be baptized.

THE JUDGMENT

Well, then, are we to judge this story to be true or not? It does come down, as do all singular historical facts, to accepting testimony. And on this basis I do not see any reason not to accept it. Deitz has been consistent in the telling of the story over the years. Moreover she has no reason to lie, nor can I tell from an association that goes back to 1981 that she has ever shown herself to be given to deliberate untruths. She herself has made not attempt to gain from the story—on the contrary, she has consistently avoided attempts to get her to become more public about it. Finally, she has not been at all interested in contributing to a hagiography. She has always been concerned that people see Weil as she really was; on that account, Deitz thinks, she was *not* a saint. She has no special case to plead. Thus there is no reason to think Deitz would lie.

This means that the only other possible way to discredit the story is to argue that it is inconceivably out of character for Weil to have consented to being baptized. Yet there is plenty of evidence to show that Weil did *not* categorically reject baptism; indeed, she inquired about it regularly. Although her major personal reasons against baptism are important—namely, that she believed baptism would involve submission to the Church and an undue restriction of thought—she may have, in the end, reached a personal accommodation on this issue (she was, after all, a bit overscrupulous in her concerns expressed in "Letter to a Priest"), although we will probably never know what finally went on in her mind on this issue.

ASSESSMENTS

If, then, the story is true, what are we to make of it? The answer is not necessarily one that simply leaps out at us, and with respect to analyzing Weil's standing as a philosopher and, perhaps to a large degree, even as a theologian, it may make no particular difference. But there are still important issues to be considered and reconsidered in light of this story. Just what they are can be seen first by looking at what Rabi made of the story and then examining how it affects a recent retelling of Weil's life.

Rabi believed the story of the baptism. He even agreed that on the Church's own definition that the baptism was valid. But this gave him cause to offer a very astounding conclusion. He claimed that while valid, the baptism was of no significance since it was performed while Weil was unconscious or nearly so and that, therefore, she did not consent to it. The fact that the Catholics had such a hard time believing the story, and why they had made no attempt to publish it, was because, Rabi said, Weil was such a theological "hot potato" (*charbon ardent entre les mains*)[17] and the baptism took place under such irregular circumstances. Rabi concluded, despite her anti-Jewish sentiments, that Weil was "actually one of us," a point he had been trying to make for some years in other publications.

Rabi's conclusion that Weil was unconscious or did not consent to the baptism is forced and scurrilous, I think. It can be easily disputed. As Michele Leleu responded in a letter printed in the next issue of *Les Nouveaux Cahiers*,[18] how did Rabi know if Weil was unconscious or not? He was not there. Moreover, Rabi was not even consistent on this issue insofar as at the same time he has Weil no longer in control of her faculties, he also has her in his article saying some very lucid things. Yet while Rabi's conclusions should be dismissed, they do point out that this issue is not unambiguous. And one of the chief foci of the issue is the one he brings up: Weil has been a hot potato for both Judaism and Christianity. Indeed, for many people she seems to be a touchstone for many of the issues surrounding the relations of the two religions. Just how can be seen by looking at Thomas Nevin's *Simone Weil: Portrait of a Self-Exiled Jew*.

Nevin's supercilious presentation of Weil is a master exercise in dismissing his subject by marginalizing her, a strategy he does not hesitate to spread around the history of Christianity: Augustine becomes a "hatchet man against heresy," and Protestants are put to the side as apparently having "a horror of comfort." More to the point, Weil is marginalized by being treated as woman, sickly, and finally Jew. In Nevin's presentation Weil apparently was merely trying to "pass" as a Christian. His evidence is his own peculiarly uninformed theological judgments about her theological opinions, but also a repeated insistence that she is best characterized as Jewish. Her religious experiences in the mid-1930s are described as examples of a shekinah, for example, despite her own description of them as having personally experienced Christ. This is not simply a matter of subjective feeling, either; let us recall that that experience occurred after reciting Herbert's explicit christophanic poem, "Love" (see chapter 7 below). Why Nevin assumes himself to be capable of judging what she saw and did not see in 1937 is not clear, except to the degree that he may believe that there was nothing to see anyhow.

Nevertheless, Nevin certainly has a point that bears stressing. Weil's background was Jewish and even in the assimilated, free-thinking family in which she grew up, that background undoubtedly caused her to look at the world differently than a Catholic *paysan* or *bourgeois* would. But, oddly, Nevin does not mine *this* point. Rather he insists that her Judaism is something she simply could not escape. To wit: "Having been born a Jew, a Jew by ancestral destiny, she did not have the freedom to choose to be a Jew."[19] Or, apparently, to choose not to be one. To be a Jew, Nevin adds, is to belong to a club "one does not quit."[20] It is clearly an essential quality, and Nevin uses it as such to discover "Jewish" traits in Weil such as "vagabondage," a "passion for justice," and "independence." She had, he suggests, "an *anima naturaliter judaica*."[21] (Nevin is clearly comfortable with gross racial and religious characterizations as "essential.")

What could possibly be the point of claiming that someone had a "natural Jewish soul?" Although few people speak that way any more, the least obnoxious point would be to use her Jewish background as a way of explaining Weil's distinctive and often unorthodox contributions to Christian thought. To the degree that Nevin does this, however, almost the entire stress is upon the "unorthodox" part, with a consequent and implicit recommendation that Christianity see Weil as a foreigner and no contributor at all to Christian thinking. Preying upon latent Christian anti-semitism, he thus can cause Weil to be dismissed from Christian halls. But that is not to claim her for Judaism, as Rabi wanted to do; it is to deliver the wayward daughter who had so many unkind things to say about Judaism to the town elders for chastisement. Thus she becomes exiled at Nevin's decree from both Christianity and Judaism. She is not a person to be taken too seriously, as she is little more than a brilliant fraud whom Nevin has ferreted out.

Now the point of looking at Nevin here in the context of the story of the baptism is this: if the story is true, then Nevin's characterization is plain and simply wrong. But it is wrong in a very particular way: that if Weil was baptized—and because the baptism is valid by Christian lights—then Weil was not "passing." She died a member of the holy, catholic Church. She may have been weird, misguided, heterodox, or any number of things; but none of them matter on this issue. She could have been all of those things and still be a member of the Christian Church. And this seems to have been the valid part of Rabi's point; to accept the story would be to admit to full membership a person whom, Rabi thought, the Catholics would themselves have *preferred* to see as an outsider.[22] In this respect one of the real challenges that the story of the baptism raises is the challenge *to the Church* to admit that people such as Weil really are a part of it, that by its own doctrine, it has admitted them, "hot potatoes" or not. That is precisely the point that Nevin has missed on a grand and systematic scale. It is a point that others miss on a smaller scale.

More, though, needs to be said, for simply noting that the baptism is valid, thus making Weil actually a Christian does not take away all ambiguities. It even increases some.

The first thing that needs to be added is a theological point. This last-hour baptism, like every other one, is a demonstration that grace can be present at any moment of our lives. Weil herself says that someday she might ask for baptism for "the action of grace in our hearts is secret and silent"(WG 50). Here the baptism may be an experimental proof of what she has written on grace. This decision, as all such decisions, is singular, and not a conclusion deduced from universally valid premises. It is the result of a movement of the will, a movement that began in a spiritual journey many years before. We know Weil often characterized her life in terms of a journey, and spirituality in general in those terms. There is no reason to think she did not know what she was talking about. This does not mean, of course, that everything in that journey is sanctified, as Augustine knew when he described his journey. It does mean that God directs it to a conclusion, often startling to the one undertaking it.

There is another side to this movement of the will, though, beyond the fact that it led her to be baptized. Given that the decision was a singular movement of will that completed a personal journey, we are obliged to take Weil's own personal motives seriously in such a decision. We need to see where they are precisely that: personal and not universal. Thus we cannot take Weil to be providing a universal example for those who will not consider entrance into the church, and, who would consider Christianity within and without the Church all of a piece. If we had not taken it seriously before, given her baptism, we are obliged now to take seriously Weil's insistence that her remaining outside the Church was a personal vocation, and one of obedience, for that matter.

There are also a number of more unsettling things to see as well. For example, we cannot claim that her particular objections to the Church ever really changed. And on this score her objections to the Church are not entirely unexceptionable.

Weil thought that entering the Church would mean complete subscription to everything it taught, and, so it seems, she thought that meant pretty much in the verbal form in which it was taught. She could not give that subscription, because she regarded most of these formulations as simply commentaries on the faith which the church has imposed as an object of belief. "Thus," Weil says, "she exercises her power to deprive people of the sacraments" (GTG 72). Weil certainly understood that in actual practice catechumens were not and could not be expected to know *The Manual of the Decisions and Formulations of the Councils* and that "it is impossible to discover by asking priests what is and what isn't 'the strict faith'" (GTG 74). But what is actual practice, she thought, ought to be official practice. Therefore the Church ought only to provide judgments "on a few essential points . . . but only as a guideline of the faithful" (GTG 72).

In part, there is a naivety in assuming that the church really is as inflexible on doctrinal formulations as Weil thought, although her own era and her contacts with Dominicans may have encouraged her in this. She, in this sense, is just not very savvy on the inner workings of the Church. But, on the other hand, she was also quite aware of what she was doing. Father Perrin in an interview in 1979 said that while Weil was constantly seeking a priest who would admit baptism without insisting on such and such a teaching, the real question at issue was whether Christ left a teaching authority to his own, or whether Christians are left to their own to fabricate their faith. "I believe," he said," therein lies the true problem. She never posed it to herself that way."[23] Perhaps she did not pose it to herself that way, but the outcome might not have been any different if she had. It is easy to imagine her admitting the authority in the abstract, but still disputing the particulars. Weil, who claimed she would not pick up her salvation if it were lying on the table in front of her if doing so meant disobedience, understood obedience quite well and must have understood how far subscription might have to go. She wanted a clear answer on this point before she found herself in a position of compromise.

It is exactly this sort of issue that is not changed by the fact of a baptism *in extremis*. And, of course, none of what she wrote before the baptism is changed either—and that is everything she wrote. It may change the way we read some of those writings, of course, on issues such as whether she categorically refused baptism and the consequent image we have of her, but that is another matter. There is, however, another interesting question that the baptism raises and that is the personal nature of Weil's claim that the Church's many formulations are an obstacle to the free play of the intellect.

We might note first her point about the Church's social nature. In her second letter to Father Perrin she says she is frightened of the Church as a social structure, because it is so tempting to be "influenced by anything collective"(WG 52). Pointing to saints who approved of the crusades, she writes: "If I can think that on this point I see more clearly than they did, I who am so far below them, I must admit that in this matter they were blinded by something very powerful. This something was the Church seen as a social structure"(WG 53). She goes on to say that if it blinded them, how much more likely would it blind her? And, of course, clarity of vision was what she wanted.

But when she writes this, she is not giving just a general answer; she is giving a very specific and personal one. And here the story of the baptism may give us some cause to speculate on some of the reasons why she, Simone Weil, saw the social nature of the Church as such an obstacle.

The fact of the matter is that when Weil complains about the social nature of the Church, she is not doing so by making the gripe of the discontented. To be discontented you have to be on the inside. She says she realizes the saints had a profound love for the Church and that she sympathizes with it, but, she adds, "they were nearly all born and brought up in the Church"(WG 50). She was not brought up in it and was not on the inside. She, in other words, did not elect to go outside; rather, she chose to stay there.

Father Perrin has said that when he first met Weil, she knew nothing about the Church, and he is correct in one sense. If she had known it from the inside, perhaps she could have been more flexible in her thinking about doctrine. In that regard, her thoughts on the matter are a theological hot potato for people on the inside because she raises issues based on half-truths and objections on hypothetical cases that are unlikely to arise. But once again this is only half the story. For at the same time we say this we must also say that she knew the Church in a way that Perrin and most of us do not—and that is as an outsider.

It is here that both Rabi and Nevin have a real point in wanting to claim Weil as a Jew. Pétrement tells us that her maternal grandmother once said that she would rather see Simone dead than see her marry a gentile. Her mother was the one who forbid mention of the story of the baptism, although she spent long hours typing Weil's writings on Christianity and seeing that they were published. Weil herself was reminded of her ethnic heritage by people on the street, by the anti-Jewish laws of Vichy France, and by those to whom she applied to be parachuted into occupied France.

Now we must be more than a bit subtle here in assessing the influence of this background. Weil, in considering baptism, would not have thought herself as about to betray Judaism by going over to a group that had consistently persecuted Jews. It is clear that she had little, if any, sympathy with Judaism. I do not think we can even say, with Giniewski,[24] that her anti-Jewish feeling was a form of self-hatred. Simply, Judaism was a dead issue for her. Nevertheless, she was associated with a group that had never fared well with the Church. She would have been well aware of criticisms of the Church that come from outsiders. As with all subordinate groups, this one can sometimes see the dominant group a lot more clearly on certain issues than the dominant group sees itself. In this regard, Weil's fears about free thought being stifled in the Church may not have been just a general worry, but the result of looking at the enclosed nature of the Church and what it has actually done to those on the outside. This is not because of having a "natural Jewish soul;" it is because of having Jewish experience. It was this that undoubtedly caused her sympathies to lay with groups such as the Albigensians who did not fare well with the Church.

Weil was a person who looked very carefully at the Church from the outside and who had cause to look at it carefully. It would have been with a great deal of personal trepidation that she would consider entering it, because she could easily feel that it would involve a major alteration of what she was doing. In this sense her objections were not entirely matters of overscrupulousness and half-baked notions. They were rooted in a definite understanding of the Church and what she might be required to give up in order to enter. This, combined with the certainty of faith, which was hers by mystical dispensation, could easily allow her to say that her refusal was not a matter of pride but was a refusal of what she saw as an unnecessary capitulation.

An outsider's perspective cannot fully define what it is like to be on the inside and in this respect some of what Weil says about the Church is half-baked and does not a convincing objection to those on the inside. Nevertheless, the outsider can have objections that are not just the result of ignorance of the insider's knowledge. One place that this seems to have been true in Weil's case is when she noted that the Church is Catholic by right but not in fact. In turn, the perspective she offers in the difficulties she had in coming to baptism may be helpful, if we pay attention to them, in helping it to be Catholic in fact.

For the difficulty in accepting the story of Weil's baptism may, in the end, mainly may be the difficulty of accepting an outsider, with valid and invalid criticisms. And there may be a great irony here. Weil criticized the Church for not being catholic in fact, and for nearly all her life preferred to stay outside it formally, in solidarity with those who are excluded. But by her baptism *in extremis* she may force Christians to accept that, like it or not, the Church in fact also includes all sorts of outsiders, including Jews, and all sorts of journeys that are not forgotten after arrival.

2. NO LONGER
ON THE MARGINS?

SIMONE WEIL not only is a *religious* outsider, she has been an outsider to the *philosophic* community as well. For example, although her understanding of what it is to be a human being is profound, it does not play much of a role in philosophical or theological discussions. This is in part because the questions she discusses are far more broad than the questions usually examined in English-speaking philosophy. For example, Weil treats the relation of work to human freedom, and what human beings need in order to live well, whereas in English-speaking philosophy the concept of a person is largely concerned with the refutation of Cartesian dualism, and the pros and cons of determinism. Unless Weil's remarks directly relate to Cartesian dualism or determinism, they are irrelevant to a philosophic discussion of the concept of a person.

Even when her remarks are relevant to these two topics, they are imbedded in discussions considered beyond the pale. For example, for her, two of the most pressing facts about human life are suffering and the desire for good. She is also devoted to a transcendent good, and the overcoming of illusions that prevent us from the discernment of justice and its relation to a transcendent good. In contrast, recent moral philosophy has largely been concerned with specifying what makes something right, and with defending human rights. She is concerned to become humble and obedient, which is largely out of fashion in theological, much less in philosophic, circles. In addition,

Weil's understanding of people has deep ontological roots. Recent moral philosophy firmly rejects the relevance of ontology to ethics.

We suspect it is Weil's attention to what is needed for humans to live well, the power of egotism, the emphasis on the need for spiritual nourishment, and the analysis of our personal and social condition that makes her appealing to many of us, and certainly to us, the authors. Yet it is precisely these features that put her outside the boundaries of so much present-day philosophy.

One of the reasons why Charles Taylor is relevant to admirers of Simone Weil is that his book, *Sources of the Self*,[1] promises to widen the scope of English-speaking philosophy. Taylor has a great deal of prestige and acceptance among professional philosophers. He has so effectively exposed the limited scope and interests of present-day English-speaking philosophy, using its own idiom, that he may succeed in getting topics and ideas onto the philosophic agenda that have been ignored for a long time. Then a forum will have been created in which Weil's thoughts may be presented for serious consideration by professional philosophers and perhaps theologians as well. We have therefore chosen to examine Taylor's concept of a person, not so much because all that is important in Taylor is new to people who have read Simone Weil, but to show how Taylor's work may help prepare the way for a wider appreciation of Weil.

It is not easy to summarize just what Taylor is trying to do. The book is in part an intellectual history describing how we in the West have arrived at our idea of what it is to be a person. He argues that a narrow understanding of what it is to be modern has cut us off from the roots of our own identity. He therefore shows the importance of Plato and Augustine for the development of our sense of individuality, and stresses how Christianity has given us our sense of the importance of ordinary life. He describes the best and worst features of the Enlightenment and Romanticism in contributing to our understanding of ourselves, and lastly argues for the value of modern art as yielding epiphanies that open us to intimations of greater significance than can be found in our prosaic world. Such wide-ranging exploration is in harmony with Weil's method of seeking a deeper understanding of human beings.

He seeks to show that we have improperly been cut off from these rich earlier sources of self-understanding by a misguided moral philosophy that relies on the natural sciences as its model of proper reasoning. A substantial part of the book is devoted to refuting this improper model of practical reasoning. This is why he calls his work one of retrieval; it is reminiscent of Weil's efforts to reclaim substantial parts of our Western heritage.

The book is also a prelude to a future book. Taylor promises to substantiate what he here only claims is true—namely, that our understanding of what it is to be a person, formed over many centuries, affects our epistemology and philosophy of language. Like Emmanuel Levinas, Taylor says that the self does and should obtrude in these areas in spite of present-day claims that it does not and should not. In other words, our discernment of what we think is true is affected by our understanding of what is good, and how to achieve a good life. It should be obvious from this summary that Taylor, like Weil, is not narrowly focused.

More importantly, the core thesis of Taylor's book connects with Simone Weil's main approach to the concept of a person— namely, a focus on good. Taylor claims that what it is to be a person is inextricably intertwined with what we take to be good. This is very like Weil, and very different from the focus of recent English-speaking moral philosophy.

> This moral philosophy has tended to focus on what it is right to do rather on what it is good to be, on defining the content of obligation rather than on the nature of the good life; and it has no conceptual place left for a notion of the good as the object of our love or allegiance.[2]

The echo of Weil we hear in the phrase "has no conceptual place left for a notion of the good as the object of our love or allegiance" is not an illusion. Although Taylor cites Iris Murdoch as the source, those who know Murdoch know how much she is indebted to Simone Weil. It bears Weil's hallmark.[3]

Taylor's characterization of present-day moral philosophy also indicates how many of Weil's concerns are beyond its narrow scope. The question of what makes life meaningful and worth living is usually ignored by present-day English-speaking philosophy, and so philosophy does not provide any way to judge whether a person is living a life that is really worthwhile. Yet for Taylor and Weil a life that is not worthwhile is condemned in the name of a standard independent of our personal tastes and desires. Such a judgment involves discriminations of good from evil, better from worse, higher from lower, which are not merely a matter of desires, inclinations, or choices.

Taylor focuses on the dignity of human beings and on what underlies that dignity. He organizes his case around an intuition of the dignity of people and the need of a framework or ontological account that goes with the intuition. This is very like Weil. According to Weil, we sometimes come to such a moral intuition through a recognition of the horror of human degradation, especially as it occurs in soul-destroying labor, in great suffering, and in social humiliation. Our recognition of human dignity is greatly assisted through a reduction of our egotism. Weil connects human dignity ontologically to the love of God (NR 5-6). For Taylor that is one possible account of human dignity, and one that he personally endorses, but he points to other possible ontological accounts, such as Plato's and Kant's. He does not, however, elaborate on any of them. Rather, he concentrates on the propriety of ontological accounts of our moral intuition of human dignity.

Let us look more closely at the pattern of argument Taylor uses for his position—intuitions and then ontological accounts:

> Perhaps the most urgent and powerful cluster of demands that we recognize as moral concern the respect for the life, integrity, and well-being, even flourishing, of others these are the ones we infringe when we kill or maim others, steal their property, strike fear into them and rob them of peace, or even refrain from helping them when they are in distress. Virtually everyone feels these demands, and they have been and are acknowledged in all human societies.[4]

These moral reactions to people are, on the one hand:

> Almost like an instinct, comparable to our love of sweet things, or our aversion to nauseous substances, or the fear of falling; on the other, they seem to involve claims, implicit or explicit, about the nature and status of human beings.[5]

One strand of contemporary moral philosophy recognizes the dignity of human beings, but declares that an ontological account of the nature of human beings is dispensable or irrelevant to morality. It rests content with the fact that we have these moral reactions toward people. The ontologies that give rational articulations to the propriety of these reactions are regarded as so much froth from a bygone age. Nonetheless, sometimes this stance is combined with a sociobiological explanation for our having such reactions, such as the claim that they have evolutionary utility.

Taylor seeks to refute such a sociobiological account. He points out that reactions of respect for people differ significantly from responses such as our taste for candy, or nausea from certain smells. In both cases:

> Our response is to an object with a certain property. But in the one case the property marks the object as one *meriting* this reaction; in the other case the connection between the two is just a brute fact. Thus we argue and reason over what and who is a fit object of moral respect, while this doesn't seem to be even possible for a reaction like nausea.[6]

He presses this argument home with other observations:

> The whole way in which we think, reason, argue, and question ourselves about morality supposes that our moral reactions have these two sides: that they are not only "gut" feelings but also implicit acknowledgements of claims concerning their objects. The various ontological accounts try to articulate these claims. The temptations to deny this, which arise from modern epistemology, are strengthened by the widespread acceptance of a deeply wrong model of practical reasoning, one based on an illegitimate extrapolation from reasoning in the natural sciences.[7]

Our moral reactions have been set aside by a false analogy to physical explanations. With physical explanations we supposedly start from facts identified independently of our reactions to them. We then try to show that one underlying explanation of them is better than another. But when we do this in moral philosophy, we lose from view the fact that ontological accounts articulate claims *implicit* in our reactions to people. Remove the implicit ontology, and no argument can move a person from a neutral stance toward other people to a moral one. Only within a world shaped by our deepest moral responses do moral arguments and moral explorations take place.

> If you want to discriminate more finely what it is about human beings that make them worthy of respect, you have to call to mind what it is to feel the claim of human suffering, or what is repugnant about injustice, or the awe you feel at the fact of human life. No argument can take someone from a

neutral stance towards the world. . . . We should treat our deepest moral instincts . . . as our mode of access to the world in which ontological claims are discernible and can be rationally argued about and sifted.[8]

It is interesting to compare Jean-Paul Sartre's views with English-speaking moral philosophy on the point of ontological backing. Iris Murdoch points out in the conclusion of her study *Sartre: Romantic Rationalist*, that Sartre is greatly distressed because he cannot justify his deep conviction about the value of people. There is no such anguish in English-speaking philosophy, as it believes it has disposed of any need for an ontological backing. Taylor believes both that there is a need, and that however uneasy we may be today about the complete success of any account, we can still draw upon the rich sources of Western civilization in our continuing explorations.

Taylor's arguments, if they are at all successful, reopen previously closed vistas. We are to explore those views of our spiritual nature and predicament that help make sense of our response toward people as deserving respect. Since every moral theory in Western civilization assumes that people deserve respect, we are not to dismiss as irrelevant our ancient, medieval, and modern heritage that has contributed to our view of what people are. He points out that articulations of our moral intuitions are both difficult to understand and controversial. Not only is there more than one theistic account, but they clash on many points with purely secular accounts. Taylor candidly confesses that he himself, like many others, cannot subscribe with complete conviction to any particular larger framework. But this situation of perplexity, confusion, and a continuing search is far preferable to a suppression of moral ontology.

Weil's understanding of our spiritual nature and predicament is largely theistic, not to say Christian. But not narrowly so. As we all know, she draws upon ancient Greek thought, mathematics, technology, physics, art, great literary figures, various religions and ancient mythologies. If anything, her range, though focused on a theistic understanding, is even wider than that of Taylor, who limits himself to Western civilization. But if Taylor's position that ontology is inescapable and vital for our concept of a person, then Weil's work is philosophically relevant, even if largely theistic in inspiration. (Part IV, "Persons and Community," of our book is especially devoted to an account of Weil's effort to retrieve the reasons we are to respect people, and the social significance of that respect.)

There is another aspect of Taylor's account of the concept of a person that is particularly important for establishing a more favorable milieu for Simone Weil's thought. Taylor claims that much of our self-understanding and moral energy comes from narratives, such as the Jewish, Christian, Marxist, and liberal humanist accounts of history. To see one's life in a pattern carries tremendous moral power. One of Taylor's major purposes is to lift the embargo on narratives from moral philosophy. Narratives not only enable us to retrieve and draw upon past achievements, but also put us in contact with the sources of good in our universe. This helps restore a view of life as a journey or a pilgrimage. The exclusion of narrative from the philosophic consideration of the concept of a person automatically excludes much of Simone Weil from the domain of philosophic concern. For Weil, as for Plato, Plotinus, Spinoza, and all the major religions of the world, life is considered to be a movement from illusion, error, or sin to enlightenment, truth, or regeneration.

Taylor writes and reasons in an idiom acceptable to present-day philosophers, even though what he argues for has been largely ignored in philosophy for some time. If he is at all successful, what Weil has to say, for all its theistic orientation, cannot be set aside as mere mysticism, as it so often is, and treated as philosophically irrelevant. Chapter 4, ("The Concept of Reading"), and chapter 5, ("Winch on Weil's Supernaturalism"), as well as all of Part III ("Journey of the Soul") of this book exhibit the philosophical significance of seeing one's own life and human life in general in a larger, narrative pattern, according to Simone Weil.

In spite of Taylor's own theistic commitment, he looks especially to twentieth-century literary artists to reinspire us with their highly personal presentations of moral sources. The epiphanies they engender are in a "subtler language," as he puts it, because they are imbedded in the artist's personal language, unlike those of theistic, Enlightenment and Romantic writers. Appropriation of the values and access to the ontological depths modern artists open to us require an immersion in each artist's personal medium, and they cannot properly be presented outside those personal media.

As we all know, Simone Weil had a passion for the fine arts as revelatory. She is far more eloquent than Taylor, but once again Taylor's prosaic approach may open doors for Weil that she herself cannot open. In our book, chapter 8 ("George Herbert and Simone Weil"), we will illustrate the role of the fine arts in Simone Weil's spiritual journey.

We think, however, that Taylor, in contrast to Weil, has overdrawn the contrast between artistic and other moral sources. He seems to think that artistic work is less accessible than nonartistic presentation, because artistic work has a distinctive vocabulary that is *essential* for it to yield epiphanies. But Christian spirituality, in both Eastern (for example, Maximus the Confessor) and Western (for example, Bonaventure) versions, requires a profound repentance, and moral and spiritual purification *before* one can even hope to discern vestiges of God in nature and the image of God in human nature. To achieve these discernment it is not possible *fully* to dispense with the language of Christian spirituality.

A much more serious reservation arises over the ease with which Taylor claims that it has always and everywhere been recognized that people are worthy of respect. He speaks as if the differences in views of the worth of people is only a matter of how far this recognition extends.

> The boundary around those beings worthy of respect is drawn parochially in earlier cultures, but there always is such a class. And among what we recognize as higher civilizations, this always includes the whole human species.[9]

It is true that with the ascendancy of Christianity, every ethical theory in Western culture acquired the conviction that *all* people are worthy of respect. But it must also be noted how difficult it is to defend this conviction *without* Christianity. For example, Kierkegaard in *Works of Love* powerfully shows that love of neighbor, not just good will and the like, but *love* of neighbor cannot be sustained on the basis of *human* motivation, nor on the basis of any ethical theory. Basil Mitchell argues in *Morality: Religious and Sacred* that our Western conviction in the sacredness of every human being not only has Christian sources but also cannot be sustained by any present-day secular theory. He fears that this central conviction of our civilization is now likely to be lost. M.F. Burnyeat, the Cambridge classicist, said of Gregory Vlastos's defense of the equal worth of people as people, "That is an extraordinarily difficult idea to swallow. . . . I myself doubt that anyone could begin to comprehend the idea if they did not have an appropriate religious background."[10]

These writers suggest that there is a great chasm between the recognition of the value of *some* people and the recognition of the value of *all* people. To think that the difference is only one of scope, as Taylor claims (see, for example, *Sources of the Self*, p. 4), is to have failed to see that the recognition of people *as* people is not present *at all* when only some people *but not others* are recognized as having worth. We will see how Weil seeks to open our eyes to the sacredness of people and how difficult it is for us to come to this awareness.

Closely connected with this point is Taylor's apparent belief that the moral intuition of the worth of people, indeed of all people, is fairly easy to come by. Both Christian teaching and personal experience amply testify to how hard it is to come to an awareness of another person *as a person*. It is so rare that W.H. Auden in the introduction to *Protestant Mystics* describes it as a mystical experience. A glance at Auden's account of his unexpected and overpowering experience of the infinite worth of three colleagues should make one pause whenever someone starts talking about the worth of people, and make one ask whether he or she understand what he or she is saying.

But to take Taylor to task in this way is perhaps to have crossed the boundary of accepted intellectual inquiry and to have entered the forbidden territory of apologetics. Taylor carefully goes to the edge of the boundary again and again, always pulling back just in time so that his voice will not go unheard in university precincts. We admire that ability, and in our present climate of opinion, it is necessary for many to employ it. But it is also one indication and measure of the violation of the very idea of the university: a commitment to free and open inquiry. Taylor is struggling to get onto the agenda of public inquiry many matters in our heritage, both Christian and secular, that the university now excludes. Should he succeed, as he deserves to, he will have written a landmark book.

Taylor's voice, however, is not a lone one. Because of the crisis in our intellectual culture and civilization at large, Taylor's voice is part of a larger chorus. There is a growing body of literature produced by distinguished thinkers from various nontheological disciplines that uncover the naturalistic assumptions that dominate their respective fields of inquiry. They all show the inadequacies of naturalistic assumptions and argue that these assumptions cut us off from rich cultural resources, including religious ones, for understanding ourselves and our world. This naturalistic creed dominates Western intellectual culture, and has not only aggressively cast aside a theistic vision of the universe, but is also making it impossible to sustain a meaningful vision of human life. According to all these writers, it has produced an increasingly serious intellectual crisis in Western culture.

This literature includes George Steiner's *Real Presences* (deconstructionism in linguistics, philosophy, and literary criticism); Robert Bellah's (et al.) *Habits of the Heart* and *A Good Society*; Glenn Tinder's *The Political Meaning of Christianity*; Michael Waltzer's *Spheres of Justice* (social and political philosophy); Alastair MacIntyre's *After Virtue*; Basil Mitchell's *Morality: Religious and Secular* (moral philosophy); Peter Winch's *Simone Weil: The Just Balance*; Leszek Kolakowski's *Modernity on Endless Trial*; and Hilary Putnam's *Reason, Truth and History* (all in the tradition of analytic philosophy); John Milbank's *Theology and the Social Sciences* (sociology and psychology); and perhaps even Isaiah Berlin's *The Crooked Timber of Humanity* (intellectual history). Of all these efforts to free us from the asphyxiating confinement of a naturalistic creed, Charles Taylor's is perhaps the most wide-ranging.

Nonetheless, we want to finish this chapter by calling attention to Kolakowski. Unlike Kolakowski, Taylor does not portray the contradictory forces in modernity that have led to its present impasse. Kolakowski argues that there are two competing tendencies in our civilization: the tendency to make claims to final and ultimate truth, and a critical attitude that so undermines all claims to truth that we tend toward skepticism, relativism, and even nihilism. It is from these two competitive tendencies that his book takes its title: *Modernity on Endless Trial*.

Kolakowski argues that when a culture loses all sense of limits, it is open to every form of intellectual and political totalitarianism. Having thrown off the limits imposed by religion in the name of autonomy and utopian hopes of perfectibility, modern society's repeated failures lead to disillusionment. The idea that society and people are "endlessly flexible things" sanctions force and violence, and finally despotism and the destruction of culture. The seeds were sown with the rejection of the sacred and of the reality of evil. We are restrained from the twin tendencies of our secular culture by religious faith.

Religion is the human way of accepting life as inevitable defeat:

> One can accept life, and accept it, at the same time, as a defeat only if one accepts that there is a sense beyond that which is inherent in human history—if, in other words, one accepts the order of the sacred.[11]

For all Taylor's insights and achievements, this dynamic is not apparent in his work. It is one with which Simone Weil would have been at home, for it is with limits and the sacred, as we will see, that she above all wrestles with. But the main point of this brief consideration of Taylor and Kolakowski, and the mention of some other books, is to indicate that because of developments in our intellectual culture a forum is being created in which Simone Weil's ideas may be presented for consideration by those engaged in academic enquiry. Let us now turn to examine those ideas in detail.

PART II
Nature and Necessity

3. DIVINE NECESSITY:
WEILIAN AND PLATONIC CONCEPTIONS

NECESSITY IS CLEARLY one of the most important concepts in Simone Weil's thought, appearing in all her religious, philosophical, and social writings. Its importance is underlined by Weil herself when she writes of it "as the material common to art, science, and every kind of labor," and as "the door by which Christianity can enter profane life and permeate the whole of it" (SN 195).

But what is necessity in the works of Simone Weil? This is no easy question, for necessity in those works exhibits a paradoxical character. At one and the same time, it is that which crushes us and yet allows us life. It is incommensurate with the Good and yet, if we consent to suffer it, it is a medium through which God touches us. Furthermore, God abandons the creation to its governance, and yet necessity is the will and providence of God.

One of the better brief formulations of Weil's conception of necessity is A-A. Devaux's when he says: "necessity presents itself therefore to us under two aspects: according to the *regard* that one bears on it, and also according to the *place* from where this regard is brought to bear."[1] We can either regard necessity according to the perspective of the self or not; similarly, we can regard it from the earth or from the heavens. Much of the paradoxical nature of necessity is therefore contingent upon us and upon our attention and its degree. This is crucial to note, for although necessity is crucial for understanding Weil's concepts of nature and supernature, the issues involved are clearly not simply exegetical and descriptive; they are also hermeneutical.

Before dealing with the hermeneutical and interpretive issues of what Weil means by nature and supernature (taken up in later chapters), it is important, though, to come to some descriptive and exegetical understanding of necessity as it is found in Weil's writings. Necessity is *not* simply a code word for an inflexible set of natural laws, as Peter Winch sometimes tends to claim.[2] Rather, it involves several sorts of relations between the created world and God. It is the purpose of this chapter to uncover the relations of necessity. It shall do so by comparing them to Plato's doctrine of creation in the *Timaeus*, for this is a work that not only inspired Weil but is also one upon which she drew heavily to describe the relations of necessity. If, therefore, we can see what Plato is doing in the *Timaeus*, we should then have easier access to Weil's thought.

Weil in the essay "Divine Love in Creation" makes the comment that Plato's *Timaeus* "comprehends a theory of artistic creation." She is entirely correct in this assessment, for the *Timaeus* is an account of how mind brings form and life to shapeless and inert matter. Indeed, the *Timaeus* is an account of the roles that mind and matter respectively play in creation. This is a fact that is easily seen from the three major divisions of the dialogue—namely, the works of reason (29d-47e), what comes about by necessity (47e-69a), and the cooperation of reason and necessity (69a ff.). The roles of both mind and matter, however, are dialectically related throughout the entire dialogue and for this reason a number of relations obtain between them. These relations are then all subsumed under the analogy of artistic creation.

Plato opens his account of creation by simply stating that everything that is made comes from a creator. Furthermore, he adds, when something is created, the creator has two choices of pattern on which the creation can be modeled—the unchangeable or the changeable. If the former is chosen, then the creation will be beautiful; if the transitory is chosen as the model, then the creation will not be beautiful. It is Plato's opinion, however, that the creator of this world has chosen the unchanging as the model, for as he says when he treats the question of why God creates at all: "He was good, and the good can never have any jealousy of anything. And being free from jealousy, he desired that all things should be as like himself as they could be"(29e).[3] Therefore, because God wished that all things be good and because God saw that the intelligent is greater than the unintelligent and that without soul there is no intelligence, then "for which reason, when he was framing the universe, he put intelligence in soul and soul in body, that he might be the creator of a work which was by nature fairest and best . . . (thus) we may say that the world came into being—a living creature truly endowed with soul and intelligence by the providence of God" (30b). It is clear that this fair creation is made after a transcendent model.

This account tells us why God created and which model was used. But *how* did God make this creation the fairest and best possible?

Plato answers this by first describing how God creates the body of the universe by fixing the *qualities* of the elements in a certain definite proportion patterned after a mean proportion of unity, "the fairest bond" (31d). (In order to be strictly accurate here, it is necessary to note that in this construction of the world body, God is *not* here creating matter or the mechanical forces found in the world; that is left to "the works of necessity." Instead, God is here creating the bonds of geometrical proportion that the elements display when God has worked on them.)

When God had thus proportioned the body of the world and given it the shape of a sphere so that it would be able to comprehend within itself all other figures, then:

> In the center he put the soul, which he diffused throughout the body, making it also to be the exterior environment of it, and he made the universe a circle moving in a circle, one and solitary, yet by reason of its excellence able to converse with itself, and needing no other friendship or acquaintance. Having these purposes in view he created the world a blessed god.(34b)

Plato then goes on to discuss the composition of the soul of the world. He admits, however, that the order of the presentation should not be taken to disparage the soul, since the soul is "in origin and excellence prior to and older than the body, to be the ruler and mistress, of whom the body was to be the subject" (34c).

When God made the World Soul he did so by taking from unchangeable being and from the sort of being found "in bodies" and fashioning from them a third and intermediate sort of being. He did likewise with sameness and with difference. Taking, then, these three compounded intermediate forms, he blended them into a single form, which he subsequently divided, according to a mathematical formula, into proportions that form a musical scale. By so dividing the World Soul into a scale, a harmony obtains among all things to which the World Soul gives life. When God had then completed this division, he divided the entire compound lengthwise into two parts, which he joined at the center like the letter X and then bent them into a circular form. It is now when the World Soul has been thus framed that God forms within her the corporeal universe and unites the two.

What is Plato's point in this complicated description of the World Soul? It is at least threefold. First, the World Soul gives being and thus (for Plato) form and intelligibility to the world, especially mathematical intelligibility. Second, by virtue of its harmonic division and consequent dispersal throughout the body of the world, it allows a relation of each created thing to every other created thing, and thus gives an overriding harmony to creation as a whole. The World Soul's mathematical function is, as Weil says, that of "an ensemble of laws of variation determined by fixed and invariant ratios"(FLN 86). Third, it is a mediator between God and the world of becoming, since it partakes of the being of both and because it is the mean term in the relation between God and the world.

There are also two further points of significance that are seen when this account of creation, as it has so far been described, is understood in the light of artistic creation. On the one hand, the motivating reason and purpose of creation, its beauty, truth, and life, and its model all exist in God in unity and actuality before the world ever comes into being. Said otherwise, God creates out of God's own being and life. The creation is thus a work of art in which the artist has created a being of perfect goodness equal to himself through his own good nature and the inspiration of a model of perfection. On the other hand, as Weil rightly notes, when we understand God's creation in this way, the very human activity from which the account has taken its analogical departure must be reinterpreted. This is to say, the good human artist is a person who imitates God's activity on a finite level. A good artist is one who chooses to reproduce the perfection of reality and who also chooses to give his creation a fullness of life as nearly equal to his own as is possible. It is this manner of activity, Weil says, that should be the goal of all science, knowledge, and labor.

The artistic theory of creation therefore has profound significance on many levels—mathematical, theological, and technological. There is, however, one crucial feature to the account that is missing—namely, the role of the material upon which the artist works. Artists do not produce a work of art completely by their mental processes, no matter how good they are. Instead, they must always take into consideration the material upon which they work, for the plasticity of the material will very much determine what they can create. The sculptor must take into account the hardness and malleability of stone and metal; the painter must take into account the canvas and pigments; and the poet must stay within a recognizable vocabulary, grammar, and syntax of his or her language (although he or she may try to extend their limits). Indeed, art is never *ex nihilo*; instead, artists must seek to persuade the matter to the desired form.

Plato is fully cognizant of this requirement of his analogy of artistic creation and therefore in the second part of the *Timaeus* he turns from the rationalist account of the "works of reason" to consider what comes about by necessity (*ananke*). [4] The Creation for Plato is not simply an extension of God's thought; rather, it is something that is at least partially ontologically independent of God. Creation is, as he says, the combined work of reason and necessity.

But what then is necessity? The word that Plato uses in the *Timaeus*—*ananke*—which we translate as "necessity," means something quite different than that which we normally understand by that term. Whereas necessity for us means ordered natural laws or fate, it does not mean either of these things to Plato in the first instance. Necessity for him is something that stands opposed to reason. Thus it is not strictly equivalent to matter, since for Plato matter has distinct properties and qualities open to the sight of intelligence. Clearly mind has something to do with this. Despite this assertion, however, necessity does play an important role in the creation of matter for it is a *donnée* with which the Creator has to work. Perhaps the best way of putting the case at this point is in the manner of many modern commentators who claim that the influence of necessity is discerned in the "brute facts" inherent in matter. What is meant by 'brute fact', though, must be described in stages.

Necessity, Plato says, can only be reached by a "bastard reasoning." Since the entity in question cannot be grasped by intelligence, lacking as it does the qualities that intelligence needs for discernment. But given this qualifier, Plato then goes on to say, as best he can, what necessity is. It must be a third entity other than the intelligible pattern or the created being which is an imitation of the pattern. Yet, what can this be? It is space:

> ". . . it is the receptacle, and in a manner the nurse, of all generation." (49a) . . . (it) receives all bodies—that must always be called the same, for, inasmuch as she always receives all things, she never departs from her own nature and never, in any way or at any time, assumes a form like that of any of the things which enter into her; she is the natural recipient of all impressions, and is stirred and informed by them, and appears different from time to time by reason of them. But the forms which enter into and go out of her are the likenesses of eternal realities modeled after their patterns in a wonderful and mysterious manner . . . " (50c).

If this is all there is to say about necessity, it would be straightforward enough and *ananke* would appear as a sort of ancient version of Descartes's view of matter as extension. Plato, however, goes on to say that space does not exactly exist as something empty; rather, it has "happenings" (*genesis*) within it. These happenings, he says, give rise to certain appearances; yet they are strange, various, and without any sort of form or order. Here necessity appears as a sort of chaos of primordial forces. It is this chaos that God fashions by form and number.When God fashions this chaos, he does so by first establishing the elements by resolving them into triangles, then putting them in proper proportion and then using them to build the three-dimensional solids that make up the figures of the inhabitants of creation. Necessity is here in the Pythagorean terminology, which Plato later employs in the *Philebus*, the *apeiron* or unlimited, which receives limit (*peras*) from outside to give rise to created being.

Necessity as the primordial chaos or *apeiron* is not graspable by the human mind. It would not even seem to be a thing of any particular importance when it appears to be so easily formed into the elements and creatures. Yet it is not only a mythical, and therefore negligent, part of creation. Where it plays a role in creation is when it gives rise to unexplained "brute fact" in phenomena. "Brute fact" is indeed fact since it is graspable by mind as having form and number; but it is brute because no reasonable explanation can be given of its purpose, either by its own being or by the being of things on its own level. *Within* the creation, or within certain levels of creation, things taken individually or in certain groupings may display form and order; certain recognizable physical laws may even pertain to them. But taken as a whole, they defy efforts to think them as an organized whole, and no account of them as a whole can be given as to their purpose. In fact, they may even serve to suggest that there is no overriding purpose. In this sense, they are recalcitrant to reason, and necessity is witnessed precisely in this recalcitrance. Necessity here gives rise often to contradiction in thought.

It is when necessity (*ananke*) is structured by form and number, and we have brute fact, that we also arrive at what matter is in Plato. Matter, as such, for him is not a preexistent amorphous mass of stuff, but is definite material that can be described mathematically. Yet while matter does have a certain form and order that can only have come from the influence of reason, it is, nevertheless, something that comes from necessity. Although matter *has* form and number, it is not the immaterial limit as such. It is, instead, necessity persuaded by goodness.[5] It is only when this concept of matter is arrived at that we truly have the material on which God works in order to complete the analogy of artistic creation, for it is only when the account of "what comes about by necessity" is completed that we can juxtapose it with the account of the "works of reason."

The description of the constitution of matter is a description of how necessity is first persuaded by goodness. This description, however, is not the only persuasion of necessity by goodness. We can also see a second persuasion taking place when we juxtapose the "works of reason" with "what comes about by necessity." When the World Soul is placed in the center of the material world and spread throughout it, the World Soul performs the operation of harmonizing the brute factors of material necessity. Thus in the transcendent life of the World Soul, the world is given a divine purpose it does not have on the level of necessity. Here we can then see that matter, which is a persuaded necessity, is further persuaded by an "ensemble of laws of variation" in which the brute facts of nature are harmonized and incorporated within a single being who is the divine purpose of the world. It is this final harmonization that gives the world its beauty, and it stands for that which we want to read as the "book of nature," discussed in the next chapter.

The final result of the juxtaposition of the works of reason and what comes about by necessity in Plato is that there is a dual causality for all that occurs within creation. There is, on the one hand, the variable cause of necessity by which forces arise, clash, and retreat. On the other hand, there is the causality of the Good, which first gives limits to these forces, making matter of them, and then incorporating them within the harmonious life of the World Soul in whom they are made to subserve the Good. In this way the analogy of artistic creation is satisfactorily completed for both the mind and purpose of the Maker and the nature of the material have been taken into account. The creation is the will of the Maker, but insofar as it is not simply an extension of the Maker's thought, it also really exists in its own right. When we view the creation, then we must see it as the result of these two causes. But we must also see these two causes in their proper roles and in the order befitting them. Plato says:

> Wherefore we may distinguish two sorts of causes, the one divine and the other necessary, and may seek for the divine in all things, as far as our nature admits, with a view to the blessed life, but the necessary kind only for the sake of the divine, considering that without them and when isolated from them, these higher things for which we look cannot be apprehended or received or in any way shared by us. (69a)

When we thus look at creation in this way, as Plato does, we ought to see three essential relations of necessity and goodness. The first is when we regard necessity in the sense of chaos. Here necessity is contrary to reason and goodness. Necessity in this sense is not a positive force that *actively* opposes good (Plato is not a Manichaean); it is simply distinct from good, being without good's qualities. While there is an irreducible mythological element to this sense of necessity, it is important to maintain as, in John Locke's words, "that something-I-know-not-what," that distinguishes the creation from the creator.

One finds the second relation between the necessary and the good in the creation of matter. There necessity receives limits and order in its individual parts and within certain limited structures. Necessity in this relation to goodness comes very close to the modern sense of necessity as the laws of physics, at least insofar as physics has individual *laws* pertaining to different phenomena and no one overarching law of physical explanation. Here again this sense of necessity is contrary or incommensurate with goodness, for it is one that does not allow full harmony or the sort of purpose that belongs to the divine good.

The third relation between necessity and goodness is the one in which the disparate elements of necessity are taken up and harmonized in the overarching order of the World Soul. This relation of all things to each other in the unity of the World Soul gives the creation its divine purpose and life. Here necessity, while not having purpose itself, is persuaded to subserve the purpose of the good.

When we have concluded highlighting these three relations an important corollary appears, for we can now see *two* essential mediations between the Good and the necessary. There is, first, in the limits of matter, a mediating term between chaos and the World Soul. Second, in the World Soul there is another mediating term between matter and God, and, thus, ultimately between God and all-that-is-not-God.

Let us now turn to look at Simone Weil's account of creation to see the roles that necessity plays in it. This is an account that very much depends upon her analysis of the Cross in her essay "The Love of God and Affliction," which we take up in chapter 5, "The Enigma of Affliction." It is also an account, however, that bears marked structural similarities to Plato's view of creation in the *Timaeus*. If these similarities between Weil's central religious symbol and Plato's doctrine of creation are made apparent, then we can proceed to show further, in the next section of this essay, the great degree to which Weil's description of necessity coincides with Plato.

Weil begins with a consideration of God before the act of creation. God "produces himself and knows himself perfectly"(SNL 176). God is all in all, and outside God there is nothing. Yet above all, God is love and in the persons of the Trinity there is a unifying love. It is this love between three equal persons that gives God's very definition of unity for "between the terms united by this relation of divine love there is more than nearness; there is infinite nearness or identity"(SN 176). The Father loves the Son and the bond between them forms a third person, which is both love itself and loved. There is no inequality in the various terms of the relationship for the love of either the Father or the Son is in no way diminished by their love for the Spirit, which binds them. The Trinity therefore is a perfect harmony, which is equality and perfect joy.

There is no more fullness of being or goodness than the Trinity. Yet, although God is all perfection, God chose to create a world of creatures who are not God and who have an existence distinct from his. Weil asks: "Why did God create? It seems so obvious that God is greater than God and the creation together" (SNL 194). However, to see the "how?" of creation is to begin to understand the "why?" In creating, God willed that beings other then himself should live. If God is all, however, the only way in which this could be done is by abdicating the full exercise of power. In this way, Weil sees creation not as an act of power or as an expansion of God's being, but one of the renunciation of power.

This is one of Weil's most distinctive—and characteristic— theological contributions:

> Because he is the creator, God is not all-powerful. Creation is abdication. But he is all powerful in this sense, that his abdication is voluntary. He knows its effects and wills them . . . God has emptied himself. This means that both the Creation and the Incarnation are included with the Passion. (FLN 120)

Thus in the very act of creation there is a "crucifixion" in God. But if creation is an abdication, what then is the stuff of which the creation is made, since there is nothing outside God? Weil says it is matter and the necessity that governs it. But here we must tread carefully for, we argue, Weil uses necessity in two different senses. On the one hand, she sees God's abdication as an abandonment to the forces of matter and necessity, which are the stuff of this world. "God abandons our whole entire being—flesh, blood, sensibility, intelligence, love—to the pitiless necessity of matter and the cruelty of the devil, except for the supernatural part of the soul"(FLN 103). In this sense creation has an independent existence, and necessity is truly distant from goodness. On the other, she views necessity as an order of immaterial relations without force. It is our duty to submit to it in the manner of the Stoic *amor fati*. But how do these two senses of necessity go together?

An answer to this question can be obtained by distinguishing not only the two senses of necessity but also two of "renunciation." In creating, God does abandon the world and allows it its own existence by withdrawing in favor of a "conditional necessity."[6] This sort of necessity can be equated with natural forces per se. It is conditional, however, in that it depends on God's withdrawing in order for it to exist. It is force without limits and a sort of unregulated chaos. Weil, however, did not see creation only in this sense where God simply withdraws to an inaccessible corner of the universe, allowing chaos to reign in his place. At the same time he withdraws and renounces the full exercise of his power, there is also a crucifixion in God himself whereby the Son is separated from the Father and incarnated in the body of the world. The withdrawal is this "crucifixion." When the Son is so "crucified" he then becomes the *Logos* or order of the world, which is precisely necessity in Weil's second sense; "God makes himself into *necessity*" (NB 190).

We are now in a better position to understand Weil's notions of God's governance of creation through a providential necessity, which he furnishes for it. The creation has its own proper forces, but through the crucifixion of the Son these forces have rigorous limits imposed on them. They then admit of an order through the interaction of their limits, for "limit is only inscribed in a relation between several conditions which compensate each other, in an order"(NB 515). Weil often used the balance to symbolize this idea, for a balance puts opposing forces into an equilibrium around an immaterial mathematical point. The point, being without magnitude or force, exercises no force, while at the same time it is a necessary relation between forces, which forces obey. When this principle is applied on the cosmic scale, the "*Logos* Necessity" is seen as "an ensemble of laws of variation determined by fixed and invariant relations." Because the ensemble is capable of being regarded as a single entity pervading all the laws of variation, and one, in fact, from which they all proceed, Weil feels justified in taking this immaterial structure as the *Logos* of the world.

In this way, Weil, like Plato, postulates a dual causality of goodness and necessity to all created phenomena. There is on the one hand the causality of conditional necessity, which is the individual blind forces making up the matter of phenomena. On the other hand, there is the causality of the Good, which is reflected in the form of order of the matter. The form and order, however, are not the Good itself, although they are caused by the Good and bear a relationship to it, a relationship that can only have proceeded from the Good itself. This relationship is found in the *Logos*, the crucified Son of the Father. This is to say, the *Logos*, taken in relation to conditional necessity creates a new necessity, which bears a mediatory relationship to the transcendent Good. She also puts it this way: *"In order that Good may pass into existence, Good must be able to be the cause of what is already entirely caused by Necessity"* (NB 99). The cause of the Good is seen in the order of the world which cannot be divorced from the world of which it is an order and which can not be equated with any part of it.

We can now see that Weil uses "necessity" in at least two senses—first as a mere aggregative term representing the natural forces found within the world, and then as the immaterial ensemble of all physical laws. Her concept of necessity, though, is not based on an equivocation; instead, like necessity in Plato's *Timaeus*, it embodies a series of relations and mediations between God, humans, and matter. Weil discusses these relations at length in "The Pythagorean Doctrine." This essay, which is an attempt by Weil to translate the spiritual inspiration of the Pythagoreans, especially Plato, is more than historical speculation on her part. It is also the most detailed exposition in one place that we have of Weil's understanding of these relations.

There are two parts to "The Pythagorean Doctrine," which are germane to the present discussion. The first is the second form of harmony which harmonizes "the opposition between creator and creature . . . [or] between that which limits and that which is unlimited, which is to say that which receives its limitation from outside" (IC 168). The limits in question, Weil says, are number.

It is important to recognize here that Weil is only talking about a unique relation between the creator and the creature (that is, the creation), and not about the more specific relations between God and creatures. In short, she is concerned with a mediating relation between the contraries of God and *all*-that-is-not-God. This relation she says is found in Christ in his function as *Logos* wherein he becomes a World Soul similar to that of the World Soul in the *Timaeus*, which gives form, order, and life to the creation as a whole.

There is a problem, however, for, she adds, any relationship in God must be a person and matter is not a person. The problem is solved and the harmonization realized, though, when the person becomes matter—"this is a human being at the moment of death, when the circumstances preceding the death have been brutal to the point of making a thing of that person" (IC 169). Christ is the *Logos* because he is crucified upon the whole of time and space wherein he suffers the full extent of the forces of matter, while at the same time never ceasing to love the Father, even in absence. He thus forms the limits of force, because they can never exceed his capacity to love and thus they can never thwart the divine purpose and goodness. The *Logos* is therefore the mediator between God and the material of the world, for it partakes of the nature of both and persuades matter to serve the purpose of the good.

The fifth form of harmony deals with things and human relations to them *insofar* as humans are also things of matter. In this fifth form of harmony there is again a set of contraries, which need to be harmonized, and these contraries are *related* to (but not the same as) the previous contraries of limit and unlimited. A careful distinction needs to be made here to understand exactly what Weil's point is. Previously she had spoken of a mediation of the contraries of God and all-that-is-not-God; that is, the limiting and the unlimited. Here, however, she is not so much concerned with that relationship as she is with the relation of created things to each other, particularly humans as natural beings related to the rest of nature, and their relations to the whole, which is to say to the natural order of necessity. There is, of course, a bridge between these two sets of contraries and this bridge shall show the final structure of necessity.

The contraries of limit and unlimited as they pertain to our relation to natural things appear when the Pythagorean dictum, "Everything is number," is applied to the way in which we know things. It is by number that we know anything at all and in this sense, it is even number that gives things a body, as Weil quotes Philolaos. In order to comprehend this claim, it is necessary to see the way in which "number" is used.

Number for the Pythagoreans, Weil says, is not just the enumeration of quantity, for this clearly would not give us an understanding of all relationships. Number for the Pythagoreans also included the notion of function, which is a quantitative law of variation. "The function is what the Greeks called number of relation, *arithmos* or *Logos*, and it is what constitutes limit" (IC 179). The gnomon of Pythagorean mathematics shows this notion of function.

A gnomon originally was the vertical arm of a sundial, which remains immobile while its shadow varies. Its mathematical usage as "function" comes about because a mathematical relationship obtains between the invariant stem and its variable shadow. That is the gnomon as function. This same idea of function can be applied to anything, active or inert, in the natural world, and a rigorous formula of a function that defines the object can then be obtained, Weil thinks.

Weil says that it is somewhat surprising to hear that it is number that gives things a body. Yet, she adds, it is literally true and "the relations of quantity which play the part of the gnomon do indeed constitute the body of the object" (IC 178). Although in perception we never see, for example, all sides and angles of a cube and their interrelations, nevertheless we understand "the form of the cube is that which determines the variation of the apparent form" (IC 179). It is this unperceived, yet understood, form that is indeed the body of the object for us. It is this understanding then that differentiates perception of the real world from hallucination and delusions. It is also a contact with necessity:

> Necessity always appears to us as an ensemble of laws of variation, determined by fixed relationships and invariants. Reality for the human mind is contact with necessity. There is a contradiction here, for necessity is intelligible, not tangible. Thus the feeling of reality constitutes a harmony and a mystery. (IC 178)

The reality of the universe is therefore the necessity constituted by the gnomic laws of variation. But this is not the entire story. The necessity with which Weil is concerned is itself conditional[7] and needs to stand on a base. But what is this base? Weil says that we really cannot have a conception of it, for if intelligibility is determined by number, then the base, which is not number, cannot be known. Nevertheless, the Greeks did have a word for this base (*apeiron*), which means "indeterminate" and "unlimited." Our physical world is therefore composed of both the gnomic laws of variation and the unlimited. *Full* contact with necessity is contact with things that are unlimited but have received a limit. We see here how Weil admirably reproduces Plato's account of matter.

The relation of things to things is therefore the mathematical relation between gnomons. But how is this linked with divine creation?

The question is most easily answered if we consider human activity. Human activity in the natural world is for the most part also a mathematically describable gnomon subject to necessity. Even methodical work is ultimately subject to necessity in this way, since the human will, which determines the goal of work, is under necessity. The one exception, however, is that which appears in the act of mind by which humans think necessity under its conditional (that is, mathematical) aspect. Here the thinker "is not present under any heading, he has no part in it outside the very process by which he thinks it"(IC 181). This is to say, the mind itself is not forced when dealing with conditional necessity to think it in any particular way determined by necessity; rather, mind *comprehends* conditional necessity and necessity is only present to mind in the mind's act of thinking things according to necessity. For the mind "the purely conditional progression of necessity is the progression of demonstration itself"(IC 181). At this level "necessity is for man no longer either an enemy or a master"(IC 181), for necessity does not stand above the mind, as it does over the will, determining its function. But neither is any human the master of necessity at this level, for in thinking necessity, one does not and cannot change it.

When intellectual attention rises to contemplate the necessary order of the world, it still only produces half of reality, for it only produces the ordered mathematical necessity under which things operate. It does not see nor does it consent to the purpose of necessity. Nevertheless, intellectual attention is extremely valuable for the human being, because "mathematical necessity is an intermediary between the whole natural part of man which is corporeal and psychical matter and the infinitely small portion of himself which does not belong to this world"(IC 182). It is this intermediary because at one and the same time the faculty that thinks mathematical necessity thinks this world and yet is not of this world. It is also this intermediary because when the mind reproduces reality under its ordered mathematical aspect, it forms the object to which we may give our supernatural consent. Thus we may pass from this side of the heavens to the other side, and from order to purpose:

> This liberty is not actual in him except when he conceives of force as necessity, that is to say, when he contemplates it. He is not free to consent to force as such. The slave who sees the lash lifted above him does not consent, nor refuse his consent, he trembles. And yet under the name of necessity it is indeed to brute force that man consents, and when he consents it is indeed to a lash.(IC 182)

It can now be seen that humans through the mediation of their intellectual activity can pass beyond the limits of creaturely relations to a friendship of persons in God. This leads Weil to conclude, "Just as the Christ is, on one hand, the mediator between God and man, and on the other the mediator between man and his neighbor, so mathematical necessity is on one hand the mediator between God and things, and on the other between each thing and every other thing"(IC 185).

These conclusions raise two important questions, which have to be answered before the relations of necessity are completely illuminated: (1) What is the relation between the unitary order of necessity, which we think, and diverse things under that order? This is to say, how can there be a singly (and therefore unchanging) order to becoming, even if the individual parts of becoming are mathematically describable? (2) What is the status of this mathematical order of necessity to the purpose of the divine good? How can necessity, which is not goodness, mediate goodness?

Order means, Weil notes, equilibrium and immobility. The universe, however, is a perpetual becoming, which stands opposed to equilibrium, since the becoming of any one thing must rupture the equilibrium. Nevertheless, she says, the becoming *as a whole* can be an equilibrium "because the ruptures of equilibrium compensate each other. This becoming is equilibrium refracted in time"(IC 185).

Each little thing, each little gnomon of activity, includes a principle of destruction of a previously existing order, and on the natural level, its relation to other things is a relation of one force trying to overcome another. But each gnomon also has a relation to things through the order of the world. Each thing, by virtue of the fact that it is a gnomon, is a limited entity. And it is this entity and not another. This limit, which makes it what it is, then "puts it in relation to an equal and inverse rupture of equilibrium"(IC 186). No thing is ever an unlimited quantity that can ceaselessly expand, for it is constantly being acted upon as it acts, and this prescribes a certain limit to its activity. The actual limit of each thing's activity, however, comes from and is incorporated into an invariant union, which is the network of all limits. This network, or order, is what Weil calls the order of the world. This order, though, is not to be confused with its particular determinations, since it is the invariant determinate of all variations. In this sense, each thing as a force has its own proper existence as it seeks to expand itself, but it also has another aspect in which it is confined and obeys the overall order through remaining within its assigned limits. The fact that each thing is, is because it acts as a force, but the fact that it is this force and not another, nor can become another, is because of the world order.

This gives us two distinct aspects to the world—there is matter and there is order. But since there are two distinct aspects to the world, there are also two distinct relations of necessity, for "we conceive of God's will with regard to necessity, and with regard to matter, as being two different relationships" (IC 186). The two relations, nevertheless, are connected. God's will with respect to matter is that it should be governed and ordered by necessity. In this regard, insofar as things keep within their assigned limits with respect to other things, they are obeying necessity. Indeed as natural things they literally have no choice but to obey necessity; this includes humans in their natural relations. On this level there is no question of divine goodness, for things are what necessity makes them. But there is a second relationship, which is God's will with respect to the governing necessity; namely, that it should reflect perfectly the divine goodness. On *this* level, necessity as the overarching order of the world is the Soul of the World and the only begotten Son.

The two relations should not be confused, for they account for the difference between necessity and goodness. If things obey necessity, they do so because it is their nature to act as they do. While it is true that in obeying necessity, things are indirectly obeying God, this does not alter the sense that they are doing so blindly. On the level of obedience to necessity, there is no communion with God. Divine goodness implies communion, and in this sense, no one can claim divine goodness simply because he or she acts within the world order. The order as a whole is good, because it directly obeys God, but it does so because of its particular relation to God. It is his Son crucified.

Humans are in a peculiar position, since they can participate in the two separate relationships at once. As natural created beings they are bound in all their empirical relationships to obey necessity. At the same time they are also spiritual creatures who are meant to participate in communion with God. These two relationships are not without connection, however, for through the intermediary of intellect they can be united and harmonized in one being. By an act of mind, a human being can stand on a level with necessity when he or she contemplates it. When she or he does so, she or he is no longer simply the object of necessity, but neither is a communion established with God. What does happen, however, is that by no longer obeying necessity as a thing, she or he has the opportunity through grace to consent to it freely as the Son does and thus participate in the Mediator. This is something that what is purely matter cannot do. Humans thus can understand and consent to the relation of necessity to God, as well as physically participating in the obedience of matter to necessity.

————————

We can now see that necessity in Weil embodies a threefold set of relations that is extremely similar to the set of relations in Plato's *Timaeus*. We can see in her view of necessity a sort of *apeiron* of forces that receives form. When it is formed, it gives rise to the gnomons of matter, which are obedient to a mathematical necessity. Like Plato, Weil even recognizes what has been called the brute facts of matter, which appear when they regard necessity by the natural intelligence and find that it gives no account of its final purpose, at least for the natural intelligence. We can also see that this necessity, which things obey, is under another aspect obedient to the Good. Therefore at this transcendent level, through its obedience to the good, it mediates the beneficent purpose of God to the creation as a whole. This too is also found in the *Timaeus*.

We can now see that the concept of necessity involves a number of distinct relations that must be kept in proper order. We can also see why necessity presents two faces to us, for when we stand under necessity alone, we not only *perceive* ourselves to be in a different relation to it than when we regard it from the heavens, we actually are in a different relation to both it and God. How that is treated as a spiritual matter is the subject of the next chapter.

At this point, though, we have at least come so far as to be able to recognize just how Plato can help us better to see Weil's account of creation and necessity. There are, of course, differences between her and Plato. Weil's explicit Christianity, for instance, causes her to differentiate more sharply between intelligence and supernatural consent. She also makes more explicit who the Soul of the World is and how he performs that function in obedience to the will of the Father. But it is now plain that Plato is not only an inspiration for Weil, but also a directing influence as well, since he provides the structure of mediated relations by which Weil is able to reconcile those concepts, which she calls contrary and incommensurate, such as necessity, matter, and the Good. By careful analysis of Plato, then, we can make further sense of Weil.

Before concluding, however, an important question remains to be answered, which concerns the status of the *apeiron* or unlimited. The reason for Plato's positing of it seems clear in that he wished to give some explanation for why there is generation and corruption in a world that is supposedly created by an eternal and unitary being. In this sense, it is not a principle of evil (as some later Platonists and gnostics thought), but is simply used to account for the apparent disharmony in the world. It is therefore a principle by which we can assert that the world is other than God. This, however, leads Plato to a theological dilemma. Either there exists something in its own right other than God, which can oppose God, in which case there is an irreducible dualism; or the *apeiron* is not an active principle, in which case it seems to be an irrelevant hypothesis, for it can offer no resistance to God's purposes.

This dilemma also applies to Weil and perhaps even more so. Whereas "chaos" might have been an acceptable way of describing an aspect of creation in the ancient world and whereas creation *ex nihilo* was an unknown idea, Weil understands that the myth of original chaos is "inevitably defective." She also apparently believed in a creation *ex nihilo*. She does provide, though, an adequate answer to this problem, and in doing so adds something to the way in which we in the modern world can read Plato.

In the beginning, Weil says, God out of his goodness wished to create. But he did not want to create more of himself; instead he wanted to see an independent creation come into existence. She says: "God *thought* that which did not exist, and by this thought he brought it into being"(WG 149). In a strong theological sense, this nothing that God thought is the stuff out of which we are made. In another related sense it is also the basis of matter, at least insofar as matter is differentiated from a purely ideal set of relations. It therefore gives us a life independent from God and it is to this independent existence that God gives life through form and order by the sacrifice of the Son. In a similar way we are to give our life to that which has not the marks of existence, such as the afflicted, and thus be reunited to God.

Thus there is not any question of a sort of Manichaean dualism prevailing here. The nonbeing of which we are made is not a principle opposed to God and coeternal with him. It is the condition of our having any existence at all. Weil says: "Matter: something which is not spirit, something which is not God. What an extraordinary phenomenon! It is thanks to Matter that creatures like ourselves have being"(NB 405). But furthermore it is not irrelevant in the sense of not being able to resist God's action, for God in creating sets out to create independent beings. This independence, which he has willed, is a condition and the matter upon which he must work. The condition is one that he has set for himself and by his continual respect for it he has created a world in which there is brute fact for which no explanation can be given. Yet God in respecting this aspect of creation does not desert creation and leave it without his goodness. Instead, he gives it order and life in the form of his Son crucified upon the whole of time and space, and in this way gently persuades matter to goodness. Through this persuasion the necessity of the world becomes obedient to God's purpose. And the *Logos* becomes mediator between God and his creation in whom we may pass from life separated from God to life in God.

This much, in all its complex detail, is the structure of the concept of necessity in Weil. We shall now turn in the next chapter to what has been called the importance of the "regard we bring to bear upon it."

4. THE CONCEPT OF READING AND THE BOOK OF NATURE

THIS CHAPTER HAS two principal concerns. First, it seeks to examine Simone Weil's concept of reading (or *lecture*) from the point of view of its interconnections with other concepts in her thought—namely, necessity, order, suffering, work, and decreation. This will help show how her thoughts are organized, which for the study of Simone Weil should be of particular concern, since she so prized order.

The second concern is with the natural world. From the earliest writings and practices of the Eastern Christian Churches, from which it spread to the West, it was believed that God could be known from two principle sources: the Book of Scripture and the Book of Nature. The visible things of nature were thought to be an adumbration of the invisible God, and it was thought possible "to discern, in and through each created reality, the divine presence that is within and at the same time beyond it. It is to treat each thing as a sacrament, to view the whole of nature as God's book."[1]

We hear more than an echo of this tradition in Simone Weil's remark:

> As one has to learn to read, or to practice a trade, so one must learn to feel in all things, first and almost solely, the obedience of the universe to God . . . For us, this obedience of things in relation to God is what the transparency of a window pane

is in relation to light. As soon as we feel this obedience with our whole being, we see God. (SNL 180, 199)

According to Weil, we are always reading events and people, since all that we are aware of is invested with meaning. We shall find that for Weil the *meaning* of some things, such as a letter to a mother announcing the death of her son, can have the same effect or impact as a physical sensation caused by a fist blow to the stomach. So too can an adequate reading of nature cause a person to be powerfully but joyfully gripped by God's loving presence.

The conviction that nature mediates the divine presence virtually disappeared in Western civilization with the rise of classical physics in the early modern period. First, nature was viewed as a machine and God's existence was posited to account for the apparent design in nature (deism). Later, nature widely came to be viewed as the ultimate reality. Today, even believing academic theologians have little to say about nature mediating God's presence. In Protestant Christianity, nature as a source of knowledge of God and as part of the exercise of a spirituality that leads to intimate contact with God largely disappeared with the collapse of Hegel's philosophy of nature in Germany, and with the rise of Darwinism in the English-speaking world.

The concept of "reading" and the idea that nature manifests God come together in an examination of how Simone Weil attempts to restore or make plausible for us today a supernatural reading of nature. These two concerns are clearly connected in Weil's thought. For example, in the passage just quoted, in which Weil points out that when nature's obedience is fully felt, we see God, she refers immediately to some of the same images—a blind man's stick, and a penholder—to explain what she means by the concept of reading in her "Essay on the Notion of Reading."

A major concern of Simone Weil's life after she had a visitation by Christ was to experience the presence of God in all things. For example, she desires

A life in which the supernatural truths would be read in every kind of work, in every act of labour, in all festivals, in all hierarchical social relation, in all art, in all science, in all philosophy. (FLN 173)

At the core of the realization of this ambition is the development of the concept of reading, and in particular learning to read nature's operations religiously. This involves a recognition that many readings are debased readings, as the following passage indicates:

> Contemplation of eternal truths in the symbols offered by the stars and the combination of substances. Astronomy and chemistry are degradations of them. When astrology and alchemy become forms of magic they are still lower degradations of them. Attention only reaches its true dimensions when it is religious (GG, 120)

THE CONCEPT OF READING

The concept of reading can found throughout Weil's writings, but only one short essay of a few pages is devoted exclusively to it—namely, the "Essay on the Notion of Reading." In this essay, she takes it that we are already language users and literate. She seeks to define a notion that she calls "reading," because it is analogous to actual reading. When we read a book or a newspaper, we have black marks on white paper. But these marks are hardly, if at all, noticed, and if they are, their intrinsic features, such as the color of the ink and paper, are usually a matter of indifference to us. What matters is the meaning that we read. Furthermore, the meaning seems to be given directly. "We are not given sensations and meanings; only what we read is given; we do not see the letters" (ER 298).[2] Weil notes in passing that this is why proofreading is difficult.

Weil claims that the example of the blind man's stick, as found in Descartes, in which a blind man knows through a stick what is beyond his body, is "analogous to reading" (ER 298). She writes (switching to the example of a penholder to make the same point):

> Everyone can convince himself in handling a penholder that to use it is as if one is carried to the end of the pen. If the pen runs into some unevenness in the paper, the skip of the pen is immediately given, and the sensations of the fingers and hand across which we read it never even appear. And yet the skip of the pen is only something that we read.(ER 298)

The sensations in the fingers and hand like the black marks on white paper are hardly, if at all, noticed. It is as if we are *directly* in contact with what is at the end of the pen—namely, the unevenness of the surface of the paper on which we are writing. The unevenness is what we "read," just as the meaning of the shapes is what we read when we look at black marks on white paper. Meaning is not an intrinsic feature of signs or words; this is why the black marks on white paper are barely noticed.

We are not, of course, actually reading with a pen in precisely the same sense that we read a book or a newspaper. But it is analogous to actual reading, as the black marks on white paper in one case, and feelings in the fingers and hand on the other, are not attended to. Something else is attended to as if it is directly given (meaning, in the one case, and the unevenness of the paper's surface, in the other).

Simone Weil shows that the analogy is so strong that the name reading is suitable for every moment of our awareness. She does this by comparing the effects of actual reading to the effects of physical causes, and shows that every moment of awareness exhibits the same effects. Although black marks on white paper are themselves often not noticed or are matters of indifference when we are reading a book or newspaper, they may have the power to affect us in the same way as a fist blow to the stomach or touching something hot with our hand:

> A man receives, without being ready for it, a fist blow to the stomach; everything changes for him before he knows what has happened to him. I touch a burning object; I feel myself jumping before knowing I am burnt. Something takes hold of me. It is in this way that the universe treats me and I know it by this treatment. (ER 297)

Actual reading has some similarities to the reflex action of doubling up when unexpectedly hit in the stomach or jumping when burnt by a hot object. It is involuntary, and it is immediate. For a moment, what is real takes the whole person over; it grips one:

> One is not surprised by the power of blows, burns, and sudden noise to grip us; for we know or believe ourselves to know that comes from without, from matter, and the mind has no part in it, except to submit to it. The thoughts that form us impose emotions on us, but do not grip us so. (ER 297)

Weil stresses that our thoughts can cause us to feel emotions, but such emotions do not grip us as do the feelings that come from blows and burns. We are not surprised that the feelings caused by blows and burns grip us, because we are aware that they are caused by something outside us. But reading, in contrast to mere thinking, can have effects that are comparable to being hit by a fist in the stomach or touching a hot object:

> Some black strokes on white paper, that is very different from a fist blow in the stomach. But sometimes the effect is the same. Everyone has more or less experienced the effect of bad news that one receives in reading a letter or newspaper; one feels gripped, upset, as by a blow. (ER 297)

In addition, it is as if the pain dwelt in the bit of paper itself, just as the burning dwells in a hot object:

> Sometimes when time has lulled the pain a little, if the letter suddenly appears among the papers one is handling, a more vivid pain surges, also gripping as if it came from without, as if it dwelt in this bit of paper in the way burning swells in the fire. (ER 297)

Weil claims that black strokes on a page, because of their meaning, may affect us in the same way as physical causes:

> Two women each receive a letter announcing to each that her son is dead; the one faints at her first glance at the paper, and never again until she dies will her eyes, her mouth, her movements, be as they were. The second remains the same, her look, her bearing does not change; she does not know how to read. (ER 297f)

Weil draws the following moral:

> It is not the sensation [black strokes on white paper], it is the meaning that has gripped the first woman, in attacking the mind immediately, brutally, without her taking part, in the way that sensations [resulting from a fist blow or hot object] grip. All happens as if the pain dwelt in the letter, and leaped from the letter to the face of her who reads it. (ER 298)

Yet the pain does not reside in the black marks on white paper. And as far as the visual sensations themselves are concerned—the blackness of the ink and the whiteness of the paper—they are not even noticed. "What is given to sight is pain" (ER 298). All the examples Weil gives in the "Essay" tend to evoke strong emotions: pain, hatred, fear, a sense of being menaced. But reading is not limited to strong emotions, since we are always reading, and we of course do not always feel strong emotions. Nonetheless, we constantly feel ourselves gripped by reality.

"It is in this way that at every instant of our life we are gripped as if from without by the meanings that we ourselves read in appearances" (ER 298). It is not as if there is "an appearance and an interpretation" (ER 299). What is given to us is meaning, and we are *always* reading. It is as if the entire world is like the contents of a book. "The sky, the sea, the sun, the stars, human beings, all that surrounds us is in the same way something that we read" (ER 298f.). What is given to us is like what is given when we read from a newspaper or from a book:

> Even should we misread, we simply replace a misreading by a more adequate one. What is called a corrected illusion of the senses is a modified reading. If in an empty road at night I believe I see not a tree but a man in ambush, a human and menacing presence imposes itself on me and, as in the case of the letter, makes me tremble before I even know what is the matter; I go nearer and suddenly all is different, I no longer tremble, I read a tree and not a man. There was not an appearance and an interpretation; a human presence had penetrated by my eyes into my soul, and now suddenly the presence of a tree. (ER 299)

Weil stresses not only that we are always reading but also that the readings are involuntary and imposed on us:

> The meanings that considered abstractly seem to be simple thoughts spring up on all sides around me, take hold of my soul and change it from moment to moment in such a way that, to translate a familiar English expression, I cannot say that my soul is my own. I believe what I read, how could I do otherwise? If in a noise I read honor to be won, I run toward this noise; if I read danger and nothing else, I run away from it. In the two cases, the necessity of acting like this, even if I feel regret, imposes itself in me in an evident and manifest way, like the noise, with the noise; I read it in the noise. (ER 300)

We are gripped as if from without by the meanings that we ourselves read in appearances. "So one can debate endlessly the reality of the external world" (ER 298). Weil says that this points to a contradiction. *"For what we call the world, that is the meanings we read; this is therefore not real. However this grips us as if from without; this is therefore real"* (ER 298 [Allen translation]).

The suggestion that the world is the meaning we read and therefore not real is misleading. We are not to think of Kantian categories or schemata that render the world phenomenal and utterly block access to noumenal reality. Nor are we to think that Weil means to imply a relativism, in which social and cultural forces lead to a variety of readings and a variety of worlds, with no way to adjudicate between various socially determined readings or worlds. Her remark must be read in conjunction with her claim that we are *gripped* by meaning and what grips us is real. We see here the importance of what she chose to compare to reading. The parallel she draws between reading the unevenness of a piece of paper with the tip of a pen and reading black marks on white paper indicates that just as the former is contact with what is real, so too is the latter. The contrast between mere thinking and reading makes the same point. Mere thinking can arouse feelings, but they do not grip us as does reading. Finally, reading is compared to the sensations caused by an unexpected blow to the stomach and indicates that reading too is a contact with what is outside ourselves. Our world is the meaning we read; that we are gripped indicates that we are in contact with reality.

Both sides of the apparent contradiction ("this is therefore not real . . . this is therefore real") are important. Taken together they indicate that we read from a particular level. The meanings we receive are not always false. Given a level, often what we read is indeed what ought to be read from such a level. Painful and pleasurable sensations as such, for example, are not illusions. But because they are read from a limited perspective, they are not an adequate reading of reality. Nonetheless, we are gripped by reality.

The apparent contradiction between meaning not being real and the fact that in reading we are gripped by what is real is, therefore, resolved by the recognition that our readings are from a perspective. But we must take this contradiction into account because it impels us toward a more comprehensive perspective whereby we may, on the one hand, read more adequately, and on the other hand, understand why readings that form a limited perspective are indeed legitimate, if inadequate, readings. This is what lies behind Weil's rhetorical question, "Why wish to resolve this contradiction, when the highest task of thought on this earth is to define and to contemplate the insoluble contradictions that, as Plato says, draw us upward?" (ER 298). To be drawn upward is to be drawn to a more comprehensive perspective. What is needed is more adequate readings of that with which we are in contact, not an abolition of meanings, so that we have things-in-themselves, apart from meanings.[3]

But how are we drawn upward? By an apprenticeship that modifies our readings. When our apprenticeship is complete, we not only read differently, but we can understand how less comprehensive or inadequate readings come to be made:[4]

> I have also perhaps a power to change the meanings that I read in appearances and that impose themselves on me; but this power is also limited, indirect and exercised by work. Work in the ordinary sense of the term is an example of it, for each tool is a blind man's stick, an instrument for reading, and each apprenticeship is an apprenticeship in reading. When an apprenticeship is complete, meanings appear at the end of my pen, or a phrase in printed characters. For the sailor, the experienced captain, whose boat has become a sense to him like an extension of his body, the boat is an instrument for reading the storm and he reads it quite otherwise than the passenger does. Where the passenger reads chaos, limitless danger, fear, the captain reads necessities, limited dangers, resources for escaping them, and obligation of courage and honor. (ER 301f.)

The captain, because he has gone through an apprenticeship, is able to read more adequately than the passenger; for though there is danger, and fear in the face of danger is appropriate, the danger is not limitless, because the captain knows what can be done to avert it. The captain is able to give a more adequate reading of the reality that grips both passenger and captain. Though our world is the meaning we read, what is important is to rise to a higher level that enables us to make more adequate readings—that is, to receive other and more adequate meanings.

There are even higher levels than that occupied by an experienced captain, whose perspective enables him to make a more adequate reading of a storm than a passenger can. The higher levels reveal different and progressively more sophisticated meanings concerning the natural world; and these meanings are superimposed on each other. We are able "to read necessity behind sensations, to read order behind necessity, to read God behind order" (GG 123). To make each of these readings is to have moved to a higher level, and to receive the meanings imposed on us by that level or perspective. It should therefore be clear that readings depend on the level we are on. Given the level we are considering, the readings we have are the readings we ought to have. As we will see, they are not idiosyncratic, nor social constructs, nor one perspective out of many in the sense we use "perspectives" in a context in which we rely on the various perspectives given by a multidisciplinary approach.

Crucial to the highest reading is the ability to read nature's order as obedience to God. When we see the order of nature as obedience to God, then the natural world becomes *transparent*, as is a windowpane, and we see God.

One of the greatest obstacles to this reading is the suffering caused by the operations of the natural world. Suffering seems to contradict or at least count against the idea that the source of the universe is the Christian God. It is here that Weil stresses that in reading, the medium through which we read is itself hardly, if at all, noticed, and if it is, we are indifferent to it. The sensations of pain, as well as pleasure, are the result of the obedience of the natural world to the will of God. Painful sensations caused by untoward events can be a barrier between us and the love of God. But if we learn to read our sensation otherwise, the natural world's operations, which because they cause us pain act as a barrier between us and the love of God, actually become a passageway.

In the essay "The Love of God and Affliction," immediately after Weil speaks of nature becoming transparent to God as a windowpane is to light, she says that we have to learn how to read before black strokes on white paper have meaning. Likewise, a captain must learn to read the swell of waves for them to have a different meaning than they do for a passenger. She then applies this to learning to read God through the sensations of pain:

> As one has to learn to read, or to practice a trade so one must learn to feel in all things, first and almost solely, the obedience of the universe to God. It is truly an apprenticeship; and like every apprenticeship it calls for time and effort. For the man who has finished his training the differences between things or between events are no more important than those perceived

by someone who knows how to read when he has before him the same sentence repeated several times, in red ink and blue, and printed in this, that, and the other kind of type. The man who cannot read sees only the differences. For the man who can read it all comes to the same thing, because the sentence is the same. Whoever has finished his apprenticeship recognizes things and events, everywhere and always, as vibrations of the same divine and infinitely sweet word. Which is not to say he will not suffer. Pain is the colour of certain events. When a man who can and a man who cannot read look at a sentence written in red ink they both seen something red; but the red colour is not so important for the one as for the other. (SNL 180)

In the opening of *Waiting for God*, Weil says we must love absolutely the entire universe as a whole and in each detail, including evil in all its forms, and she uses her frequent image of a penholder to explain in what sense she intends this astounding claim to be understood:

In other words, we must feel the reality and presence of God through all external things, without exception, as clearly as our hand feels the substance of paper through the penholder and the nib. (WG 44)

In *The Need for Roots*, Weil uses as an example the meeting of two dear friends after a long separation. The friends embrace each other so hard that it hurts them. But the pain is a mark of their love for each other. So too God sometimes embraces us through the grip of the universe very hard, causing pain, but those who have completed their apprenticeship, know that it is love that grips them through the universe and, because of their detachment, they are indifferent to the pain they feel, and attend only to the love of God (NR 289).

She makes the same point with her example of a beloved waiting for a message from a lover. It does not matter whether the message when it comes is gruff; it is still treasured because it is a message from a lover. To one who has completed an apprenticeship, the pain that results from the medium of God's presence is a matter of indifference or is discounted, because there is indirect contact with divine love.

The mystery of reading is that meaning is *given* to us, by all that surrounds us. We do not create these readings; they are involuntary and are imposed on us at each level. And they are not present in the media that convey them to us (anymore that they are in the penholder, or in the sensations in the fingers of the hands). We are not really, for example, at the far end of the penholder, yet we are in contact with what is there. Even should we not read fully or adequately what is there, we are always gripped by reality. Our task is to undergo various apprenticeships so that we are capable of receiving more comprehensive readings. And we can rise to higher levels so that more adequate and more comprehensive readings replace limited ones. To read from the level of our sensations, as does a passenger, is a much more limited perspective than to read necessity behind sensations, as does a captain. Ultimately, when we read order behind necessity and God behind order, nature becomes transparent to the presence of God.

In the "Essay on the Notion of Reading," Weil says she sought "to define a notion that has not received a suitable name, and to which the name reading may be fitting" (ER 297). She raises several questions which she does not there resolve. Perhaps the most important is the nature of the apprenticeship that enables us to rise to higher levels so as both to receive more adequate readings and to be able to distinguish more adequate readings from less adequate ones. We will describe this apprenticeship by an examination of how we can learn to read nature as obedience to God's will or, in other words, see how we modify our readings and in particular how we achieve a supernatural reading of the world.

A SUPERNATURAL READING OF THE NATURAL WORLD

We will describe the apprenticeship that leads to higher levels and more adequate readings by explicating Weil's remarks that we are "to read necessity behind sensations, to read order behind necessity, to read God behind order."

Weil is concerned with the way truths from different levels make their way into our awareness. In the "Essay on the Notion of Reading" the effects of the ego on reading are ignored. But Weil believes that most of our thoughts and actions are self-centered. We stand at the center with all other people and events in orbit around ourselves. Everything is seen from our perspective and evaluated, understood, and thought about in such a way as to enhance, comfort, or protect ourselves. We do this as automatically as matter and energy perform their operations. This self-centeredness causes us to read people, events, and nature incorrectly (WG 158–60; GG 122).

One way in which self-centeredness can be punctured is by the operations of the natural world. Its reality impinges on our bodies. We are material beings, and as material beings we are subject to wear and tear, accidents, illnesses, aging, and death. When one of these impinges on us, our usual way of responding is egocentric. We say or think, "Why did this happen to me?" "What did I ever do wrong?" This is often said or felt with a sense of indignation, outrage, offense, self-pity. These are just a sample of a host of quite automatic and normal reactions to adversity.

These automatic responses can be the occasion for *reflection*. They can be the occasion to ask oneself: "Why did I think I was immune to such misfortune?" "Why did I think that pleasant and unpleasant things are parceled out according to some scheme of merit?" Such reflections can lead us to recognize more fully something we already know: we are material, and as pieces of matter, we are vulnerable to injury, illness, and decay. To realize this is to realize our status, our place, to realize what we are. It is to come to terms with a hard fact. Indeed, it is to come to terms with necessity.

Adverse contact with matter helps free us from inadequate readings caused by our egocentricity. It brings us closer to reality. To recognize that we are vulnerable pieces of matter, and that this is an inescapable fact about us, is to read *necessity* behind our sensations. It is to perceive the operations of the natural world as indifferent to our welfare. "The absence of finality is the reign of necessity. Things have causes not ends" (WG 176–77).

As we saw in the previous chapter, Simone Weil's understanding of the necessity of nature is not equivalent to the way present-day scientific laws are understood. Descartes argued that matter consists of extension and that its motions are describable by the necessary relations of geometry. Matter is completely transparent to thought. For Weil, like Plato, it is not (see chapter 3, above). She uses the ancient Greek distinction between the unlimited and limit. The unlimited is brute force, the stuff of nature. Limits are geometric ratios and proportions. The natural world is a cosmos— that is, an ordered and beautiful whole because of geometric ratios and proportions. The mind can grasp ratios; nature apart from ratios is not capable of being grasped by the mind. This means that the stuff of brute material force, the unlimited, is unthinkable. In addition, the ratios or limits that enable the universe to be cosmos, orderly as a whole and in its parts, are themselves immaterial. This ought to be evident in present-day science:

> The operations of the intellect in scientific study makes sovereign necessity over matter appear to the mind as a network of relations which are immaterial and without force. Necessity can only be perfectly conceived so long as such relations appear as absolutely immaterial. (NR 290)

This analysis of the natural world in terms of the unlimited and limits enables Weil to make a transition to the world's operations as exhibiting obedience to God:

> Forces in this world are supremely determined by necessity; necessity is made up of relations which are thoughts; consequently, the force that is supreme in the world is under the supreme domination of thought. (NR 191)

One of the controversial issues of the modern world has been the question whether we need to make reference to an intelligent source of the order of the universe, or whether the laws of nature, which science discovers, account for the operations of the natural world without any need to infer an intelligent source. In this dispute most attention has been devoted to the argument from design.

According to the argument from design, the order of the universe so strongly resembles artifacts designed by human beings that it is probable that the universe has been designed. Now and again among the discoveries of science, some arrangement is discovered for which no scientific explanation is available. The only options seem to be that the arrangement is the result either of chance or of superhuman design. But when a scientific explanation for the arrangement is eventually found, *both* chance and design are dropped. Scientific explanations of natural phenomena by eliminating chance seem to eliminate the grounds for inferring superhuman intelligence to account for them.

To claim, as Weil does, that nature consists of a network of necessary relations also seems to eliminate the possibility of supreme intelligence as the source of nature's order. For to show that the relations are necessary seems to have reached a terminus of explanations. If the relations are necessary, in the sense that they could not be other than they are, then the reason they are as they are is because there is no alternative.

But Simone Weil does not rely on the argument from design, nor does she use the term "necessity" in the sense that the relations between members of the universe (the laws of nature) logically cannot be other than they are. They are necessary in the sense that human beings are subject to them, and human beings are not their source and cannot alter them. But this does not mean that the natural world is the ultimate or final reality. The crucial point for Weil is that the necessary relations we grasp with our minds in our study of nature are *immaterial*.

This is easier to see if we think in terms of pure mathematics, and in particular pure geometry. A line in pure geometry is without any physical force, and unlike any line we draw, it has no width. It cannot be sensed; it is conceivable only in thought. The immaterial relations described in pure geometry are necessary relations, and only in thought do we have the relations of logical necessity. Yet it is by means of geometric relations that we grasp the natural world and understand its operations. The pure relations themselves have no force, yet the material forces of the world are subject to them.

Simone Weil's reasoning, therefore, seems to be as follows. Matter as such is unthinkable. What makes nature thinkable is the logically necessary relations of mathematics, especially geometry. But logically necessary relations are the product of thought, not matter. This means that matter, which is unlimited or indeterminate, is encountered as formed in a harmonious and orderly cosmos, because it is governed by relations that are themselves immaterial and the product of intelligence. The brute force of nature is under the supreme direction of thought or mind:

> Brute force is not sovereign in this world. It is by nature blind and indeterminate. What is sovereign in this world is determinateness, limit. Eternal Wisdom imprisons this universe in a network, a web of determinations. The universe accepts passively. The brute force of matter, which appears to us sovereign, is nothing else in reality but perfect obedience. . . . That is the truth which bites at our hearts every time we are penetrated by the beauty of the world. That is the truth which bursts forth in matchless accents of joy in the beautiful parts of the Old Testament, in Greece among the Pythagoreans and all the sages, in China with Laotse, in the Hindu scriptures, in Egyptian remains. (NR, 285)

The necessary relations that produce a cosmos—that is, a harmonious, balanced set of relations—are evident to our senses in the beauty or splendor of the universe. When the operations of nature hurt us, we are aware of nature's brute force. When the operations are pleasant to us, we do not notice its brute force. But if nature were nothing but brute necessity, and not beautiful and obedient to God, we could not love it as a totality. We would hate nature when it hurt us. But we are able to modify this reading.

When our thoughts are not dominated by our desires and needs, we may see nature as perfectly obedient to God and its operations as the results of Eternal Wisdom. Brute force is ordered by thought, but clearly not by human thought. We are subject to nature's force, and we can modify it to achieve our ends to a very limited degree, as does a ship's captain. But as thinking beings, we are on the same side as that which dominates nature's force. This happens when we detach ourselves sufficiently from our egocentrism to see nature as a network of necessary relations. The human mind is then not subject to force: to being driven by lower readings of its pleasures and pains, desires, and wants. The human mind is functioning so that it is subject only to truth. It is then that the human mind is grasped by Eternal Wisdom; Eternal Wisdom is perceived in the universe as the balance of necessary relations, and enjoyed in the beauty of the universe. Beauty is the radiance of truth:

> So long as man submits to having his soul taken up with his own thoughts, his personal thoughts, he remains entirely subjected, even in his most secret thoughts, to the compulsion exercised by needs and to the mechanical play of forces. If he thinks otherwise, he is mistaken. But everything changes as soon as, by virtue of a positive act of concentration, he empties his soul so as to allow the conceptions of eternal Wisdom to enter into it. He then carries within himself the very conception to which force is subjected. . . . He is certainly not lord and master of creation . . . but he is the master's son, and the child of the house. . . . A little child belonging to a wealthy home is in many respects under control of servants; but when he is sitting on his father's knees and identifies himself with him through love, he has shared in the father's authority. (NR 291)

MEANINGS SUPPLIED BY THE SOCIAL ORDER

Egocentrism and the suffering caused by the operations of the natural world are not the only reasons we do not read as accurately as we might. We must also rise above those meanings supplied by the social order, especially those meanings supplied by the social groups to which we belong, such as a Marxist trade union that invests events with revolutionary significance, or a fascist political party that invests a leader with messianic powers. As Rolf Kuehn puts it, "There has to be a *deconstruction* of all the received and elaborated meanings of the collective."[5]

Kuehn rightly places Weil in the tradition of Kantian Critical Philosophy. He cites Alain's comment on Weil's early essay, "Reflections on the Causes of Social Liberty and Oppression," that her work is "Kant continued." Kuehn reminds us that according to this tradition:

> Any perceived reality, including those of the historical and social fields, is based on constructed representations and that criticism of this power [faculty] requires a demonstration of a symbolizing "mechanism" which explains the signifying origin of what seems natural to immediate consciousness and ruling institutions. [6]

Simone Weil stresses the *constructed* nature of readings supplied by the collective in the social order, and exhibits the forces of egotism and "gravity" that produce these constructed representations, but she does not share Kant's view that appearances are phenomena that block access to noumenal reality, as we mentioned earlier.

To approach social institutions from the perspective of Critical Philosophy is indeed to continue Kant. But Weil is not unique in this. It has been done, and continues to be done, in various ways by different thinkers, most of whom are influenced by Hegel, Marx, and Nietzsche. Where Weil exhibits distinctiveness, perhaps, is that there is no demarcation of reason into "speculative" and "practical," with the passions essentially separated from both, as in Kant. This is perhaps most evident in concrete cases of perception, as in Weil's telling example of a French person who sees a Nazi soldier after the fall of France. What is read is not a soldier *and* hate; what is read is hate. (NB 1)

Simone Weil may also be said to represent an advance on Kant because it is from an analysis of some concrete situations that she gains access to what is not constructed by us. It is precisely the emotional effects produced by representations that enable us to realize that we are gripped by reality, even when our reading is inadequate.

Above all, by criticism we can find more adequate representations to give us more adequate readings. This is the basis of her objection to algebra. Algebra consists of a set of signs that are unsuitable for contact with reality. The signs and their transformations may give us accurate results, but the connections in reality between the operations of the signs and the results of the operations are not apparent to our minds. We do not have contact with reality through the signs used in the operations:

> Algebra: the method is in the signs, not in the mind . . . these automatic applications of method lead, of themselves to something new; so one invents without thinking—that is what is so bad. (FLN 27)

Simone Weil, therefore, preferred geometry to algebra, because it is conducive to readings that give us contact with the notion that nature consists of a tissue of limits and ratios, ideas which we have already seen are so rich in aesthetic and religious significance. She claims that it is the use of geometry by the ancient Greeks in their science that largely accounts for the intimations of Christianity among the Greeks.[7]

It is the same with our work in a complex economic system. We are paid for performing tasks, but the money we receive does not enable us to read the relations between our work and what our money can buy. Money is analogous to magic: money provides us with goods as an incantation executes a magician's wishes:

> We must accept that our actions shall be only *indirectly* connected with the satisfaction of needs; but let the intermediate stages be sufficiently few for the relation between cause and effect to be perceptible, although indirect. Aim: that the conditions of existence should be such that AS MUCH AS POSSIBLE IS PERCEIVED.
>
> People used to sacrifice to the gods, and the wheat grew. Today, one works at a machine and one gets bread from the baker's. The relation between the act and itsresults is no clearer than before.
>
> That is why the will plays so small a part in life today. We spend our time in *wishing*. (FLN 19)

Machines can also destroy thought, or take the place of thought. Instrumental machines, because they are adaptable for all sorts of tasks, are analogous to a sailor with his ship. But automatic machines leave a person nothing to do but to tend them. The thought it took to *design* the machine is now built into the machine, so to *operate* it requires no understanding of it and no genuine thinking. An automatic machine, like algebra and money, is not conducive to more adequate readings of reality. "Money, mechanization, algebra. Three monsters of contemporary civilization" (GG p139).

GRASPING AND BEING GRASPED

The "Essay on the Notion of Reading" is a late one. But we find Weil wrestling with the same problem of our knowledge of reality in her very early work on Descartes, *Science and Perception in Descartes*. In that diploma essay, Weil started from the side of thought or mind and progressed to knowledge of external reality through directed action. Four years later in her *Lectures on Philosophy*, she began at the opposite end. She tried to interpret all reality from a materialist point of view, until thought or mind, becomes evident from directed bodily movement or action. In the *Lectures* she pointed out that it is *concepts* that are used in a fashion analogous to a blind man's stick to give us a grip of the world. Concepts or thoughts employed by the body in manual work put one into contact with reality, just as a blind man's stick enables him to touch and feel, as if directly, the contours of the world. In manual work we use our minds and thoughts. In this fashion, although the contact is mediated contact, it is experienced as direct contact.

Personal or direct contact with reality took on a new dimension in the late "Essay on the Notion of Reading." Here it is not we who grasp reality, but reality that impinges on us and grips us. In the earlier writings that we have mentioned, freedom was understood primarily in terms of having an understanding of the operations needed to overcome some obstacle and to achieve some goal, and selecting the means to the goal, even if one did not have a say in the setting of the goal. This was before her experience of factory work, in which she learned that such limited freedom was impossible under the prevailing working conditions, especially with fragmentation of the work process and machine minding. Her experience with affliction led her to abandon her previous Kantian position that one could keep one's moral personality intact even in impossibly oppressive external conditions. One can be reduced to the point that one does not think that one has a right to any consideration (WG 66–67).

One indication of the effects of her religious conversion is the way it modified her view of how reality is to known—by being gripped—and her view of how individual human value can be sustained. Weil's religious conversion introduced her to a kind of force that elevates us, even though we are utterly subordinate to it. It modified her ideal of freedom. No longer is it modeled exclusively on the craftsperson. Now freedom is consent to being integrated into the flow of the created order. She cites the utter obedience of brute matter to the divine will as the image of perfect obedience. Manual work (along with death) are seen as the best ways of reentry into the flow of matter.

In *Waiting for God* Weil tells us that she had three vital contacts with Christianity. The first was in Portugal, where she witnessed a religious procession in a very poor fishing village. It made her realize that Christianity is preeminently a religion of slaves—that is, for people who are wretched. The second event took place in Italy at the church in Assisi devoted to St. Francis. She felt herself forced to her knees by a gracious love. Wretchedness and love came together in her third contact at Solesmes during Holy Week. While reciting George Herbert's poem "Love," at the culminating point of a violent headache, she had a vistitaion by Christ.

The visitation only half-convinced her mind, but the experience of a force she henceforth referred to as grace or love completely won her heart. It motivated her search for a religious understanding of reality, which would finally convince her mind. A way to deal with the question of God, which previously she considered to be an insoluble problem, eventually became evident. It was a matter of receiving or waiting, not of grasping but of being grasped.

Waiting, however, is not utter passivity. It involves the activity of an apprenticeship, of which suffering and manual work are a major part, and which modifies our readings:

> Man places himself outside the current of obedience. God chose as his punishments labor and death. Consequently, labor and death, if Man undergoes them in a spirit of willingness, constitute a transference back into the current of supreme Good, which is obedience to God.
>
> Death and labor are things of necessity and not of choice. The world only gives itself to man in the form of food and warmth if Man gives himself to the world in the form of labor. But death and labor can be submitted to either in an attitude of revolt or in one of consent. They can be submitted to either in their naked truth or else wrapped around with lies. (NR 300–301)

Our apprenticeship has as its result what Weil calls "decreation." Decreation is a rich notion with several aspects. The one that is particularly relevant to our concern with reading is that in decreation it is not we who do the reading. Rather, we ourselves become like a pencil, or a stick, or like marks on paper so God can perceive the created universe through us. Rather than God's streaming through the natural order to us as light through a windowpane, now it is we who become transparent as a windowpane for God's love to pass through us to other creatures:

> To be what the pencil is for me when, blindfold, I feel the table by means its point—to be that for Christ. It is possible for us to be mediators between God and the part of creation which is confined to us. Our consent is necessary in order that he may perceive his own creation through us. With our consent he performs this marvel. If I knew how to withdraw from my own soul it would be enough to enable this table in front of me to have the incomparable good fortune of being seen by God. God can love in us only this consent to withdraw in order to make way for him, just as he himself, our creator, withdrew in order that we might come into being. This double operation has not other meaning than love, it is like a father giving his child something which will enable the child to give a present on his father's birthday. God who is no other thing but love has not created anything other than love. (GG, 35–36)[8]

Weil is not speaking of annihilation. Rather it is that we are creatures of God, yet we live as though we are unrelated to God. "God allows me to exist outside himself. It is for me to refuse this authorization. Humility is the refusal to exist outside of God" (GG 35). God loves this refusal to use our power for self-expansion, since this is the acceptance of ourselves as God's creatures, dependent for our being on God's own. We refuse to live outside God.

We also think of ourselves as the prime value around which to judge the value of everything else, as it gratifies our wishes and desires. "The self is only the shadow of sin and error cast by stopping the light of God, and I take this shadow for a being" (GG 35).

It is this shadow that is to disappear in order that through our love for God, God's love may pass through us unhindered to his creatures, both human and nonhuman, in our vicinity:

As Creator, God is present in everything which exists as soon as its exists. The presence for which God needs the co-operation of the creature is the presence of God, not as creator but as Spirit. The first presence is the presence of creation. The second is the presence of decreation. (GG 33)

Paradoxically, the problem of individual worth finds its resolution here. We have such a limited perspective, responding to the universe on the level of our sensations of pain and pleasure, and to all things from ourselves as beings independent of God. We seek to elevate ourselves and thereby suffer debasement, by occupying too limited a place:

> A woman looking at herself in a mirror and adorning herself does not feel the shame of reducing the self, that infinite being which surveys all things, to a small space. In the same way every time that we raise the *ego* (the social *ego*, the psychological *ego*, etc.) as high as we raise it, we degrade ourselves to an infinite degree by confining ourselves to being no more than that. When the *ego* is abased (unless energy tends to raise it by desire), we know we are not that.
> A beautiful woman who looks at her reflection in the mirror can very well believe that she is that. An ugly woman knows that she is not that. (GG 29)

It is only by consenting to allow a universe to exist without the distortion of oneself that one can live in God and know God as Spirit, loved by God and loving the universe as God does. "I do not in the least wish that this created world should fade from my view, but that it should no longer be to me personally that it shows itself" (GG 37).

It is in *The Need for Roots*, in particular, that Weil develops the concept of this essential identity all of us share as the foundation for her social and political philosophy. It is because we have been made to receive God's presence as Spirit that we have absolute value, and this is also the reason we are all worthy of respect. (This will be examined in Part IV.)

Prior to her conversion, Weil had only known forces that restrict human freedom. Even on such an abstract philosophic topic as our knowledge of the external world, Weil read Descartes with an eye on the social oppression inherent in a division between the class of people who have the capacity and opportunity to know in terms of the dominant model of science, and those who are debarred from such knowledge because of the lack of capacity or opportunity. A different conception of science, one modeled on that of the thought and perception of a craftsperson, would enable all manual workers, were they allowed to organize their work, to have a degree of freedom from the social oppression of the savant.

But after her religious experience of a force that is gracious, nourishing, and uplifting, Weil came to see the network of relations that make up the universe as a symbol of divine love. Earlier we saw that, according to Weil, brute force is not sovereign in this world. Rather, the necessities of the universe are the result of limits imposed by an Eternal Wisdom. Brute force that is supreme *within* the world is *under* the supreme domination of thought. We can come to realize that nature is obedient to God when we empty ourselves of all personal thoughts, and thereby come to realize that nature is obedient to God, and thereby come to be obedient to Eternal Wisdom ourselves.

Decreation involves a nonreading. That is, as we become transparent to the divine love, we achieve such detachment that we notice only the divine love, paying no regard to all the readings from lower and less comprehensive perspectives, to which we could attend if we wished:

> We also find here the reason for the paradox that a perfect reading is impossible. To think of a reader of a true text that I do not read, that I have never read, is to think of a reader of this true text, that is to say God; but at once there appears a contradiction, for I cannot apply to the being that I conceive when I speak of God this notion of reading. (ER 302)

God does not read, because God does not have a perspective. When we, by our consent, become transparent to the divine love, we do not read. Because our reading is always from some level, and God, who does not read, knows reality perfectly, we have the paradox that a perfect reading is impossible.[9]

Finally, there is also a nonreading to be sought in relation to people. We are not to use people as extensions of ourselves to read the rest of the universe.

> The relationship between me and another man can never be analogous to the relationship between a blind man and his stick, nor to the inverse relationship either. (NB 24)

This is because another person is "another point of view under which all things appear" (NB 24). Another person is capable of giving his or her consent to God. We may not, therefore, seek to change their readings by force, whose extreme form is war, but only by education (NB 23–25; ER 302). To love another person is to feel with one's whole self the existence of another point of view able to consent to God. One does not read another in terms of accidents—for example, in terms of their appearance and their status in the social order—any more than we notice the color of ink in which a message is written.

SYMBOLS

According to Weil, there is another proof that nature's necessity is in actual fact obedience to God:

[The proof] consisted in the symbols attached to the relations themselves, as the signature of the painter is affixed to a picture. (NR 291)

Geometry thus becomes a double language, which at the same time provides information concerning the forces that are in action in matter, and talks about the supernatural relations between God and his creatures. It is like those ciphered letters which appear equally coherent before as after deciphering. (NR 292).

Today, science, history, politics, the organization of labor, religion even, in so far as it is marked by the Roman defilement, offer nothing to men's minds except brute force. Such is our civilization. (NR 295)

Similar remarks are to be found throughout Weil's writings, especially after her conversion. They are indeed very alien to our civilization today, and impossible to evaluate here. They call for a specific study in their own right. But at the very least they suggest a deeper way to study ancient Greek civilization, and indeed, the fables and myths of ancient cultures that she took so seriously. She believed, they showed that ancient peoples regarded the universe as mediating a reality not contained by it.

Simone Weil's more fundamental argument that nature's necessities are actually obedience to God, which we have considered, is less foreign and clearly quite plausible. We do see nature as a tissue of necessary relations, save on the quantum level, and mathematical relations are immaterial on all levels. Weil gives a religious reading of these facts by pointing out that since we are not masters of the universe, nature's necessities are not *our* thoughts, and the beauty that is a result of necessity calls forth our love. This line of reasoning enabled Weil to claim that, given the level from which they are made, various readings are accurate. Thus we may say:

> It is one and the same thing, which with respect to God is eternal Wisdom; with respect to the universe, perfect obedience; with respect to our love, beauty; with respect to our intelligence, balance of necessary relations; with respect to our flesh, brute force. (NR 295)

And given a person who can move successively from sensations to necessity, from necessity to order, from order to God, we have:

> A life in which the supernatural truths would be read in every kind of work, in every act of labor, in all festivals, in all hierarchal social relations, in all art, in all science, in all philosophy. (FLN 173)

5. WINCH ON
   WEIL'S SUPERNATURALISM

IN 1978 HUGH PRICE'S translation of Simone Weil's *Lectures on Philosophy* was published with an introduction by Peter Winch. While the *Lectures* are, in reality, the result of a remarkable effort of notetaking by one of Weil's students and not from the pen of Weil herself, Winch in his introduction recognized in them not only the genuine marks of the lecturer but that herein lay "the hard and systematic philosophical thinking out of which grew the character- istic ideas in [Weil's] later writings which have justly attracted so much attention." With rare exception, however, that insight has not been mined until Winch's own carefully considered and thoughtful publication of *Simone Weil: The Just Balance* in 1989. It is one of a very small handful of works that systematically engages Weil as a philosopher.

In that book Winch's account of Weil's philosophical develop- ment begins in the quasi-cartesian meditation of her diploma essay "Science et perception dans Decartes." There Weil, unlike Descartes, roots knowledge in activity. For Weil *"je puis donc je suis"* replaces *"je pense donc je suis."* This, Winch argues, is a vast improvement over Descartes, who, once he has systematically doubted everything, is hardly entitled either to the content or connection of thoughts from which he deduces his existence. Yet, Winch continues, even if activity is a more promising beginning point, by remaining within the sphere of the isolated individual, Weil is left with some very deep cartesianlike problems. For example, he argues, by beginning with the "I" Weil opens herself to "the temptation to substantialize the "I" (to which Descartes had notoriously succumbed) [which] precisely *is* the temptation to substantialize, or hypostatize order."[1] She herself saw the problem of this hypostatization, but at this point did not seem to be able to avoid it.

The *Lectures*, however, he believes, constitute a remarkable revolution in her starting point and hence in the overall character of her thought. For it is there that Weil begins her consideration of human knowledge and activity *within* the context of the material and social world into which one is born. It is a world that is already ordered, particularly by language. We do not discover and apply a preexistent necessary order in thought; we participate in a material and social world in which thought occurs.

Despite this promising beginning, Winch contends, the earlier view is not entirely eradicated and continued to cause Weil difficulties in her social philosophy, notably the essay "Reflections concerning the Causes of Liberty and Social Oppression." There she seems to have reverted to a position where thought is conceived as separate and distinct from bodily activity and as primarily instrumental. It is this approach, Winch claims, that keeps her from finding the equilibrium she so earnestly sought in human relations. He is right; the project amounts to trying to find satisfactory social relationships to fulfill persons while at the same time insisting that persons are essentially unrelated to each other and hence able to be fulfilled without reference to their social world. Although Weil seems somewhat aware that freedom is limited—it is the freedom to work out means for given ends—she does not always take into careful enough consideration that the givenness of those ends are part of a social context. To be sure she is able to critique them as such, but then often writes as if there could be ends that are not socially given. Although Winch does not try to find the origins of this problem, it seems that it may well be due to her beloved Rousseau. For it was Rousseau who, unlike most of his contemporaries, was keen enough to see that all virtues and vices are *social* through and through, and completely distinct from what one might be able to say of humans in the state of nature, and who yet, at times, once having reached that insight, treated it as a problem to be solved, instead of a starting point.

But, according to Winch, Weil did not stay stuck with this problem. Rather, in the second half of his book, by means of a subtle and sensitive reading, he attempts to show the great degree to which

Weil takes to heart the insights that began to dawn on her in the *Lectures*. As he puts it in dealing with crucial concepts such as justice and beauty:

> Earlier attention was focussed almost exclusively on the agent's immediate project with little attention to the context of his action. It was almost as though Simone Weil wanted to *construct* that context by bringing together a collection of autonomously acting individuals. But now that context is the starting point of the discussion.[2]

The important upshot of this concentration on the context of human activity and knowledge in the case of concepts such as justice is that while justice is clearly something to be striven for, it is not so much a thing out there to be noticed like tables and chairs, but an epistemological concept:

> A point of view from which alone a certain sort of understanding of human life is possible. . . . The understanding that is in question is not independent of one's moral, social, religious viewpoint; not one therefore which can be used as a foundation for such a viewpoint. It is rather a mode of understanding that presupposes the viewpoint in question.[3]

(This approach, which allows us to see justice as a balance between knowing subject and known object, needs to be to kept in mind when we discuss the supernatural, below.)

Winch's point is subtle, but a grasp of it is crucial to understanding the character of Weil's later thought. Two brief examples will help in showing just how apt and crucial it is. The first can be seen in how Weil's political philosophy differs from Hobbes, and, indeed, the tradition of liberalism in general (a point we will develop at much greater length in chapter 9.) Hobbes believes that political philosophy is a matter of applying preestablished rules and principles; Weil, on the contrary, recognizes that there are no meaningful principles *outside* human social activity to apply. Or, put another way, the rules and principles cannot be separated and then examined separately from the playing of the game. Winch makes the point clearly himself in contrasting Weil's procedure with that of John Rawls's attempt to calculate social justice by attempting to negotiate the social contract from behind a "veil of ignorance." We quote at length:

Rawls' contract is an entirely abstract construction, a theoretical device. Normally the point of saying that a common arrangement must be arrived at by "negotiation" is that one must wait on the result of the negotiation in order to know what the arrangement is going to be. One may, of course, make more or less well-founded and shrewd predictions about the likely outcome, but such predictions must await verification or falsification by events. There is room for surprises. Rawls, however, does not say: put the interested parties together, set suitable limits to the kinds of consideration to be deemed relevant to the negotiation, and then retire to see what happens. He *calculates* the result. In other words the outcome is not a genuinely negotiated one at all: the idea of a "negotiation" is nothing more than a logical device for presenting a certain form of argument, the conclusion of which can be appraised by anyone. This is of course connected with the fact that Rawls' contracting parties are not human beings at all, but rational constructions. And the notion of "reason" or "rationality" that is deployed is a purely *a priori* one: not derived from any serious examination of how such terms are actually used.[4]

For Weil, on the other hand, justice is not brought into the realm of politics or human relations from somewhere outside; it is not a calculation that could be done by an unjust person. Justice is precisely the way one approaches other human beings, and cannot be divorced from that interaction with them without loss of meaning.

A second example can be seen in the contribution Winch's point can make toward understanding an important Weilian theory—and, conversely, how that theory can provide confirmation of Winch's claims. Some years ago Springsted sought to explain what exactly Weil meant by her frequently used borrowing of the Greek word *metaxu*.[5] The term, which translates as "intermediary," is used by Weil throughout her notebooks to signify things that serve, indeed, as intermediaries or bridges between the human spirit and God. These bridges are also intermediary in a second sense: they form our world of intermediate value. At first blush Weil's use of the term seems *merely* metaphorical. Springsted, however, argued that Weil's use of the term involved the use of a real theory that she seems to have developed from ancient Greek mathematics. It is a theory that has an upshot of presenting what might be called a "sacramental" view of the world, for all sorts of things that one encounters in the world can, according to it, serve as purveyors of God's grace. As such, it appears a bit like medieval theories of the *vestigiae*, those traces of God and God's design to be discovered in the world. (This can, of course, be trivialized, as in Abbot Suger's claim that God had intended melons to be eaten *en famille* because he had so clearly marked how to cut them in pieces to be shared.)

Weil, on Springsted's account, however, differs from the stereotyped medieval theory (many medievals, such as Bonaventure, actually had very sophisticated understandings of the *vestigiae*) in that she is clearly not interested in setting out clear, objective criteria of what might make any object a *metaxu* or not. In fact, it appears that she muddies the water by considering not only objects—which sometimes are and sometimes are not *metaxu*—but subjective states as *metaxu*. Moreover, he claimed:

> An object is . . . only efficacious as a *metaxu* for the subject when it is related to the subject's own attention. For this reason nothing is capable of serving as a *metaxu* simply by physical possession or proximity. But through attention the object, whether it is a thing, state or act, can serve as a *metaxu* when it causes one to direct the soul beyond the represented finite good towards the unrepresentable transcendent God.[6]

On this account it should be noted that at least part of the reasoning behind this theory is that the theory itself works within a framework of thought, which is faith.

Now the relation of Winch's point to this theory is at least twofold. In the first place it keeps one from reading the theory of the *metaxu* as a sort of mystic's (or metaphysician's) map of the spiritual galaxy. We do not believe that Weil ever intended to provide such a map. Rather, the genius of the theory is that it points out the *uselessness* of such maps (even if they were possible) for what makes anything a *metaxu* or not, what makes it spiritually meaningful, is a *relation* between that thing or being and a human subject. We, of course, are necessary to that relation, in the sense that it requires our attention. But it also ought to be well noted that to pay attention for Weil is to let a thing exist in its own right. Then there is a spiritual relation. So spiritual meaning does not occur, for Weil, apart from that relation. By adding his voice in the way he does, Winch does not let us turn aside from this aspect of Weil's thought and thus makes a significant contribution to reading Weil correctly. But secondly, insofar as this is Weil's theory, it then provides corroboration for what Winch is trying to tell us about Weil.

So far so good. But now we run into a problem that has sorely troubled many otherwise sympathetic (and unsympathetic) readers of Winch. That problem has to do with his remarks on the role of the "supernatural" in Weil's thought.[7] The term, frequently used in Weil, is obviously crucial to understanding her. How it is used is closely related to many of the points we have already noted that Winch raises, and to that degree we believe that he makes another important contribution to reading Weil in this context. But Winch has not always been so read.

One specific sort of criticism is often leveled against Winch's last chapter, "A Supernatural Virtue?" This objection can be described in this way. In that chapter Winch notes that Weil has a tendency to talk about rare and beautiful actions as if their rarity were proof that they could only originate in an "outside" power. Thus, he claims, she appears to use the concept of the supernatural as a metaphysical foundation, taking what amounts to an a priori approach and abandoning her otherwise clear understanding of the meaning of concepts as rooted in human social activity. As pointing to such an "outside" foundation, he thinks, rarity, even extreme rarity, is hardly convincing, for clearly human actions that are rare, still remain with the realm of human possibility in some sense. So what use does the concept of the "supernatural" have in Weil? According to Winch, it is "a way of expressing the connections between various attitudes, interests, strivings, aspirations which are all part of our 'natural history.'"[8]

The criticism that has frequently been offered of this interpretation is that after a very sensitive reading for two hundred pages, we are at the very end given a very un-Weilian, reductionistic one. Without going nearly so far, even Richard Bell in a quite sympathetic review thinks Winch's view is a "secular" one (and, without prejudice, deliberately so) that needs supplementing. For, he notes, "at times, however, Winch sounds as if Simone Weil's religious view is "merely" perspectival, i.e. providing us with a certain way of thinking about things . . . or "a certain orientation."[9]

The first of these criticisms—that of Winch presenting a reductionistic reading—is very implausible. It simply seems incredible that Winch, after spending two hundred pages trying to get us to believe that Weil genuinely advanced in her philosophical thinking because she quit thinking in foundationalist ways, would then himself recommend, explicitly or by oversight, a foundationalist sort of conclusion. On the other hand, though, the second criticism seems to be on firmer ground. A genuine question does stand behind Bell's observations. But, before trying to deal with it head on, we must first try to see what it is and what it is not.

On the surface the problem is straightforward enough. Purposely Winch has tried to present a "secular" account, because, he says, he wants to see how far one can go in these terms, and not because he thinks religious terms are inappropriate. This, of course, somewhat limits what he can do, and, to that degree, supplementing his account by the use of "religious" terms is perfectly appropriate. It may even be quite necessary, for he seems to have applied a distinction that he does not really believe has, in the end, a great deal of value, or, at least, he does not think entirely appropriate to the subject at hand.

One example of where such supplementing might be appropriate would be to say something about the role Weil's discovery of affliction and subsequent experience of Christ played in causing her to discard her views involving a quasi-cartesian, substantialized "I." After all, we suggest (see "The Enigma of Affliction," chapter 6 below) the experience that caused her to doubt that the "I" is always capable of self-esteem may be integrally linked to that discarding. It was that shocking and unexpected discovery and experience, therefore, and not simply the intellectual solving of certain otherwise unresolved tensions in her philosophy that launched her into her later views. We also suspect that Winch would have no particular problem with this supplementing.

At a deeper level this supplementing is not so innocuous, however. While Winch, as a Wittgensteinian, ought not to have insuperable objections to bringing in religious examples to which the concept of the supernatural rightfully applies, at the level at which he is working, to do so may well be a sort of *deus ex machina* and quite misleading. For, as we shall see momentarily, what Winch sees as crucial in Weil's concept of the supernatural is that it is not an explanation of certain events, attitudes, and so forth, just as "justice" is not a mental meaning mapped onto certain events, attitudes, and so forth, but is precisely our approach to events. In this regard Winch rightfully is suspicious of bringing in language forms that, without examination, may be taken for explanations. To simply use this sort of language runs the risk of obscuring the very point he is trying to make in the first place.

But now another sort of very serious problem is raised, for if Weil understands the concept of "supernatural" well—that is, has something important to tell the rest of us about it—it becomes difficult to see how much of religious language, or perhaps better put, theological language, is even possible. Such language certainly appears explanatory at times. If the charges of reductionism against Winch are unentertainable per se, they do at least witness in a muddled way to this problem. It is difficult to see how one can move from understanding the supernatural as the Winchian Weil seems to present it, to the sort of religious language that believers are quite used to and which uses words such as "outside" quite naturally. Now we suspect that this is less a problem in Winch's presentation, or a contradiction in Weil, than it is in the very way that philosophy and religion have divided themselves. In this sense a problem, a deep problem, is being presented. It is less our concern to solve it in any rigorous sense than it is to locate what Weil is saying in relation to it, and thereby to come to a fuller comprehension of what she is saying. But even to do that much is to point to something like a solution.

———————

Let us begin by reexamining Winch's claims concerning the concept of the supernatural in Weil, and let us begin by asking how one might best characterize the supernatural. At least according to many of Weil's own statements, to talk about the supernatural is to talk about a good that is "outside this world." But what exactly does this mean? Well, according to Winch it certainly is "neither to make an existential judgement nor to comment on the whereabouts of some existent: it is simply to redirect one's love."[10] As Winch insightfully quotes Weil, "The Gospel contains a conception of human life, not a theology."[11] To say that it contains a conception of life does not mean that it gives us a picture of a properly good life or a recipe for living such a life; it means that having such a conception—by living life in its *light*—we know how to live life, and how not to.

Now what exactly is being said here can be illustrated quite well by two points, which will be even further developed in the next chapter, "The Enigma of Affliction." The first is that affliction, according to Weil, even though it can be the occasion for a perfect contact with God, is *not* to be thought of as a "divine educational technique." This is to say that God is not trying to get a point across to us; it is also to say that merely knowing about the existence and horror of affliction will do little to keep one from being destroyed.

This is because, second, what opportunity affliction provides for contact with God depends upon one's love even in situations where, as Weil says, there is nothing left to love—and psychologically and socially no subject left to do the loving.

The point to be made here about the supernatural is this: that what we say or do about affliction does not depend upon having a certain sort of knowledge about affliction that anybody could, in principle, have. It is to act a certain way toward others, toward the universe and toward God when afflicted. It is, as Winch aptly quotes Weil, to say "that earthly things are the criteria of heavenly things."

Now while there is certainly a temptation here for one to say that the reason one can love in such circumstances is because of God's grace, because of "outside" help, as Winch points out, while religiously appropriate to do so, this sort of language is also *religiously* misused when taken as an explanation. It makes a believer into a philosopher, which she, as believer, is not and does not have to be. Winch argues (against a passage of Weil's where she herself seems to have fallen prey to this temptation) that this is:

> The succumbing to a temptation to take the language of the supernatural in a metaphysical way. This does not merely misconstrue such language; it turns its original thrust through 180 degrees. To speak in the terms of this language is, as she herself says, to express faith. Faith does not consist in the holding of a theory based on argument, in thinking that a certain view is justified; it involves thinking in a way to which one recognizes questions of justification to be irrelevant.[12]

To use the example of affliction again, one's love does not depend upon something one knows about the world—it does not depend upon "the hearing of ear"—it simply is the extraordinary response of love in an unlovely situation. It depends not upon argument, but on love, pure and simple.

The aptness of Winch's subtitle—"The Just Balance"—can also be brought into evidence at this point. It is apt because, on Winch's account, if the concept of the supernatural operates in Weil as he says it does, then the supernatural may best be pictured by the illustration of a balance. For in a balance two forces constitute a harmony around a center, which is itself not a force that is directly played off against the other two at all. Forces balance, especially in the case of intelligent creation, by a certain respect for each other, which also constitutes their relation to the center. But they balance *each other*, and it is only by coming into that actual relation with each other that balance is achieved. In human relations particularly this occurs only when one actually takes the other into account as he or she is. As pointed out in chapter 7, this is why the distance of friendship is not coldness, but essential for deep friendship. For others are not to be figured out, they are to be loved. The same may even more appropriately be said about God.

To read the metaphor of balance as being at the heart of Weil's writings on the supernatural is to understand her thought much better. She is not simply one more would-be cosmographer; indeed, even those who take her to be a sort of cosmographer also tend to react to her writings as something more than objective maps of the spiritual universe insofar as they *respond* to them. Her writing and thinking is meant to evoke a response, a response of profound love and faith. They are such a response themselves.

That, of course, is why Weil continues to be read with profit. But it also helps us understand why so many of her readers have seen affinities between her and other thinkers such as Plato, Augustine (at least when he was being meditative), Kierkegaard, and Wittgenstein. Each knew better, as Plato put it, than to put the unsayable into a "fixed form" such as words. They sought, as we argue in the Epilogue, to find the Word behind the words. But having to use words to find that Word, they used them in the form of dialogues, spiritual meditations, pseudonymous authorship, or constant questioning of the reader, each trying to reform the *thinking* and not just the opinions of his or her reader.

To see Weil in this light, as we think Winch is trying to have us see her, is pretty much to do away with anything seriously damaging in the claim that what Winch is presenting is a "mere perspective." What he is trying to present is the reaction of love and faith, which may to the unfaithful *seem* like a simple difference in perspective. Yet a problem still remains, which may be the real problem behind the "mere perspective" charge. For while it needs to be thoroughly understood that the language of faith is not, as Weil herself says, the language of a geometrical theorem, nor is religious belief in God like believing in the truth of the Pythagorean theorem, nevertheless it is at least arguable that some forms of religious language are, in some sense, objective.[13] Indeed, while much of the language of faith is response or calls for a response, it is also used to teach and to describe. Is there any way in which to conceive it as legitimately fulfilling that more public function without betraying its crucial inner quality? Can people like Weil—or Kierkegaard, for that matter—simply say what they mean without having to be so very and maddeningly indirect all the time?

Winch himself has not ever said she could not, although he has expressed a preference that she avoid her tendency to generalize and to present matters in quasi-objective theoretical way. He has argued for simply retelling the stories that astound us in their depths, and compel a response of love and faith. But he has also appropriately noted that at the end of the first section of the *Philosophical Investigations*, Wittgenstein after having shown the nonsense of taking "meaning" to consist in a specific mental activity, nevertheless makes this concession: "It would be possible to speak of an activity of butter when it rises in price, and if no problems are produced by this it is harmless."[14] Similarly, it might be argued that religious language that *appeared* in explanatory guise may really be no problem, if nobody takes it to be an explanation or to think a question had just been asked that is most appropriately answered by an explanation.

That is one possible response to the problem. However, we maintain Weil herself had an answer to the problem, which if used to understand intellectual constructions generally and religious formulations specifically, allows us to use words in an objective way without betraying the essential hidden nature of the Word behind them. Weil's answer, in brief, is this: In the crucial, but dense essay "The Pythagorean Doctrine," a relatively late essay (written in Marseilles), Weil distinguishes between the intellect and what we might call the spirit, and between them and the body, with the intellect serving as a mediator between the spirit and the body, and with the spirit (or faith, which is the function of the spirit) serving as a mediator between God and the lower functions of the human being.

At first blush this sort of talk appears to be exactly the spawn of Weil's occasional wild generalizing tendencies that worries Winch so. However, careful attention to Weil's real point shows she is after something far different. For, she maintains, it is the function of the intellect to generalize and to construct methods by which it can grasp and hence act in the world. But, she points out, it is precisely this furthering of a universal method that denies the intellect access to God, for the soul's access to God, as to a real friend, is always a particular relation of consent. But this does not mean that the world of ordered intellectual construction is antithetical to the world of the spirit. It can genuinely act as a mediator between the spirit and the body. For example, while the universalizing intellect has a necessarily limited understanding of the world (it does not comprehend God in the way only faith can), nevertheless, given a world to which the spirit has given its assent as something truly good, it can order a world for bodily action. On the other hand, whenever the intelligence grasps the world as an ordered whole, Weil maintains, it suggests to the spirit the possibility of a transcendent creative purpose, which the spirit itself may then grasp and penetrate. (This is precisely where her seemingly "metaphysical" views on necessity discussed in chapter 3 actually become matters of reading, discussed in chapter 4.)

The upshot of this proposal is twofold. First, it means that for Weil intellectual constructions and explanations are necessarily limited by virtue of the fact that the intellect, a natural function, is itself limited. In this sense we can never take them to be the final word, as it were. In this respect she follows a well trod path in Christian theology, which has always insisted on caveats against taking intellectual constructions to be too descriptive of God. This is true even of Aquinas.[15]

Second, more positively, insofar as these constructions are responsive to faith they allow faith to become incarnate in the world. Even if they are only tentative or half-solutions, they can prepare one to accept the world in faith by regulating bodily and intellectual activity. In this sense, they are *metaxu*, things themselves limited but which, nevertheless, really allow us access to grace.

But here Weil can make an even stronger claim: insofar as they are *metaxu*, these constructions (or most intellectual constructions, for that matter) cannot be characterized apart from love and faith. Just how they cannot may be seen in a comment Wittgenstein himself makes about doctrines (which are subjectively *and* objectively of faith). He writes:

> In religion every level of devoutness must have its appropriate form of expression which has no sense at a lower level. This doctrine, which means something at a higher level, is null and void for someone who is still at the lower level; he *can* only understand it *wrongly* and so these words are *not* valid for such a person. For instance, at my level the Pauline doctrine of predestination is ugly nonsense, irreligiousness. Hence it is not suitable for me, since the use I could make of the picture I am offered would be a wrong one. If it is a good and godly picture, then it is so for someone at a quite different level,

who must use it in his life in a way completely different from anything that would be possible for me.[16]

To put things in quite this way—that is, that intellectual constructions cannot be characterized *apart* from faith or that their validity depends upon the faith that reads them—allows us to add a converse to Winch's claim that the "supernatural cannot be understood apart from our natural history." That converse is that our natural history cannot be understood apart from our *supernatural history*. This is not to say for Weil that there are two things—nature and supernature—to be played off against each other, or which explain or are explained by each other. Rather, to understand anything well involves seeing its natural and supernatural histories. *And to see that one has a supernatural history and that one's life is not adequately described apart from it, is precisely to see one's natural history in a certain light as well.*

The most obvious example to be cited here is, of course, Augustine's *Confessions*, and a brief commentary on it is in order to illustrate our point. Explained in Winch's terms, Augustine's conversion cannot be understood apart from the events of his earlier life, which is not to say by any stretch of the imagination that it is *explained* by those events. At least it would not be explained for Augustine, Weil, or Winch, or us. Nor on Winch's or our account should we take the supernatural to explain those events either, even when Augustine talks as if they were caused by an agent other than himself. That is the understanding of unconverted pagans. Rather the supernatural, which appears as an operative concept at the conversion, appears appropriately there because it does express "the connections between various attitudes, interests, strivings, aspirations, which are all part of [Augustine's] 'natural history.'" But it appropriately appears and expresses those connections because, for Augustine, those connections involve a very different sort of history, a history of which he was not even aware until his conversion—that is, what he might have called his "spiritual biography." His conversion is the *recognition* that he has such a biography, and that lets him see his natural history in the way he does after the conversion. That supernatural history does not attempt to explain anything, at least not in the forbidden sense—and Augustine certainly does not take it to do so; it is simply the best account that Augustine can give of his life. And to fail to see it in those terms, he would say, is to fail to understand it very well at all.

Now it seems that Weil herself does not often use the explicit biographical and historical categories that Augustine does in the *Confessions*, although her own spiritual biography can also be aptly described in them. Indeed, she herself does use them there. But even beyond that instance, we give throughout this book some reason to challenge the perception that these were foreign categories to her. We explore some of the ways in which she does use history in Part IV, and especially highlight the crucial roles of spiritual journeys and histories in chapters 7 and 8. We do think that such categories are important for understanding Weil.

For example, the very schema of implicit and explicit loves that is central to the very important essay "The Implicit Forms of the Love of God," relies on something like them (see also chapter 8 on this point). The point of talking about implicit loves in that essay is that even at a relatively highly developed level of spiritual awareness one is not explicitly aware what it really is that is developed. One is, as it were, still undergoing an apprenticeship in "reading." While much more can be said about what occurs when the love of God has become explicit, at least this much can be said: that for the love of God to be explicit is to see explicitly the spiritual nature of all the individual loves that preceded it, even though one may have been unaware that that was what they were.

This can be put another way by putting it in terms of Weil's notion of "reading." Reading in Weil is not exactly an interpretation of things, at least not in the Enlightenment sense where we interpret data that provide neutral and objective foundations and measuring sticks for our interpretations. Rather, as discussed in the chapter on reading, reading is a function of having learned how to read. It is the result of an apprenticeship. When reading we indeed read what is there in front of us, even though there may be several ways of doing so. In this sense when Weil, for example, tells us that we are to respect our communities because they are "nourishment" to the soul, she really sees them as nourishing. She also sees us as having souls. She is not just talking in a fancy way. That is what she reads in our lives.

But we need to stay aware of the fact that our reading is a function of the attention and the sort of attention we pay to something. That attention is the result of an apprenticeship. In the spiritual realm, this apprenticeship can be described as the result of a contact with God and the growth of the seed of God's grace in us. At least Weil so describes it. Thus for Weil there really is a God responsible for the "seed" in us. In that sense there is a cause of our spiritual life and it is appropriate to talk about it as such. But that "cause" does not replace talk about natural causes, which continue to operate (see chapter 3), and should not be confused with it. Indeed, as we saw there, Weil's own account of necessity puts this sort of "cause" at a very different level, one that is incommensurate with natural causes. Rather the "cause" is a relationship, a contact, and the beginning of a spiritual journey. Even our understanding of it is dependent on this relationship and contact.

Thus we are suggesting for Weil that, indeed, the supernatural does express important connections between various aspects of our lives that have little meaning apart from our "natural history," and that they are essential for understanding the "supernatural." But we are also suggesting that to see these connections is also to see "natural history" in the light of having a very different sort of history that is not separate, but yet distinguishable from natural history.

To see intellectual constructions and explanations in this way, we suggest, meets Winch's objections and caveats. For built into Weil's understanding of the intellect is a claim that the intellect is necessarily limited. Sometimes it is even inappropriate in certain areas of faith. But noting the negative and limited aspects of Weil's theory is only half of it. Intellectual constructions are also positively, *metaxu*—intermediaries in the spiritual life. They are not these sort of spiritual mediators simply because they exist; they act in this way only because we approach them in a certain way. Which is to say, it is only because of the response to the world that is appropriately called "supernatural" that they are effective for conveying grace.

So far we have stayed rather strictly within the confines of Weil's and Winch's texts. It is possible, though, to stand back briefly to appreciate what Weil's theory of the *metaxu* might even be thought to do. At first it simply appears fideistic, or worse, a matter of begging the question. For it seems that to appreciate this theory, one must already share its viewpoint; the theory seems to presuppose the moral standards it means to judge. And to a degree, it does. But how it does is crucial, for whatever circularity exists is not vicious, but a simple matter of consistency; it seems quite absurd that one could actually pronounce on spiritual and moral matters without in some way sharing that viewpoint. That in fact seems to be part of Winch's objection to Weil's so-called "universalizing" tendency, because when she shows it, she seems to expect her reader to appreciate her point simply because of its rational luminosity, as if one could, say, appreciate "justice" without being in any sense just. That, of course, is rarely, if ever, the case, no matter what some philosophers might say. But how can one defend more generally this intuition that moral theories must somehow be moral and spiritual theories spiritual?

Many of the clues and views Weil herself provides to answer this direct question are treated elsewhere in this volume. In order not to repeat ourselves, we shall not therefore tackle her own views directly any longer at this point, but briefly consider what we suggest is an argument that at least enlightens the sort of theory at stake. It is an argument by the Canadian philosopher Charles Taylor, who has already been introduced in chapter 2.

Taylor, in his *Sources of the Self*, while pointing out that a platonic sort of argument to the Good may now be impossible philosophically, nevertheless argues:

> Nothing prevents a priori our coming to see God or the Good as essential to our best account of the human moral world. There is no question here if our ever being able to recognize this by prescinding from our moral intuitions. Rather our acceptance of any hypergood is connected in a complex way with our being *moved* by it.[17]

By "best account" Taylor means precisely that: an account of the moral life, which is not the same as offering a "basic reason." Such an account is an attempt to articulate our moral vision, and any moral vision is, of course, something that "involves our changing, a change which is defined as 'growth,' or 'sanctification,' or even 'higher consciousness,' and even involves our repudiating earlier goods."[18] Although we have over the last two hundred years or more been misled into trying to construct theories along lines similar to theories in the natural sciences where our own moral reactions are beside the point, once we drop the *expectation* that moral theories should parallel scientific ones, we begin to see that, as Taylor suggests, moral theories *always* involve our vision of the Good, whether we can argue to that good or not. Thus what makes one account better than another is not its arguments per se, but its ability to incorporate and articulate— and increase and make life possible under that vision. In short, as we have put it elsewhere in this volume, a theory needs to be able to be thought from the perspective of the first person and not just that of the third person.

It is a similar thought, we suggest, that gripped Weil's mind in her coming to treat intellectual constructs as *metaxu*, and, even more radically, in coming to devise a theory that says as much. That she did so, for example, in the context of a commentary on Pythagorean texts, which she was hardly naive enough to believe either actually described the world to a scientific literalist's satisfaction or competed with theories that would, indicates how nuanced her thought on this issue really is. It is for this reason that we should like to suggest that Winch's concern about Weil's backsliding into universalistic and rationalistic theories, while not misplaced (she was indeed capable of it), is perhaps over cautious. For, we suggest, Weil herself understood about her own thinking on the supernatural exactly what Winch has been so helpful in bringing to light for her readers: that it is part of our natural history, and not an explanation.

But we also suggest she also goes further than this. In concerning herself with tying our thought of the supernatural to our natural history, we believe that she was also trying to get us to understand something about the morally self-referential nature of thought. For thought both reflects our moral and supernatural history, and also guides us—sometimes haltingly—through that history. In that sense it cannot be divorced or understood apart from that spiritual history.

That is to go further than Wittgenstein's suggestion that such talk is "alright on occasion;" indeed, it seems Wittgenstein himself went beyond it. For what we think Weil is saying is that some advancement of the Good actually (but not necessarily) takes place in talking about the supernatural. What good that is, is an indirect one. Insofar as it is not an absolute good, it can be misused—because the user is morally limited as are his words. But insofar as such talk is a function of faith, and hence comes from or is a certain self-understanding, it may be an important way by which the intellect is actually incorporated and healed by the life of faith.

PART III
The Journey of the Soul

6. THE ENIGMA
OF AFFLICTION

WE HAVE READ Simone Weil's essay "The Love of God and Affliction," several times, and each time with profit. It is, however, with the reading of Epictetus, especially his chapter "Of Providence,"[1] that we have come to realize the significance of two major convictions that she shares with him. When the operation of these two convictions in her thought is made explicit, we can see why and in what ways affliction posed such a challenge to her and drove her to the Cross of Christ for illumination.

These two convictions are not biblical ones. Their use by her forcefully illustrates how Christianity at its central point—the crucifixion of Christ—is profoundly enriched by nonbiblical convictions. When these are connected to her other views, she can explain how the Cross of Christ is the prime mediation between God and human beings, and how human affliction is a witness to his Cross in those times and places where Christianity is or was not known.

We do not claim that Epictetus is the direct source for these two convictions in Weil. Even though she always mentions him and Greek Stoicism with approval, she seldom refers to him by name, and references to Greek Stoicism are relatively few compared with references to Plato or even Aeschylus. Nonetheless it is clear that she shared these convictions with Epictetus.

In her essay, Weil delineates the nature of affliction as a specific form of suffering. It is not primarily physical suffering; it can be caused by physical suffering, if that is very prolonged or frequent; and it has physical effects, such as when one has difficulty breathing at the news of the death of a beloved person. If there is a complete absence of physical pain, there is no affliction, because our thought automatically flees from affliction. For there to be affliction, there must be some event or events that uproot a life and affect it physically, socially, and psychologically. Physical distress keeps the mind fastened to one's affliction; but the source of affliction is primarily social. A person is uprooted from the fabric of social relations, so that he no longer counts for anything. There is social degradation, or at least fear of it.

Even more horrible, psychologically the afflicted person inwardly feels the contempt and disgust that others express toward one who is socially of no account. An afflicted person feels self-contempt and disgust, and even guilt and defilement in proportion to his or her innocence!

For those who are unprepared, affliction prevents them from performing the act of "decreation" for themselves. It turns them into "nothing" by crushing them from the outside, instead of allowing them to become "nothing" by their own action. For the unprepared, its presence takes from them their one vital freedom: the freedom to give their "consent" or concurrence to the existence of the universe in spite of all the negativities they find in it. To "consent" is to love God, even if only implicitly. "That is why those who plunge men into affliction before they are prepared to receive it are killers of souls" (SNL 173).

But to see the full force of the challenge that affliction posed for Weil, we need to consider two convictions she shared with Epictetus. The first conviction is that *all things have a purpose.*

For Epictetus this meant the teleological ordering of all things. Just as the sword is fitted to the scabbard and the scabbard to the sword, so too are colored objects and light fitted to our vision and our vision to them.[2] Everything in nature has some use, and so each item helps to make our universe a cosmos—a harmonious whole. Each creature fulfills its purpose by acting according to its nature; human beings, because they have reason, have the task of discerning these purposes and rendering praise for the gloriousness of the ordered whole.

But all does not go well for human beings. This brings us to the second shared conviction: *we can make use of whatever befalls us.*

In Epictetus, the goodness of the cosmos is not that everything goes according to our will, with each of our desires catered for; but if we take a comprehensive view of the entire order of the universe, we will see that we are but one item among many in a vast interconnected whole. Many pleasant and unpleasant things occur to individuals because of the interconnections, but in every instance we have the ability to endure what comes to us. We have received from the cosmos the faculties to bear whatever happens to us "without being degraded or crushed thereby."[3] We can wipe our nose because we have hands; we can accept being lame as a small sacrifice toward the rest of the universe; we can even endure an unavoidable death from the hands of either nature or the social order without degradation.

This is achieved by recognizing necessity and by exercising the only real freedom we have. Our position in the physical and the social world is that of but one reality among many in a system of interconnected events, most of which are utterly beyond our control. What is beyond one's control can sometimes injure one's wealth, one's social position, one's body, and even bring utter destruction. In such circumstances an individual's only real freedom is the manner in which she or he responds to events beyond her or his control. She or he can complain about misfortune; she or he can bear whatever comes, even death, without degradation, by seeing its necessity and yielding to it courageously and magnanimously.

One thus makes *use* of whatever befalls, by using it to bring out these qualities of character. A person can thus be grateful to providence, whatever happens, for providing her or him with the capacity to recognize the universe as an ordered whole and for the capacity to yield to the adversity it brings—even death—with courage and dignity. Thus Epictetus can exclaim:

> Bring now, O Zeus, what difficulty Thou wilt; for I have an equipment given to me by Thee, and resources wherewith to distinguish myself by making use of the things that come to pass.[4]

Weil does not argue for the goodness of the cosmos on the basis of such a simple teleology as that of Epictetus, with such analogies as the fit of a sword and a scabbard. She employs a more sophisticated understanding of events as connected by a necessity that can be expressed in mathematical relations. Nonetheless, she shares with Epictetus the essential idea that the cosmos is a gloriously ordered whole, and that it is our function to perceive the goodness of its order and to praise God for it. As she puts it:

> It is our function in this world to consent to the existence of the universe. God is not satisfied with finding his creation good; he wants it also to find itself good. That is the purpose of the souls which are attached to minute fragments of this world. (SNL 193)

She also shares Epictetus' outlook concerning suffering brought on by things over which we have no control, and which result from the order of the universe. As she puts it:

> The world's beauty gives us an intimation of its claim to a place in our heart. In the beauty of the world harsh necessity becomes an object of love. What is more beautiful than the effect of gravity on sea-waves as they flow in ever-changing folds, or the almost eternal folds of the mountains?
>
> The sea is not less beautiful in our eyes because we know that ships are sometimes wrecked. On the contrary this adds to its beauty. If it altered the movement of its waves to spare a ship it would be a creature gifted with discernment and a choice, and not this fluid perfectly obedient to every external pressure. It is this obedience which makes the sea's beauty.(SNL 178)

So, like Epictetus, she can face lameness or even death, and yet praise the cosmos whose order causes them.

But there is one phenomenon that Epictetus did not consider or apparently know about: affliction. Epictetus' final refuge against adversity is that no matter how bad it is, it need not degrade us or crush us. We have the power to retain our dignity, whatever happens to us. No matter what happens to us, we can give thanks for the order of the universe, our power to perceive its order, and our power to yield even our life to it. A person can find reason to praise the goodness of the cosmos and all its events because there is this final refuge of dignity. Although it takes great courage and nobility to bear our own destruction, it is that very capacity that gives us dignity. So we have reason to render praise for the order of events that gives us the occasion to actualize or exercise our powers.

But in Weil we find that this final refuge is not impregnable; for the condition of affliction is one in which we *are* crushed or degraded. Affliction fills us with self-contempt, disgust, and a sense of guilt and defilement. If we are unprepared for affliction, we are overwhelmed by it. It crushes us. There is nothing of us intact whereby we could nobly yield to it. But even if we are prepared for it, there is no question of acquiring nobility by consenting to self-disgust and a sense of defilement! So there is no way to encounter affliction and to keep from either being crushed or degraded in our own eyes. Simone Weil therefore writes:

> The great enigma of human life is not suffering but affliction. It is not surprising that the innocent are killed, tortured, driven from their country, made destitute or reduced to slavery, put into concentration camps or prison cells, since they are criminals who perform such actions. It is not surprising either that disease is the cause of long sufferings, which paralyse life and make it into an image of death, since nature is at the mercy of the blind play of mechanical necessities. But it *is* surprising that God should have given affliction the power to seize the very soul of the innocent and to possess them as sovereign master.(SNL 171–72)[5]

That such events should lead the innocent *victim* of them to feel self-contempt, disgust, and even guilt, and a sense of defilement, instead of the *criminal*, is an arrangement that baffles her. What purpose is served by having someone not only battered, outraged, and uprooted, but having them regard *themselves* with loathing and a sense of defilement?

Although affliction is a phenomenon never considered nor perhaps even recognized by Epictetus, Weil seeks to reconcile it with convictions she shares with him: (1) that all things have a purpose, and (2) that we have the capacity to make use of whatever befalls us. Were she not convinced that the universe is wellordered, and that we can make use of all that occurs to us—including adversity—affliction of the innocent would not be so enigmatic and would not press her to find its purpose and how we can make use of it. She writes, for example: "Often, one could weep tears of blood to think how many unfortunates are crushed by affliction without knowing how to make use of it"(SNL 198).

But what use could be made of affliction? What could be the point of consenting to degradation? To determine how one may make use of it, one must know its purpose. She claims that this is precisely the question that a person suffering affliction asks with persistence. "So soon as a man falls into affliction the question takes hold and goes on repeating itself incessantly, Why? Why?"(SNL 197). The question has no answer within this world:

> The afflicted man naively seeks an answer, from men, from things, from God, even if he disbelieves in him, from anything and everything. Why is it necessary precisely that he should have nothing to eat, or be worn out with fatigue and brutal treatment, or be about to be executed, or be ill or be in prison? If one explained to him the causes which have produced his present situation, and this is in any case seldom possible because of the complex interaction of circumstances, it will not seem to him to be an answer. For his question "Why?" does not mean "By what cause?" but "For what purpose?" (SNL 196)

The events that occur can only give us the causes of affliction and not its purpose; for other adversities enable us to actualize or exercise noble qualities. However difficult, a good can thus always be realized in face of all other adversities caused by the physical and social order of the universe, and realized in the very person who endures the adversity. Thus Epictetus can say, "From everything that happens in the universe it is easy for a man to find occasion to praise providence."[6] Affliction must have a purpose for its victim for us to accept its existence. And unless its existence is acceptable, we cannot praise or love a cosmos that produces affliction. But events that cause affliction provide no occasion for a good to be realized in the victim. So to the victim's question, "Why?," a reference to society and to the workings of the universe only specifies *causes* of the affliction without giving the victim any *purpose* for it:

> So there can be no answer to the "Why?" of the afflicted because the world is necessity and not purpose. If there were finality in the world, the place of the good would not be in the other world. Wherever we look for final causes in this world it refuses them. But to know that it refuses, one has to ask. (SNL 197)

If then affliction has a purpose, and not just a cause, this purpose must reside outside the universe. If one holds firmly to the conviction that everything has a purpose, then affliction compels one to say that if it has a purpose, the purpose cannot be within the cosmos.

We are thus driven in our demand for finality to a reality that is not this cosmos of necessity. If everything added up to harmony in this world, we would never look beyond this world for light. If everything added up in this world, the world's lack of purpose for affliction would not function to *lever* us beyond the world. That is, to raise us to a supernatural level.

The finality for which we search is outside the cosmos of necessity; we ourselves, however, are utterly encompassed by necessity. "The infinity of space and time separates us from God. How can we seek for him? How can we go towards him?"(SNL 181). "Distance" is given its concrete meaning in terms of what is above a nexus of necessary relations in which all things are related by compulsion and what is enmeshed in such a nexus and thus subject to it. We are thus separated from finality by the cosmos of time and space, by its principle of operation: necessity or compulsion.

We are now confronted with a new enigma. We can find the purpose of affliction—the good it brings—only by contact with something beyond the realm of compulsion; but we ourselves cannot escape the realm of compulsion.

Resolution is found by relating the two enigmas: *affliction* is to be the bridge between the finality that is outside the cosmos, and creatures subject to necessity! The purpose of affliction—the good it brings—is *contact* between that which is outside necessity and that which is subject to necessity.

How is affliction to be conceived of as a form of contact? The nexus of necessity, which is what is meant by "distance," is what causes affliction. So affliction is a mark of distance. Then what is above or not subject to necessity is conceived of as the *ruler* of necessity, so that the cosmos obeys God in its operations. That which is outside this cosmic order of compulsion is thus the cause of affliction through the medium of the cosmic order. Affliction is thus a *contact* between the ruler of the cosmos and those creatures who can be afflicted by means of the cosmic order. People who are afflicted are feeling God touching them through the cosmic order which the Creator wields!

This indeed gives a way to conceive of *contact* between what is outside the cosmic order and what is subject to it. But how is that contact a *good*? Unless it is a good, even though we have got beyond this world, we still only have a *cause* of affliction and not a justification for it. Unless contact is a good, affliction cannot be "an occasion to praise providence" or a reason to be grateful.

How then is the contact felt as affliction to be conceived of as a good? It is only possible to conceive of affliction as a good by turning to the Cross of Christ—to his affliction—and to the related notions of Trinity and Incarnation:

> God produces himself and knows himself perfectly, just as we in our miserable way make and know objects outside ourselves. But, before all things, God is love. Before all things God loves himself. This love, this friendship of God, is the Trinity. Between the terms united by this relation of divine love there is more than nearness. There is infinite nearness or identity. But through the Creation, the Incarnation, and the Passion, there is also infinite distance. The interposed density of all space and all time sets an infinite distance between God and God.(SNL 176)

The Son enters the created world so that he is subject to the nexus of connections that form the cosmos. The Father and the Son are thus separated by the cosmos: by what is under the sway of necessity. The Son is thus exposed, as are all human beings, to the possibility of affliction through the might of the cosmic order. Indeed, the Father wills that the Son be afflicted:

> God created through love and for love. God did not create anything except love itself, and the means to love. He created love in all its forms. He created beings capable of love from all possible distances. *Because no other could do it, he himself went to the greatest possible distance, the infinite distance.* This infinite distance between God and God, this supreme tearing apart, this incomparable agony, this marvel of love, is the crucifixion. Nothing can be further from God than that which has been made accursed. (SNL 174–75, our emphasis)

Despite this distance, the Son is connected to the Father. Love is the bond between the Father and the Son in the Trinity. Even though separated by the distance of the cosmic order—one being under its sway and the other above it, and even though separated by the distance of the affliction produced by that cosmic order—they both still love. Love is at each end of the universe that is between them: a universe that is being pressed down onto the Son by the

Father, with affliction being produced through its pressure. The Son responds to this event as the will of the Father. So they are still connected by love, but connected through the medium of a world that produces affliction. They are connected because the Son accepts this medium, as one through which the Father's love is expressed; for he believes that the affliction is sent by the Father, and the Father is above all love.

So it is still the Father's love that is being felt and received, although it is felt and received *as* affliction. To be afflicted is the touch of the Father's love through a cosmos that produces this condition in the Son. The acceptance of affliction as from the Father is a response of love, even though in the condition of affliction one feels cursed and forsaken. But to continue to trust the Father is to be turned toward him as love and to receive this affliction as his loving touch:

> God is so essentially love that *this unity*, which in a sense is his actual definition, *is a pure effect of love*. And corresponding to the infinite virtue of unification belonging to this love there is *the infinite separation over which it triumphs*, which is the whole creation spread throughout the totality of space and time, consisting of mechanically brutal matter and interposed between Christ and his Father.(SNL 177, our emphasis)

We thus see that *blessed* contact between what is outside the nexus of necessity and what is encompassed within it is possible by love. But love between what is outside and what is inside is expressed only *through* the medium of the cosmic order, with the Father's love at one end and a Son's love at the other. The cosmic order is *between* them, and contact is made *through* it.

The cosmic order is a medium of *blessed* contact between God and us, however, only if we at our end receive all that happens to us as the loving will of the Father:

> As Creator, God is present in everything as soon as it exists. The presence for which God needs the cooperation of the creature is the presence of God, not as Creator but as Spirit. The first presence is the presence of creation. The second is the presence of decreation. (He who created us without our help will not save us without our consent—Saint Augustine). (GG 33)

Then *nothing*, including affliction, can separate us from the love of God.

For us to be able to respond with love to God's touch, however, there must be within us a capacity to love him. This is explained by the metaphor of the "seed." God's love can reach us over the infinite distance of time and space:

> Over the infinity of space and time the infinitely more infinite love of God comes to possess us. . . . If we consent, God places a little seed in us and he goes away again . . . the seed grows of itself. A day comes when the soul belongs to God, when it not only consents to love but when truly and effectively it loves. *Then in its turn it must cross the universe and go to God.* The soul does not love like a creature, with created love. The love within it is divine, uncreated, for it is the love of God for God passing through it. God alone is capable of loving God. We can only consent to give up our own feelings so as to allow free passage in our soul for this love. That is the meaning of denying oneself. We were created solely in order to give this consent. (SNL 181, our emphasis)

God's love can reach us and plant a seed in us if there is a void—an emptiness within us; that is, when there is nothing to impede or block God's entrance. This, Weil tells us, occurs when we do not give our love to anything of this world. To withhold oneself so is painful; for it is to want, but to deny that want out of the conviction that there is nothing we can know or imagine that would satisfy us fully (WG 208ff.).

After this seed has grown (a process that requires a disinvestment of our self-interest), we effectively love. Then when the love of God touches us through the medium of the world, we at our end can respond with love. Then we are connected by love. A person who is prepared in this fashion, when pressed by the world to the point of affliction, can endure this touch of the Father:

> Throughout the horror he can go on wanting to love. . . . It is only necessary to know that love is an orientation and not a state of the soul. Anyone who does not know this will fall into despair at the first onset of affliction. (SNL 182–83)

Affliction, then, can be a good for the victim, because:

Misery gives us the infinitely precious privilege of sharing in this distance placed between the Son and his Father. . . . For those who love, separation, although painful, is a good, because it is a love. Even the distress of the burden is a good. There cannot be a greater good for us on earth than to share in it. God can never be perfectly present to us here below on account of our flesh. But he can be almost perfectly absent from us in extreme affliction. For us, on earth, this is the only possibility of perfection.(SNL 177)[7]

Because the Son has gone the greatest possible distance, we can have confidence that nothing that happens to us can separate us from the love of God. His love is present at any and every distance that we can occupy, and it reaches us no matter how much distress we suffer. Without the cross of Christ—without the Son going the greatest possible distance—we would not have this assurance. With the cross of Christ, affliction can be conceived of as a good, indeed as a way to receive our greatest good and to love God perfectly.

Affliction is not only the touch of God and a possible route for us to love God perfectly, but it is a *witness* to the Cross of Christ among those who have never heard of him:

If God had been willing to withhold Christ from the men of any given country or epoch, we would know it by an infallible sign: there would be no affliction among them. (SNL 194)

Affliction serves as a witness by leading the victim and other people to ask why it exists. If they are honest and persist, they will see that within the world we can find only its *causes* and not its purpose. Weil claims that those who endure this lack of an answer—this "silence"—participate in the Cross of Christ:

Any man, whatever his beliefs may be, has his part in the Cross of Christ if he loves truth to the point of facing affliction rather than escape into the depths of falsehood.(SNL 194)

Affliction is to serve as a witness to Christians as well:

[They] sidetrack the problem of affliction when they discuss it. All the talk about original sin, God's will, Providence and its mysterious plans (which nevertheless one thinks one can try to fathom) and future recompenses of every kind in this world and the next, all this only serves to conceal the reality of affliction, or else fails to meet the case. There is only one thing that enables us to accept real affliction, and that is contemplation of Christ's Cross. (SNL 194–95)

Affliction is a witness to Christians and to all others that all God wants from us is our love. Adversity to the point that it has no purpose within the world forces us to look beyond the world; and it finds its purpose in the contact it gives us with God, which Christ by his faithful endurance of such contact on the Cross reveals to us as our highest good. No recompense is needed for affliction to be our good (rewards on earth or in heaven); in fact to speak of them keeps us from receiving the witness of affliction. No cause (for example, original sin) is to deflect us from looking for its purpose. "If we accept death completely, we can ask God to make us live again, purified from the evil in us" (WG 224).

Weil concludes her essay with the remark that both beauty and affliction are witnesses to the fact that there is no finality in the world. Beauty, which equally with adversity and affliction is a result of the necessary relations within the cosmos, is a testimony that there is no finality in the world. Beauty does this by holding our attention and filling us with an expectancy of some good, which it always promises but never gives. The world thus suggests a finality to us, which it never gives us. So if there is a finality, it is to be found outside the world. Weil laments that we squander both beauty and affliction. We do not make sufficient use of them.

Simone Weil can consistently retain the two convictions she shares with Epictetus; for affliction does have a purpose and can be used by us. But she has far transcended Epictetus' view of the purpose and use of all things, because she believes in a good that is outside the cosmic order. Our purpose is to have contact with that good through acceptance of this cosmic order as the medium of our contact with what is outside it.

Even though she transcends Epictetus, it is their two shared convictions that show us why affliction posed such a challenge to her and drove her to the Cross of Christ for illumination. They are not biblical convictions. The Bible does describe God's creation as orderly, even though it is marred by sin. But the Bible does not have an intricate teleology of nature so that everything, by serving the world order, has a purpose. And only Epictetus claims that whatever befalls us must not only be explained as being part of the order but also be of potential use *to the person to whom it happens.* That person ought to be able to make use of it; it can become a good for him, and thus be a reason for praise and gratitude.

It is with Epictetus' convictions that Weil approaches the phenomenon of affliction, and because she so approaches it, it becomes an enigma. She is driven beyond this world to find its purpose and to the Cross of Christ as giving us access to what is beyond the world. These nonbiblical convictions bring out features of the Cross of Christ that one would not see unless one approached the phenomenon of affliction from the perspective of those convictions. They drive one to search for the good of affliction from the perspective of those convictions. They drive one to search for the good of affliction and so lead one to view both suffering and affliction as themselves the effects of God's love. Thus we can find the love of God *in* adversity itself, as well as in pleasant contacts.

Also, as we pointed out at the beginning of this essay, these nonbiblical convictions enable one (1) to conceive of the Cross of Christ as the *prime* mediation between, or way of relating, two incommensurate realities: God and human beings; and (2) to view human affliction as a witness to the cross of Christ for people in times and places beyond the confines of historical and institutional Christianity.[8]

Weil is not the only one who has made the first claim; indeed, it is Christianity itself that claims this. But she has shown a way, and indeed an original way, to conceive of Christ as the *prime* mediator. She has also shown a unique way to conceive of Christ's universal presence in human history—a claim frequently made but not often rendered conceivable—by her view of human affliction as a witness to his Cross and a way to participate in it.

We thus have a powerful example of the fruitfulness of nonbiblical ideas when used in relation to Christianity. Nonbiblical ideas were of course frequently used by the early church fathers and by theologians in the high Middle Ages. Abuses, especially in the nineteenth century, made most Protestants deeply suspicious, and sometimes openly hostile, toward this practice. But the beauty and profoundness of Weil's reflections on the Cross, assisted by some nonbiblical convictions, may help us see the value of this procedure and encourage its practice once again, especially the use of ancient philosophy.

Finally, an autobiographical point should be mentioned, as it relates to the way we view the intellectual construction reared by Simone Weil in her essay. It was only when she herself was suffering intense physical pain and was psychologically in a wretched condition that she experienced contact with God's love. It happened, she reports, as she was reciting George Herbert's poem "Love." Without realizing it, she was actually praying. She points out:

> I had never foreseen the possibility of that, of a real contact, person to person, here below, between a human being and God. . . . I only felt in the midst of my suffering the presence of a love, like that which one can read in the smile on a beloved face. (WG 69)

So it appears that the intellectual construction she reared to deal with the phenomenon of affliction did not arise merely from the desire to resolve a problem or an enigma. In this sense, as we also noted in the previous chapter, the supernatural, which alone can save one from complete and utter destruction, is not an explanation. It is something seen in the loving consent to the existence of affliction. Thus the experience of contact with love in the midst of wretchedness was known first, and only afterwards was this intellectual construction reared to render this experience of contact and some other convictions coherent with one another. But again, this is not to *explain* as such. It is to make a *metaxu* of the intellectual construction, a way to move from thinking of the world as hostile to consenting to its form and existence bodily, intellectually, and spiritually. To be able to do that renders the intellectual construction even more plausible than if it were taken as an explanation.

7. THE LOVE OF PARTICULARS

LOVE OF GOD and love of neighbor are very familiar Christian teachings. Weil follows the traditional Christian teaching that love of God and love of neighbor are possible only because of God's love or grace at work in us (WG 150, 212–13). She frequently refers to its presence as a divine seed that God plants in us (e.g., WG 163), and which we can expel, retard, or allow to grow and manifest itself in love for God and for our neighbors.

Divine love, as it becomes part of our motivating energy, is frequently contrasted with love that has natural, rather than supernatural, origins. All forms of human love are aroused by the attractiveness of the object, and usually gratify the lover's desires and needs. Divine love does not show any preference, but is universal, extending to all people whether they are attractive or not, and independently of any good that might be received from them.

Anders Nygren in his monumental and very influential book, *Agape and Eros* (1930-6), used *agape* to designate divine love and *eros* to designate human love. Even though there is no linguistic basis for this use of the words in ancient Greek, Nygren's distinction has achieved widespread currency in current discussions of love. Nygren vigorously argued that *agape* and *eros* are utterly incompatible. He even went so far as to claim that all human love is inherently selfish. All attempts by theologians, such as Augustine, to connect or even blend *agape* and *eros* are misguided and corrupt the very core of Christianity.

Nygren claims that Plato is the greatest and most influential exponent of *eros* in its sublime, rather than its vulgar, form, and thereby the thinker whose views are most easily confused and blended with a Christian view of love. For Nygren Christianity must be purified of platonism. For Weil, Plato had intimations of Christian teachings. In this Weil is on the side of theologians such as John Burnaby (*Amor Dei*, 1938) and M.C. D'Arcy (*The Mind and Heart of Love*, 1959), and philosophers such as R. A. Markus ("The Dialectic of Eros in Plato's *Symposium*" in *Plato*, vol. 2, ed. G. Vlastos, 1971), and A. H. Armstrong (*Plotinian and Christian Studies*, 1979). None of them, however, have exerted nearly as much influence in recent discussions on the relation of divine and human love as has Nygren, especially in Protestant circles.

Irving Singer, in *The Nature of Love: Plato to Luther* (1966), the first volume of his three-volume study of love in the Western world, endorses Nygren's position. He draws from it the conclusion that a human love for a particular person, because it is a preferential love, is excluded from the Christian view of love. In Christian love there is an indifference to people's individuality. People are not to be loved because of their particular attractions, which appeal to our desires and needs. They are *all* to be loved, regardless of their particularity. There is to be no love for particular human beings as *particulars*. Love that allegedly springs strictly from a divine source is a love that, like its source, is utterly indifferent to the specific individual qualities of those who are loved. The exclusion of love of particulars as particulars is especially objectionable to Singer because he considers erotic love between man and woman, when stripped of romantic excesses, to be the highest form of love and essential to the fulfillment of our human nature. Accordingly, he rejects a Christian view of love, because it has no place for human love.

We do not agree with Nygren's view of Christian love, and therefore reject the implications drawn from it by Singer. But the difference between divine love toward us or as it motivates human beings and human love in its various forms is indeed striking. Even though it is universally accepted that there is no aspect of Western civilization in which Christianity has not been a major, not to say, essential, ingredient, the contrast is so stark between a preferential and a nonpreferential love, as to make it plausible for R. G. Hazo completely to ignore Christian love in his encyclopaedic analysis of some two hundred writers on love in Western civilization (*The Idea of Love*, 1967).

Christianity did introduce a new and distinctive idea of the nature of love. The relation of divine love and human love is thus a major topic in Christian theology. It is part of the large subject of the relation between nature and grace—that is, between what we have been endowed with as creatures and what we may become and do because of the presence of God's love at work in us. Nygren's view is an extreme one but, as suggested, it is not without some basis. This is evident from Weil's own contrast of gravity and grace. They too are radically different: one is natural; the other, as she frequently says, is supernatural.

An examination of Weil's understanding of divine love at work in us and human love of particulars thus seems called for. It should illumine how gravity and grace (roughly Weil's equivalent of the traditional theological terms, nature and grace) are related to each other. Indeed, it will show that although gravity and grace are so different that Weil refers to them as natural and supernatural, nonetheless in the case of love they are so related that human love is able to overcome its own destructive tendencies only because of the ingredient of grace at work in us. Particulars as particulars can be loved properly only because of the presence of divine love at work in us. A proper balance in natural relations between our needs and the well-being of those we love is achieved because of the presence of the supernatural.

Weil has little to say about love between men and women even though she frequently compares it to our love for God (e.g., WG 126, 132–33, 137, and 171–72). She has, however, written an essay on friendship, and friendship emphatically includes an attraction to the specific individuality of the people involved. Weil's understanding of friendship also deserves some attention because it has struck astute, and sympathetic, readers of Weil, such as the theologian Rowan Williams, and the philosopher Peter Winch as bizarre.[1] Some clarification thus seems called for. We will find that her understanding of friendship has been misunderstood by both Williams and Winch, and that it is of a piece with her overall position that the supernatural manifests itself in bringing into balance necessity and good.

Weil's discussion of friendship occurs in her long essay "Forms of the Implicit Love of God." She says that the commandment "thou shalt love the Lord thy God," cannot refer only to the love "the soul can give or refuse when God comes in person to take the hand of his future bride" (WG 137). Since it is a permanent obligation, and God is not yet present in person, the love must be directed to something else in which God is present in a veiled way. There are "only three things here below in which God is really though secretly present" (WG 137). They are religious ceremonies, the beauty of the world, and our neighbor. Accordingly there are three indirect or implicit forms of the love of God.

Weil then immediately adds friendship to their number, but indicates that it is unlike the other forms of indirect love of God. Like love of neighbor, it is directed toward human beings. But it differs from love of neighbor because it is a personal and human love, and thus shows preference for a particular human being. It "is necessarily a different thing from charity. Charity does not discriminate" (WG 138, 200). As a form of the implicit love of God, friendship is in a distinctive class. On the one hand, it is one of the four ways we may obey the first great commandment, love of God, and on the other hand, since in friendship we show preference for a particular person, it is a personal, a human love. Because it is a human love, unlike the other forms of implicit love of God, an understanding of friendship will enable us to understand the relation of human love to Christian or divine love.

Although friendship, as a human love, is distinct from love of neighbor, the discussion of love of neighbor and of friendship both turn on the same issue: How is equality to be maintained? In the case of love of neighbor, this is because Weil interprets love of neighbor under the category of justice. She cites the parable of the sheep and the goats, in which Jesus calls the just those who give aid to the distressed. Weil claims:

> The Gospel makes no distinction between the love of neighbor and justice. . . . We have invented the distinction between justice and charity. It is easy to understand why. Our notion of justice dispenses him who possesses from the obligation of giving. If he gives all the same, he thinks he has a right to be pleased with himself. He thinks he has done a good work. As for him who receives, it depends on the way he interprets this notion whether he is exempted from all gratitude or whether it obliges him to offer servile thanks. (WG 139–40)

In the examples Jesus gives of love of neighbor, people are in a very unequal situation. Some give help; others, who are in deep distress, as in the parable of the sheep and goats, and that of the good Samaritan, receive help. How can there be equality when one gives and the other receives?:

> The even balance, an image of equal relations of strength, was the symbol of justice from all antiquity. . . . Its use in trade is the image of mutual consent, the very essence of justice. (WG 143)

Weil explains how there can be equality in a situation of inequality by explaining how there can be mutual consent, the very essence of justice. Even though they do not have to, benefactors consent to treat others as equals. They recognize that various forms of distress do not disbar those who suffer from respect. Not only do they help, but they help in such a way that their essential equality as people is not in the slightest degree infringed:

> The supernatural virtue of justice consists of behaving exactly as though there were equality when one is the stronger in an unequal relationship. Exactly, in every respect, including the slightest details of accent and attitude, for a detail may be enough to place the weaker party in the condition of matter, which on this occasion naturally belongs to him, just as the slightest shock causes water that has remained liquid below freezing point to solidify. (WG 143)

The person who receives help exercises consent by receiving it with gratitude. Gratitude arises from the recognition that the help given is due solely to generosity. By acting justly, the giver has not sought to oblige the receiver to servile thanks. The gratitude is not servile, but a proper response to the beauty of a just act. It thus "leaves self-respect absolutely intact" (WG 148). Both giver and receiver, then, acknowledge justice, and act on the basis of justice in their distinctive ways. What are opposites—giving and receiving— are united by a mutual consent: one consents to give, and to give, in such a way as to respect a person as a person; the other consents to such giving by receiving it with gratitude. A balance is achieved in a situation that is naturally unbalanced by the exchange of compassion and gratitude (WG 140, 148).

In friendship equality is threatened by the very love friends have for each other. Friends are attracted to each other, and the nature of their attraction is so strong that there is a tendency to infringe the freedom or autonomy of each other. According to Weil, attachments between people have two sources—desire and need:

> In a general way all possible attachments come under one of these heads. We are drawn toward a thing, either because there is some good we are seeking from it, or because we cannot do without it. Sometimes the two motives coincide. Often however they do not. Each is distinct and quite independent. We eat distasteful food, if we have nothing else, because we cannot do otherwise. A moderately greedy man looks out for delicacies, but he can easily do without them. If we have no air we are suffocated; we struggle to get it, not because we expect to get some advantage from it but because we need it. We go in search of sea air without being driven by any necessity, because we like it. In time it often comes about automatically that the second motive takes the place of the first. . . . A man smokes opium in order to attain to a special condition, which he thinks superior; often, as time goes on, the opium reduces him to a miserable condition which he feels to be degrading, but he is no longer able to do without it. (WG 200–01)

Weil says there is no contradiction between seeking our own good in human beings and wishing for their good to be increased (*pace* Williams[2]). But when the motive that draws us toward another person is simply some advantage for ourselves, the conditions of friendship are not fulfilled (WG 202). This happens when a human being is in any degree necessary to us. Our need drives us to remain attached, either by domination or by subordination. Either domination or subordination, by depriving both people of the free disposal of themselves, violates their essential equality.

There are degrees of necessity. A total deprivation of food causes death, whereas a partial deprivation only diminishes energy. Everything is necessary if its loss causes a decrease in vital energy (WG 202–3). When Weil applies this general observation to friendship, we see how the bond of friendship is itself a threat to friendship:

> When a human being is attached to another by a bond of affection which contains any degree of necessity, it is impossible that he should wish autonomy to be preserved in himself and in the other. (WG 204)

Peter Winch quite naturally takes this to mean that ideally, according to Weil, there ought not to be any need at all for another person in the bond of friendship. But, he argues, the removal of needs from friendship renders the relation completely impersonal, with no bonds of affection, and thus leaves us with a very bizarre understanding of friendship. It is very different from what many of us would ordinarily recognize as friendship.

Williams agrees with Winch:

> My value and security may come to depend entirely on my needs and wants being met by a particular kind of human relationship—by a variety of what we usually call human love. . . . I may manipulate or tyrannize over someone else, deny their right to be themselves or to have interests other than my supposed interests, and so do profound injury to them. . . . Weil's claim is that this is endemic in ordinary human relations. If I love someone as a particular individual, this means that their particularity is attractive to me. *These* features of their reality meet or gratify my expectations, they are pleasing to my standards; my selection of them as objects of love means that I have found reason to ignore or discount other aspects of their reality and to withhold love from other individuals not possessed of the relevant desirable features. Thus my love of the individual as individual is *necessarily* an attempt to "cannibalize" them, to bring them into *my* world on *my* terms.[3]

But this interpretation by Winch and Williams fails to take into account Weil's main point. The previously misleading passage from Weil continues in this fashion. "It is impossible by virtue of nature. It is, however, made possible by the miraculous intervention of the supernatural. This miracle is friendship" (WG 204).

In other words, when the bond of affection contains any degree of necessity, it is impossible by *natural* means to wish autonomy for oneself or for the other:

> When a human being is in any degree necessary to us, we cannot desire his good unless we cease to desire our own. . . . The central good of every man is the free disposal of himself. (WG 202)

Either we remove our own freedom, by becoming servile in order to get what we need, or we desire that the being we stand in need of should be deprived of this free disposal of himself or herself by becoming subordinate to ourselves. The very existence of needs prevents friendship *by natural means*. But as a matter of fact, in friendship people both need each other and also desire each other's central good—namely, their liberty, and do so by *supernatural* means:

> There is harmony because there is a supernatural union between two opposites, that is to say necessity and liberty. . . . There is equality because each wishes to preserve the faculty of free consent both in himself and in the other. (WG 204)

For Weil what is astounding about friendship, the reason she says it is a miracle, is precisely that it combines opposites: the need for the good found in each other, and at the same time a desire for the autonomy of each other. If you leave needs entirely out of the picture, there can be no harmony of opposites. According to Weil, it is precisely the harmony of opposites that forms the very essence of friendship. It is quite clear that for Weil need is in fact present in genuine friendship, and the miracle is that necessity does not "triumph" (WG 205) by driving out the desire to preserve the faculty of free consent. "Friendship is a miracle by which a person consents to view from a certain distance, and without coming any nearer, the very being who is necessary to him as food" (WG 205). Need is indeed present in friendship, in fact it is the presence of need, along with a respect of free consent that makes friendship so astounding. "Friendship is a supernatural harmony, a union of opposites" (WG 202).

Weil says that friendship is very like love of neighbor in achieving a harmony of opposites. "In both cases the contraries which are the terms of the harmony are necessity and liberty, or in other words subordination and equality" (WG 205). In the response to need (love of neighbor) and in the attraction to another (friendship) the problem is to achieve equality. In both cases equality is achieved by a supernatural love that in love of neighbor awakens compassion and gratitude, and in friendship preserves a desire for mutual freedom.

Winch correctly sees the nature of the problem of friendship in Weil. In friendship there is a preferential love for a particular human being. But, Winch points out, "in her treatment of justice in "Human Personality", she emphasizes the notion of the "impersonal" and *at the same time* insists on the identity of justice and love (in the sense of charity)"[4] If justice is impersonal, and love is identical with justice, love must also be impersonal. Since love is impersonal, how then, asks Winch, could there be a preferential or personal form of love that is acceptable?[5] The problem is essentially the same as the one raised by Nygren's account of *agape* as impersonal love and *eros* as personal love. Nygren stressed that they are incompatible, a position followed by Singer, but rejected by Burnaby, D'Arcy, Armstrong, and Marcus.

According to Winch and Williams, Weil's way of rendering friendship acceptable is to *stipulate* that *genuine* friendship is impersonal, in contrast to the way we ordinarily think of friendship. Friendship is genuine only to the extent it is free of all dependency. Winch grants, as does Williams in a passage quoted earlier, that relations based on needs may indeed become something terrible in certain circumstances. But Winch claims that Weil does not consider the possibility of other cases in which the dangers are avoided, nor consider whether the risk of such dangers is a price we have to pay for some of the greatest things in human life, such as passionate love.

Winch cites with approval Weil's remarks in her London notebook, "Real love wants to have a real object, and to know the truth of it, and to love it in its truth as it really is." He says that this "is precisely what is lacking in her account of friendship":[6]

> It has to include the possibility of recognizing for example, someone in her truth as she really is, is going to involve recognizing one's dependence on her or hers on me: in which case that dependence too will be something to be loved.[7]

So Weil is apparently involved in a contradiction. If real love is personal and attentive, as Weil claims it is, then the preferential love of friendship must include mutual dependence. But Weil has argued that where there is dependence, there is subordination and dominance. She therefore stipulates that genuine friendship is impersonal, dropping desire and need from friendship. But Winch and Williams point out that this not only makes what she calls genuine friendship different from what we ordinarily regard as friendship, but she contradicts her own stress on love as attention and her claim that real love wants a real object and to know the truth of it and to love it in its truth as it really is.

We share Winch's and William's horror of the spectacle presented by an account of friendship as something *totally* impersonal. Indeed, Allen has openly expressed this same horror elsewhere with respect to Nygren's rejection of *all* forms of human love in favor of an impersonal, divine love as the model for us.[8] But Weil, unlike Nygren, does not deserve such a reaction. As we have seen, she did not exclude mutual dependence from genuine friendship. Rather, she emphasized that its dangers are miraculously overcome by the simultaneous presence of the desire for preserving liberty in ourselves and in each other. Had she dropped mutual dependence from friendship altogether, she would indeed have given us a bizarre notion of friendship, as well as have contradicted herself. Weil described the dangers and risk involved in human love, not in order to say that we should not become dependent, but to show that it is indeed by "the grace of God" (as Winch puts it[9]) that these dangers are sometimes avoided. Ironically, Williams also voices Weil's view—that human needs do not always triumph—when he believes that he is actually posing a contrary view:

> If, by grace or hard work or both, we manage to broaden the scope of our love so that we are able to give patient attention, to respond joyfully and generously, to the presence of a wide variety of others, this suggests not that we have abandoned a point of view, but that we have learned not to let our responses be totally dictated by what we believe to be our needs, and to accept, or even celebrate as a gift, what in another person is irrelevant to my imagined need or expectation.[10]

When in an account of the bond formed by personal preference, one of the two terms in friendship is either dropped or simply not mentioned, leaving us with only the other term—a desire that liberty be maintained—then indeed a bizarre view of friendship as impersonal results. Whenever Weil does not explicitly mention both terms of the relationship in any particular passage, she is open to such an interpretation. For example, she writes:

> Friendship has something universal about it. It consists of loving a human being as we should like to be able to love each soul in particular of all those who go to make up the human race. As a geometrician looks at a particular figure in order to deduce the universal properties of the triangle, so he who knows how to love directs upon a particular human being a universal love.

The consent to preserve an autonomy within ourselves and in others is essentially of a universal order. (WG 206)

Winch points out that a geometer is indeed not interested in the particular figure as such. He rightly claims that in friendship or other kinds of personal love, such as mother and child, husband and wife, and lovers, it is the particular that we are above all concerned with and attentive to. Winch thinks that even the good Samaritan, who exhibits love of neighbor, is interested in the specific person being helped.

He is correct that Weil's words imply an impersonal attitude. But her words have this implication only because one term of the relation of preferential love—a desire and even need for the specific good that is another—is neglected. With that term in mind, however, this passage can be understood as pointing out that in friendship we can *discover* that we should love every human being. The preservation of autonomy within ourselves and in others, an element found in friendship, can be seen to be applicable to all other human beings. It is the focus on the feature of autonomy—a feature that is present in every friendship—that is compared to a geometer's discovery of universal properties in a particular figure. But this does not mean that in friendship, one does not care for a specific person. It is this care for a specific person that creates the bond in friendship. The balance between need and autonomy enables friendship to overcome all the risks and dangers of preferential love. Of itself, the ingredient of respect for autonomy is something impersonal. But it is a necessary condition for friendship and other human loves to function properly. "There is no friendship where there is no equality" (WG 204).

Consider this episode within a friendship as it happened to one of us: "Once, while walking across the campus where I teach, I met a friend coming out of one of the guest accommodations that is used for continuing education programs. We warmly greeted each other and I said to my friend, Did you just get here? He looked uncomfortable and began to explain that he had been here for nearly a week. Immediately I thought to myself: You've been here nearly a week and not gotten in touch, even though I live only a few blocks away? Are you really as much a friend as I thought? Then I stopped myself. My friend explained how tired he was from overwork and that he had come to stay at our center in order to read quietly and recuperate, but had caught the flu. Before he had finished, I had stopped my negative thoughts; because I had realized that precisely because he was a friend, he was not obliged to look me up whenever he came to town. Our friendship should not prescribe his behavior. He ought to have the freedom to do exactly as he wishes with his time when he comes to the town in which I live. A friendship ought to be strong enough to bear the fact that friends do not always want to be with each other, and that this does not mean that they do not care for each other greatly. Happily I realized this in time to let my friend know that he did not owe me an apology at all, and that I was delighted to see him."

To take the friend's explanation at face value was to take a risk. Maybe this reluctant friend's behavior really did indicate that he was not the friend he was thought to be. On the other hand, if offense had been taken at his reluctance, it is quite possible that that very understandable behavior would, nevertheless, have soured the relationship and might even have spelled the beginning of the end of the young friendship. The conclusion to the story is also relevant: "As it turned out, I was just able to recognize his otherness by controlling my need to be liked and wanted by him, and not to feel that I had been abused by his behavior. It was fortunate because I have since learned from his subsequent behavior that at that time he was indeed a friend who cared for me. I have learned, too, over the years that he is a person who needs a great deal of solitude. His work places great emotional demands on him and from time to time he needs to be alone. I had run into him on one of those occasions, not knowing about this aspect of his personality."

Winch agrees that the notion of respecting another's autonomy is very often crucial to the way we evaluate a close personal relationship. But, he says:

> It is not always relevant in the same way and does not always take the same form; and sometimes the nature of the relationship may even be such as to speak against it. An example of the latter sort of case might be that between Mary Garth and Fred Vincy in George Eliot's *Middlemarch*, where Mary's love is hardly conceivable apart from her recognition of Fred's need for her: a need which Simone Weil would certainly find offensive.[11]

But Weil's position is consistent with different expressions of autonomy in concrete cases, and need, rather than excluding the relevance of autonomy, makes its operation all the more needful to friendship. As we have seen in the example of friendship given above, each friendship has its own peculiarities. Different kinds of behavior mean different things in each friendship. In this case, the reluctant friend's failure to make contact when it would have been easy to do so did not mean what it usually does. His need for solitude, and his need for it on the particular occasion of his visit to the town in which his friend lived, was peculiar to him. Respect for autonomy in *this* instance meant the respect for his particular need. But however much needs differ, and so lead to different kinds of friendship, friendships must all have as an ingredient respect for the freedom, independence, or "otherness" of the friend.

Weil does not give a full account of the nature of friendship. There are many other dynamics she does not mention that are necessary ingredients if a friendship is to prosper and develop, rather than be arrested in its growth or even decline and die. Among them are such things as the need for tolerance, and a balance between self-revelation and privacy. Differences between male-male and female-female friendships, as well as between both of them and male-female friendships, need to be thought out, too.[12] Weil, however, is concerned with friendship as a form of the implicit love of God. Just as the failure to be just to those who suffer, failure to accept one's own vulnerability to the necessary operations of nature, and failure to be attentive in worship can keep one from loving one's neighbor, from loving the beauty of the universe as a whole, and from loving religious ceremonies, so too can our need for another person keep us from friendship.

In all four cases, the ability to love comes from God, and in loving we are enabled to love God. Although the essay on friendship is not intended to be a full study of the nature of friendship, it makes a striking contribution to an understanding of the relation between human love and divine love. The presence of a supernatural love in us creates a balance between the desires and needs found in human love and the desire to preserve the liberty of consent.

If Simone Weil thought that desire and need for another person in human loves were *always* wrong and to be disapproved of, she could not have qualified, as she did, her examples of "bonds of affection which have the iron hardness of necessity" (WG 202):

> Mother love is often of such a kind; so at times is paternal love, as in *Père Goriot* of Balzac; so is carnal love in its most

intense form, as in *L'Ecole des Femmes* and in *Phedre*; so also, very frequently, is the love between husband and wife, chiefly as a result of habit. Filial and fraternal love are more rarely of this nature. (WG 202)

If Weil's point were that the bonds of affection *always* destroyed or corrupted human love, then she would not have used the qualifications of "often," "at times," "'in its most intense form," "very frequently," "chiefly," "more rarely." Clearly, necessity does not always triumph in human relations, and this is because it is balanced by the desire to preserve liberty, which runs counter to bonds of affection in which the good of another is as necessary as food. The tension between need and respect for liberty is easily seen in the case of an elderly parent, who is in need of care and money. The parent indeed wants his or her grown child to help, but the parent wants the child to help willingly. Rather than badgering or shaming the child into giving the help that is needed, the parent would rather go without. There is a desire for mutual consent.

Winch suggests that Weil's views on friendship, which for the most part he finds unacceptable, "are in part undoubtedly an expression of Simone Weil's own experience of, and difficulties with, close personal relationships."[13] Williams makes a similar point and, like Winch, does not use autobiographical material as a reason to reject her views.[14] Were we to guess at what point Weil's own experience is reflected in her discussion of human love, we would hazard that it is in the remark that maternal love is *often* marked by the iron hardness of necessity, but that paternal love is so only *at times*. Her mother rather enveloped her children, whereas her father was rather withdrawn and played a lesser role in their lives. Even though her brother's brilliance caused her to feel inferior, she thought that filial and fraternal love were *more rarely* marred by the iron hardness of necessity than instances of maternal and paternal love.

But why is friendship said to be a manifestation of the supernatural? One of the marks of the supernatural is that it brings balance and harmony, where otherwise there would be inequality and conflict. To desire that another person be free, takes renunciation similar to God's renunciation in the creation of the universe. God draws God back, so to speak, in order to allow something that is not God to exist. Such a love is also evident in the incarnation, in which God the Word becomes subject to the forces of creation and history, and in the crucifixion, in which God the Word suffers the degradation of affliction. Friendship requires us to restrain our needs for the sake of our own and other's liberty. In the combination of need and restraint, friendship resembles divine love in creation, incarnation, and crucifixion, and this implies that friendship can exist because people, who so love, have been in contact with divine love, whether they realize it or not. Friendship is thus an implicit or indirect love of God. It has the virtue of a sacrament:

It is not the way a man talks about God, but the way he talks about things of the world that best shows whether his soul has passed through the fire of the love of God. In this matter no deception is possible. There are false imitations of the love of God, but not of the transformation it effects in the soul, because one has no idea of this transformation except by passing through it oneself.

When a man's way of behaving towards things and men, or simply his way of regarding them, reveals supernatural virtues, one knows that his soul is no longer virgin, it has slept with God; perhaps even without knowing it, like a girl violated in her sleep. That [not knowing it] has no importance, it is only the fact that matters. What is proof is the appearance of supernatural virtues in that part of its behavior which is turned towards men. (FLN 145–46)

Just as desire for the good in a person can be transformed into a need, and become destructive, so too can our need for another be transformed into a respect for the autonomy of ourselves and others by contact with supernatural love:

When the bonds of affection and necessity between human beings are not supernaturally transformed into friendship, not only is the affection of an impure and low order, but it is also combined with hatred and repulsion. . . . We hate what we depend upon. We become disgusted with what depends on us. Sometimes affection does not only become mixed with hatred and revulsion; it is entirely changed into it. (WG 207)

For this reason, Weil says, Christ added as a new commandment "love one another," to the two great commandments of the love of our neighbor and the love of God. He was not referring to the establishing of bonds, but to their transformation:

> As it was a fact that there were bonds between them due to the thoughts, the life, and the habits they shared, he commanded them to transform these bonds into friendship, so that they should not be allowed to turn into impure attachment or hatred. (WG 207–8)

Pure friendship is an image of the love found in the Trinity between the Father, Son, and Holy Spirit. They are united, so they are one God, but they remain distinct persons. The only way two people can be one, while scrupulously respecting the distance that separates them, is for God's love to be present in each of them. They are united by a love that consents to distance (WG 208).

Weil's claim that friendship is the result of a supernatural love is complex. So far we have given three aspects. First, there is a conflict between need and liberty. We are in the power of that of which we stand in need, and we cannot desire the liberty of the person we need. In friendship need and liberty are reconciled. Their reconciliation is a manifestation of the presence of another love besides human love. Second, there is a resemblance between the love exhibited in friendship and divine love as described in the Christian doctrines of creation, incarnation, crucifixion, and Trinity. Third, we can tell that individuals have been in contact with the supernatural from their behavior toward people and things, or even simply the way they regard them.

But she points out that these matters are not of themselves sufficient for us to say that friendship is a manifestation of a supernatural love. "So long as the soul has not had direct contact with the very person of God, they [friendship and the other forms of the implicit love of God] cannot be supported by any knowledge based either on experience or reason" (WG 209). A person who exhibits these loves may not realize at first that God is their source, and no one should be expected to believe that God is their source simply on the basis of the matters we have so far treated. She says: "It does not rest with the soul to believe in the reality of God if God does not reveal this reality (WG 211). It is even better that these forms of implicit love should not be associated with any belief:

> This is more honest intellectually, and it safeguards our love's purity more effectively. On this account it is more fitting. In

what concerns divine things, belief is not fitting. Only certainty will do. Anything less than certainty is unworthy of God. (WG 209)

We may put the situation this way. With the human love of friendship, you may not be aware and certainly do not know that friendship is a manifestation of supernatural love. But things change when a person knows God. Then a person sees their entire life in terms of its supernatural development, and friendship as a place where supernatural love is manifest:

> After God has come in person, not only to visit the soul as he does for a long time beforehand, but to possess it and to transport its center near to his very heart, it is otherwise. The chicken has cracked its shell; it is outside the egg of the world. (WG 209)

Direct contact of the kind Simone Weil experienced when Christ took possession of her soul (WG 68–69) is needed in order to say with certainty and intellectual honesty that the forms of implicit love are manifestations of a supernatural love. Only after direct contact can one make an intellectual analysis of friendship, such as we have examined in her essay on friendship, as a manifestation of supernatural love. One does not realize that one is implicitly or indirectly in contact with a supernatural reality with the human love of friendship until after one has a direct knowledge of God. (This point with respect to understanding the concept "supernatural" has been taken up also in chapter 5.)

God must reveal God's reality. It does, however, lie within our power to be aware that we are hungry for a final and ultimate good, and that all that we presently love is not such a good. "Everything that appears good in this world is finite, limited, wears out, and once worn out, leaves necessity exposed in all its nakedness" (WG 210). But we find it difficult to face the truth that there is no final good here below, a good not subject to necessity:

> As soon as we have seen this truth we cover it up with lies. . . .
> Men feel that there is a mortal danger in facing this truth squarely for any length of time. That is true. Such knowledge strikes more surely than a sword; it inflicts a death more frightening than that of the body. After a time it kills everything

within us that constitutes our ego. In order to bear it we have to love truth more than life itself. (WG 210–11)

To face the truth is to withdraw our love from everything. Winch rightly asks, "Wouldn't this mean that one loved *nothing*? And wouldn't *that* mean that one did not love at all?"[15] To find an answer Winch turned initially to an examination of Weil's views on friendship, since friendship for her is (allegedly) an impersonal love. But Winch did not find this of any use. In passing, he expressed his dissatisfaction, as we have seen, with Weil's view on friendship.

According to Weil, those who withdraw their love from everything, do not thereby automatically give their love to God. "How could they do so when they are in total darkness?" (WG 211). What it means is that they have a hunger for good, a realization that all that they are aware of does not satisfy them, and a willingness to endure a hunger without knowing whether there is anything real to answer their hunger:

> In the period of preparation the soul loves in emptiness. It does not know whether anything real answers its love. It may believe that it knows, but to believe is not to know. Such a belief does not help. The soul knows for certain only that it is hungry. The important thing is that it announces its hunger by crying. A child does not stop crying if we suggest to it that perhaps there is no bread. It goes on crying. The danger is not lest the soul should doubt whether there is any bread, but lest, by a lie, it should persuade itself that it is not hungry. It can only persuade itself of this by lying, for the reality of its hunger is not a belief, it is a certainty. (WG 210)

If one who holds fast to a hunger for final good, finds him or herself nourished, there is certainty that the supernatural is real. "When we are eating bread, and even when we have eaten it, we know that it is real" (WG 212). It is then recognized that God is the reality that inspires all indirect or implicit loves.

Weil illustrates what she means by "withholding our love from everything," direct contact with God, and recognition that God is the reality inspiring all indirect loves with the example of Electra's longing for Orestes:

> When she was convinced that he no longer existed, and that nowhere in the whole world was there anything that could

be Orestes, she did not on that account return to her former associates. She preferred the absence of Orestes to the presence of anything else. Orestes was to have delivered her from slavery, from rags, servile work, dirt, hunger, blows, and innumerable humiliations. She no longer hoped for that. But never for an instant did she dream of employing another method which could obtain a luxurious and honored life for her—the method of reconciliation with those in power. She did not want wealth and consideration unless they came through Orestes. She did not even give a thought to such things. All she wanted was to exist no longer, since Orestes had ceased to exist.

At that moment Orestes could hold out no longer. He could not help declaring himself. He gave certain proof that he was Orestes. Electra saw him, she heard him, she touched him. There would be no more question for her now as to whether her savior was in existence.

He who has had the same adventure as Electra, he whose soul has seen, heard, and touched for itself, he will recognize God as the reality inspiring all indirect loves, the reality of which they are as it were the reflections. (WG 212–13)

Not only do we have certainty about the supernatural source of our love of neighbor, our love for the beauty of the universe as a whole, our love for religious ceremonies, and our friendships, but our love for God is now a *personal love for a particular*, just as Electra's love for Orestes is for a particular person. After a long period of preparation through the implicit forms of the love of God, "God comes in person to take the hand of his future bride" (WG 137). The most intimate of relations, the nuptial one, is now used to describe our relation to God:

The love of God ought to be impersonal as long as there has not been any direct or personal contact; otherwise it is an imaginary love. Afterwards it ought to be both personal and impersonal again, but this time in a higher sense. (WG 200)

That is, it is a love for a particular, just as is Electra's love for Orestes; but it retains an impersonal element, because the implicit forms of love continue. Indeed, they become stronger (WG 138):

Our neighbor, our friends, religious ceremonies, and the beauty of the world do not fall to the level of unrealities after the soul has had direct contact with God. On the contrary, it is only then that these things become real. Previously they were half dreams. Previously they had no reality. (WG 214–15)

Weil, therefore, rejects the kind of spirituality in which to love God is to cease to love creatures. She says that those who do this are not true friends of God (WG 214). When we are fed by God, our love for created goods becomes real because now we know that our implicit loves are not subject to necessity. Our love for particulars—neighbors, friends, religious ceremonies, the beauty of the world as a whole—are now known with certainty to be from God, because our hunger for a final good has been assuaged.

What is meant by *supernatural love* is indicated by its being placed in the context of four loves that some human beings exhibit. In this chapter we have seen its relation to friendship. Supernatural love is what enables us to desire the equality of free consent in each other, and so prevents the triumph of necessity. That friendship is a manifestation of supernatural love becomes evident to those who are hungry when they receive nourishment. Such direct contact with God enables a person to recognize that all four forms of the implicit love of God have a supernatural source.

The ontological status of the supernatural was considered more fully in chapter 5 on the supernatural. Here we only wish to emphasize that just as in traditional Christian theology, God is known only in God's effects and not as God is in God's self, so too the supernatural is spoken of by Weil only in its relation to this world and the things of this world. For example:

As soon as we wish for this autonomy to be respected in more than just one single being we desire it for everyone, for we cease to arrange the order of the world in a circle whose center is here below. We transport the center of the circle beyond the heavens. (WG 206)

Our orientation changes completely. Everything earthly is now seen in the light of divine love:

A painter does not draw the spot where he is standing. But in looking at his picture I can deduce his position by relation to the things drawn.

On the other hand, if he puts himself into his picture
I know for certain that the place where he shows himself is
not the place where he is. (FLN 146)

The supernatural is not a member of the universe, but outside
it in the sense that a painter is not in a picture. But the supernatural
is not in a space literally outside the world, as is a painter in a
space outside a picture. The supernatural is indicated only by the
way people and things of the world are seen and treated by one
who wishes the autonomy discovered in friendship to be respected
in everyone.

In addition, the supernatural is not a metaphysical realm of
the kind to which we have access by some special faculty of reason.
Nor is the supernatural independent of its relation to the
confirmation of value we find from its illumination of the things
of the world:

Only spiritual things are of value, but only physical things have
a verifiable existence. Therefore the value of the former can
only be verified as an illumination projected on to the latter.
(FLN 147)

But a person who receives nourishment is certain that the good
received is not subject to necessity. "As Plato says, there is a great
difference between the essence of the Necessary and that of the
Good" (WG 201).

8. GEORGE HERBERT
   AND SIMONE WEIL

IT IS WELL KNOWN that George Herbert's poem "Love"[1] was extremely important to Simone Weil. She tells us:

> Often, at the culminating point of a violent headache, I make myself say it over, concentrating all my attention upon it and clinging with all my soul to the tenderness it enshrines. I used to think I was merely reciting it as a beautiful poem, but without my knowing it the recitation had the virtue of a prayer. It was during one of these recitations that, as I told you, Christ himself came down and took possession of me.
>
> In my arguments about the insolubility of the problem of God I had never foreseen the possibility of that, of a real contact, person to person, here below, between a human being and God. (WG 68–69)

Her knowledge of Herbert was more extensive than just this one poem which figures so largely in her mystical experience of the visitation of Christ. She had learned of the metaphysical poets from a young English Catholic whom she met when in Solesmes during Holy Week of 1938, during which she attended the services at the Abbey. She tells us that in reading them later on, she discovered Herbert's poem "Love" and learned it by heart. She sent a copy of it to her brother André when he was in prison and to Joë Bosquet in response to his query about her mystical experiences.

She alludes to the poem "Love" in her essay "Reflections on the Right Use of School Studies with a View to the Love of God," and there are two references to Herbert in her journals (NB 5, 138). She cites "Love" as an example of a perfect poem, and in the context of a discussion of the lack of balance between favor and gratitude, she writes, "G. Herbert. Giving to beggars *irregularly*." This last remark also indicates that her knowledge of Herbert extended beyond the one poem "Love." The connection between the poem "Love" and her mystical experience, on the one hand, and the central place the poem "Love" occupies in Herbert's understanding of Christianity, on the other hand, make a comparison of Herbert and Weil on the nature of the spiritual life both possible and instructive in spite of the paucity of references. Our procedure will be to show the place the poem "Love" occupies in George Herbert's understanding of the Christian pilgrimage, and to relate Simone Weil's ideas to Herbert's at various points.

THE CHRISTIAN PILGRIMAGE

The poem "Love" is the last of a series of one hundred sixty-four poems that make up a volume Herbert entitled *The Temple*. Each poem has a self-contained meaning and can be read apart from the others. Nonetheless, the individual poems are arranged in an order that traces the transformation of our hearts, which form a "stone altar" on which Christ is sacrificed, into hearts that yield to God's love so that we form a temple in which his love may dwell (1 Cor. 6:19–20). Herbert is above all concerned with the struggle to open our lives to the love of God, and the poem "Love" in the sequence of poems that make up *The Temple* represents this achievement.

Simone Weil has the same understanding of the goal of the spiritual life: the creation of a heart that loves God. We do not obey God from fear of punishment or hope of reward, either carnal or celestial. It is thus not surprising that the poem "Love," which represents the achievement of the goal of the Christian life, should speak to her so profoundly.

Traditionally, the spiritual life is divided into three main phases: purgation, illumination, and union. On the matter of union, or the goal of the pilgrimage, Herbert and Weil are in deep agreement. It is on the matter of purgation that Herbert and Weil differ the most. The two main divisions of *The Temple* are "The Church Porch" and "The Church." "The Church Porch" concerns our preparation for entering "The Church." The poet tells us how we must conduct our lives and discipline our desires, if we are to be free of the blindness that prevents us from perceiving spiritual realties.

Weil shares with Herbert the conviction that we are in a fallen state. For us to be restored, there are at least six characteristics we need to cultivate. There is the need for attention; the need to withhold our allegiance from all that is earthly; the need to make use of beauty, suffering, and the void; and finally the need to recognize that we are like "leaky vessels" that cannot be filled. Several of these are treated by Weil under the single concept of "gravity."

Herbert treats only one or perhaps two of these in his celebrated poem "The Pulley," in which of all the blessings God confers, he withholds only one—namely, rest. If we do not turn to God out of love, then perhaps we shall turn to him from exhaustion. But even so, this overlap with Weil's notion of withholding our allegiance from all that is earthly and the comparison of us to "leaky vessels" does not occur in the division of *The Temple* devoted to our preparation.

This difference on the matter of preparation should not be surprising, however, for every spiritual writer is concerned to some extent with the particular barriers to God to be found in a specific age or a specific group of people. Herbert is concerned with courtiers who loved to be entertained, and so he writes verse to ensnare them by means of pleasure. Their blindness is the result of gambling, drunkenness, idleness, gluttony, lust, and the like. Weil is concerned with the sufferings of ordinary people and the barriers caused by their suffering.

Let us now look at the phase of the spiritual pilgrimage called illumination or understanding. Herbert treats this in the second major division of *The Temple* called "The Church." It opens with the very short poem, "The Altar," followed by a very long poem of sixty-three stanzas called "The Sacrifice." Each stanza ends with the question, "Was ever grief like mine?" Its frequent repetition in the short four-line stanzas has the effect of an accumulating force, penetrating more and more deeply into one's heart, until at last it breaks. (Only the stanza that contains Christ's cry of abandonment on the Cross, and the last stanza of the poem, have a variation: they end with "Never was grief like mine.")

The speaker in the entire poem is Christ himself. He addresses the pilgrim whose stony heart is the altar on which he is sacrificed. Christ tells the pilgrim of the love that seeks us from the very creation of the world, and describes its treatment by the Hebrew people and its culmination in his own earthly ministry. He asks the pilgrim to perceive the grief that our stony hearts have caused him.

"The Sacrifice" is followed by a poem entitled "Thanksgiving." The pilgrim searches unsuccessfully for an adequate response to such a sacrifice. The motivation of the Christian pilgrimage is the grief we have caused God—not, as in John Bunyan's *Pilgrim's Progress*, a fear of "the wrath that is to come," nor a desire for "the celestial city." Once freed of blindness, those whose hearts now form "broken altars" perceive God's sacrifice. Their most pressing concern now becomes: What can we render that is an adequate or proper response to such love? In "Thanksgiving" the poet gives up wealth, honor, and the like, but no matter what is offered, nothing is adequate. God in his love has always anticipated our gifts with his own, greater gifts. Before the passion of Christ, the pilgrim is utterly undone. "Then for thy passion—I will do for that—/ Alas, my God, I know not what" (49–50).

There is a partial resolution in the next poem, "The Reprisal" (meaning a second thanksgiving). The poet vows, "I will overcome / The man, who once against thee fought." This is only a partial resolution because, Herbert writes, "though I die for thee, I am behind" ("The Reprisal," 3). We do not learn until we come to the poem "Love," the last of the one hundred sixty-four poems of *The Temple*, and indeed not until the last line of that poem, what is an adequate response to the sacrifice of Christ.

There is one feature of the sacrifice—God's way of winning our hearts—which deserves special attention. The spectacle that the crucifixion presents is that of God, who is almighty, once again allowing creatures to use their power to resist the good he would bestow:

> The Princes of my people make a head
> Against their Maker: they do wish me dead,
> Who cannot wish, except I give them bread;
>   Was ever grief like mine?
>
> Without me each one, who doth now me brave,
> Had to this day been an Egyptian slave.
> They use that power against me, which I gave:
>   Was ever grief like mine? ("The Sacrifice," 5–12)

God's response to our resistance is to endure it. He hopes to win us through our perception of his grief:

I answer nothing but with patience prove
If stony hearts will melt with gently love.
But who does hawk at eagles with a dove?
Was ever grief like mine? (89–92)

Herbert's point in " The Sacrifice" is that we cannot defeat
God's love and design. He describes the benefits God seeks to confer
on us, and our blindness to his generosity. But still God seeks us—
finally coming to us in the person of Christ. Our response to Christ
is rejection. But Herbert shows that this cannot defeat his love.
Our very hateful rejection is turned into a sacrifice. That is, instead
of rejecting us for rejecting him, God takes our very rejection and
turns it into a revelation. It reveals the magnitude of his love; of
his willingness to put up with our blindness, our folly, our evil.
His response to all that we are and have done is not rejection, but
painful endurance. "I, who am Truth, turn into truth their deeds"
(179).

Not only does God let us see the effects of all that we are
and have done by letting it destroy his body, but he also shows
us that all that we are and have done does not stop him. His love
cannot be turned away. Even when people killed the one who bears
the love of God, God raised him from the dead to confront us once
again and to claim us. Thus the greatest rejection of all is not able
to defeat his love, and we are to see in the suffering our rejection
causes, a precise measure and revelation of the extent and tenacity
of his love:

Herbert summarizes the core of Christian truth in "The
Agony":

Philosophers have measur'd mountains,
Fathom'd the depths of seas, of states, and kings,
Walk'd with a staff to heav'n, and traced fountains:
     But there are two vast, spacious things,
The which to measure it doth more behove:
Yet few there are that sound them; Sin and Love.

Who would know Sin, let him repair
Unto Mount Olivet; there shall he see
A man so wrung with pains, that all his hair,
     His skin, his garments bloody be.
Sin is that press and vice, which forceth pain
To hunt his cruel food through ev'ry vein.

> Who knows not Love, let him assay
> And taste that juice, which on the cross a pike
> Did set again abroach; then let him say
> If ever he did taste the like.
> Love is that liquour sweet and most divine,
> Which my God feels as blood; but I, as wine.

The Cross is a focus for Simone Weil as well because, even though afflicted, Christ continues to look to the Father and to trust him. Affliction, the greatest kind of suffering, is unable to break the bond between them, or the reality of the Father's love. Both Herbert and Weil see the Cross as the intersection of incompatibles: for Herbert, sin and love; for Weil, affliction and love. Weil, for example, tells us in her "Spiritual Autobiography" that during her ten days at Solesmes she suffered from splitting headaches. Nonetheless she was able:

> To rise above this wretched flesh, to leave it to suffer by itself, heaped up in a corner, and to find a pure and perfect joy in the unimaginable beauty of the chanting and the words. This experience enabled me by analogy to get a better understanding of the possibility of loving divine love in the midst of affliction. It goes without saying that in the course of these services the thought of the Passion of Christ entered into my being once and for all. (WG 68)

The Cross of Christ is also a place of focus for her because the crucified one offers himself to us as food. Weil tells us it was while at Solesmes that she gained her first idea of the supernatural power of the sacraments from a young English Catholic, "because of the truly angelic radiance with which he seemed to be clothed after going to communion" (WG 68). The offer and the consummation of such food is the theme of Herbert's poem "Love."

SPIRITUAL GROWTH

The process of being formed into a temple in which God's love may dwell is so demanding that in "The Temper (I)" the poet is driven to plead with God to abandon the goal he has set for human beings:

How should I praise thee, Lord! how should my rhymes
    Gladly engrave thy love in steel,
    If what my soul doth feel sometimes,
       My soul might ever feel!

Although there were some forty heav'ns, or more,
    Sometimes I peer above them all;
    Sometimes I hardly reach a score,
       Sometimes to hell I fall.

Oh rack me not to such a vast extent;
    Those distances belong to thee:
    The world's too little for thy tent,
       A grave too big for me.

Wilt thou meet arms with man, that thou dost stretch
    A crumb of dust from heav'n to hell?
    Will great God measure with a wretch?
       Shall he thy stature spell?

Oh let me, when thy roof my soul hath hid,
    Oh let me roost and nestle there:
    Then of a sinner thou art rid,
       And I of hope and fear.

Yet take thy way; for sure thy way is best:
    Stretch or contract me thy poor debtor:
    This is but tuning of my breast,
       To make the music better.

Whether I fly with angels, fall with dust,
    Thy hands made both, and I am there:
    Thy power and love, my love and trust
       Make one place evry'where.

A central theme of Simone Weil's conception of spiritual growth is that of waiting. God, she claims, plants a seed in us and it grows of its own accord. Our contribution is to endure its growth, for it destroys all that we are accustomed to call "I." This includes the destruction of carnal desires, the love of social prestige, and all self-sufficiency. So our "waiting" for God is not sheer passivity, for we can hinder the growth of the seed by holding onto those things that its growth would drive out, or we can release them and thus give the seed of love more room for unimpeded growth. We can even come to so regret that the seed of love ever got into us so that we can expel it. Both Herbert and Weil, then, consider that spiritual growth is so demanding that it is common for us to be tempted to renounce God's intention of permeating us with his love.

The course we travel in our formation into a temple in which his love may dwell is actually made visible by the very pattern of the printed words of the poem "Colossians 3:3":

> *My* words and thoughts do both express this notion,
> That *Life* hath with the sun a double motion.
> The first *Is* straight, and our diurnal friend,
> The other *Hid*, and doth obliquely bend.
> One life is wrapt *in* flesh, and tends to earth.
> The other winds towards *Him*, whose happy birth
> Taught me to live here so, *That* still one eye
> Should aim and shoot at that which *Is* on high;
> Quitting with daily labor all *My* pleasure,
> To gain at harvest an eternal *Treasure*.

There is a double motion in the Christian pilgrimage. Our daily life goes along a horizontal course, like the printed words of the poem, and like them has a meaning. But more is taking place in our lives, for as we move through our daily tasks, our hearts are being shaped so that our desire is for Christ, our treasure. This is shown by the diagonal line that connects a word from each horizontal line.

This means that the Christian pilgrimage, whereby we are formed into creatures in which God is pleased to dwell, does not follow a direct course. Directly we go to church, hear sermons, take part in the liturgy and music, pray and receive the Eucharist. As part of our vocation, we engage in our work as labor undertaken for God's glory. In Herbert's own case it is to be both a priest and a poet. Another aspect of the horizontal is our own inner moods of peace, anxiety, hope and fear, elation and distress. They are not to be identified with our spiritual progress or state. They too are part of the direct, observable part of life, and they can be very erratic. But through church observances, work, and inner experiences we are being so formed that we may desire Christ as our treasure. We may not see how they contribute to this formation. But it is only be moving along the horizontal as best we can, obeying God by making use of the benefits of his Church and the discipline of our work, and offering to him in both our praise, that we provide the building blocks for the construction of that life which is hid with Christ in God, and which finds in him our treasure. Thus every moment of dismay and dryness, as well as times of elation, makes a contribution to the life that is being formed, but is not visible to us, especially when we are in states of distress.

Herbert then does not identify the spiritual life with the interior life. It, like church going and work, belongs to the horizontal or the observable. The structure of the poem also indicates that for Herbert some of God's work in forming us is open to view. Thus Herbert does not treat spiritual growth as utterly hidden from view, as does Kierkegaard in his earlier works such as *Fear and Trembling*. There Kierkegaard identifies the spiritual life with sheer "inwardness." Spiritual growth for Herbert does not take place independently of the visible. Yet from what is visible, we cannot observe all that is taking place.

The refusal to identify the spiritual life with our subjective consciousness is strikingly different from the way people commonly think of spirituality. But on this point Weil is wholly in agreement with Herbert. As we saw in chapter 7 concerning friendship, the reality of God or the supernatural is made evident in the course of our natural history. Our natural history is the life described by the horizontal lines of the poem. But once we are converted or have faith, we start to read our natural history as a supernatural one, which in the poem is the diagonal line.

As we see from Weil's "Spiritual Autobiography" in *Waiting for God*, the supernatural history is now the one that counts. She now presents her life as one of preparation for direct contact with God, in which Christ himself becomes present to her. She says that she previously had thought that the problem of God was insoluble and had "never foreseen the possibility of . . . a real contact person to person, here below, between a human being and God" (WG 69). After this direct contact with God, she is then able to describe love of neighbor, love of the beauty of the world as a whole, the love of religious practices, and friendship as implicit or indirect contact with God. She is also able to embark on the intellectual task of understanding myths, folklore, philosophers such as Plato, work and social reform in spiritual or religious terms. She begins to read (see chapter 4) all things religiously.

For Weil, not only does one not know one has a supernatural life until after conversion, but that supernatural life is not independent of a natural history (see chapter 5). In other words, even though the diagonal and the horizontal are not identical, the diagonal cannot and does not exist without the horizontal. The supernatural is realized in and through the natural.

In Weil, as in Herbert, the spiritual life is a divine work. As Weil puts it, the seed of love, which is planted in us, is planted in *secret*. That is to say, it is not perceptible to other people nor to our introspection. It is planted in what Weil calls "the void," and it begins to grow of its own accord without our awareness. Only when it has grown sufficiently large does it begin to impinge on our awareness and show itself in our behavior:

> When a man's way of behaving towards things and men, or simply his way of regarding them, reveals supernatural virtues, one knows that his soul is no longer a virgin, it has slept with God. (FLN 145–46)

Moreover, the seed of love is not identified with our person or personality. The spiritual life is not our *possession*. It is the result of divine love at work in us. Our task is to *consent* to its presence and work, rather than to impede it, regret it ever got into us, or even to reject it as we have seen.

WORK

Herbert, because he has poetic talent, has the vocation to offer praise through poetry, and thus enable others, in the joy poetry gives, to join in praise. This employment, along with the vocation to be a priest, is what he is called to render to God. But Herbert in common with all Christians has to tread a course between two extremes. On the one hand, we must not think that our identity is the same as our work. On the other hand, we must resist the temptation to reject our work as irrelevant to our true life. Work is the horizontal, mortal life we lead. If we identify ourselves fully with what we create there, our true life is lost. But such work must be done with all our heart, mind, soul, and strength as our praise of God. Then it supplies the material for the hidden life that is a heart, which finds in him our treasure. The Christian is thus not to be a hater of this world. Herbert's sacramental view of work is especially strong in his poem "The Elixir," which represents his penultimate resolution of what we can render unto God for all his benefits, especially for his sacrifice:

Teach me, my God and King,
In all things thee to see,
And what I do in anything
To do it as for thee:

Not rudely, as a beast,
To run into an action;
But still to make thee prepossest,
And give it his perfection.

A man that looks on glass,
On it may stay his eye;
Or if he pleaseth, through it pass,
And then the heav'n espy.

All may of thee partake:
Nothing can be so mean,
Which with his tincture (for thy sake)
Will not grow bright and clean.

A servant with this clause
Makes drudgery divine:
Who sweeps a room, as for thy laws,
Makes that and the action fine.

This is the famous stone
That turneth all to gold:
For that which God doth touch and own
Cannot for less be told.

Work for Weil is an essential part of our formation, or as she puts it, our "de-creation." People often interpret Weil's notion of "decreation" as harsh and life-destructive in contrast to a life-affirming idea. We may gain some help from Herbert in understanding the meaning of this difficult notion.

For Herbert work is an appropriate response to the passion of Christ because God is a builder. God not only made the heavens and earth and gives all things their proper employment in the functioning of an orderly cosmos, but he is also building us into a temple in which his love may dwell. Since God is a builder, our proper response to him as his servants is likewise to be engaged in building or in work. Work renders him praise; work contributes to his creation; work contributes to our being made into a fit dwelling for his love. This is why there are several poems in which Herbert laments that others have work, but he has none. (These may reflect the long period in which he was without any employment before his ordination. See "Employment II" and "Business.") For Weil work is a way we become obedient to God. For her the physical universe is perfectly obedient to God. We, by our work, insert ourselves into the chain of necessary relation that hold between the forces of nature, and so integrate ourselves into its perfect obedience. We thus become "de-created."

Even when Herbert has employment, both as a poet and priest, he complains that we are often unfaithful in our labor, and he frequently finds himself running dry as a poet. (See "Affliction IV.") But work, even when done faithfully, is inadequate. We are forever debtors, as we depend utterly on God for all our powers:

> I threat'ned to observe the strict decree
> Of my dear God with all my power and might.
> But I was told by one, it could not be;
> Yet I might trust in God to be my light.
>
> Then will I trust, said I, in him alone.
> Nay, ev'n to trust in him, was also his;
> We must confess, that nothing is our own.
> Then I confess that he my succor is:
>
> But to have nought is ours, not to confess
> That we have nought. I stood amaz'd at this,
> Much troubled, till I heard a friend express,
> That all things were more ours by being his.
> What Adam had, and forfeited for all,
> Christ keepeth now, who cannot fail or fall. ("The Holdfast")

The progression of thought here is from seeking with all one's own strength to be obedient, to reliance on trust, to a realization that trust is not within our own power and that even a confession that trust is not within our own power is not enough. We are not to *confess* that we have nothing, but *are* to have nothing. The paradox that we have naught is resolved when we see that God seeks to be our benefactor, and that our task is to receive. But we can receive from him on whom we utterly depend only to the extent to which we are in a condition in which we not only see that we are dependent on him but actually do become dependent on him. *The entire Christian pilgrimage is a process in which we are being so shaped and formed by him that we indeed not only confess that we are dependent on him, but actually become dependent on him.* Thus the poems on such themes as guilt, repentance, thanksgiving, dryness, temptation, rebellion, peace, affliction, praise, as well as poems on worship during the daily offices of the Church (such as "Matins") and the church year (such as "Easter") are the movements of the Christian as he or she is being formed or shaped to fully receive God's benefits.

Herbert thus can help us understand Weil's notion of "de-creation." De-creation is not destruction. In Weil's own words, destruction is "to make something created pass into nothingness" (GG 28). To become "decreated" is to have renounced self-sufficiency, not as an idea or a firmly held conviction, but in fact. It is "to have naught." Free of all possessions, there is room for divine love to enter; to be our treasure; to be our life. De-creation, then is not destruction, but it is, again in Weil's own words, "to make something created pass into the uncreated" (GG 28). This passing into the uncreated need not be understood as absorption, but following Herbert, it is for divine love to dwell in us as a temple.

The poem "Time" nicely brings out the distinction between "destruction" and "de-creation." Our spiritual formation takes time, and Christ's coming transforms time for the pilgrim. Formerly time was an enemy, for if time is all that there is, then the passage of time is a fearful thing. But with Christ's coming, time is no longer a scythe cutting us as crudely as a dull hatchet, but a pruning knife. "Christ's coming hath made man thy debtor, Since by thy cutting he grows better" (11–12). This makes very good sense in light of the poem "Colossians 3:3"; increments are added to the diagonal line by the passing of our daily life. Time has been transformed from an executioner to a gardener, as our movement to greater and greater dependence on Christ's love with the passage of time is growth into that never-failing life. Cutting things away is not an act of destruction but a de-creation, because Christ is the Lord of time. Now our passing life is leading us to our end or goal.

Just as Herbert can help us understand Weil's notion of "de-creation," Weil in turn can help us understand Herbert's reformation doctrine that we depend on God's grace utterly. To say that we "have naught" makes sense in terms of Weil's notion of "gravity." For Weil all that is created is gravity, in contrast to God who is grace. Gravity is not to be identified with evil; it is simply earthliness. Each one of us consists of gravity, surrounding a void or "nothing."

That void cannot be filled by anything that is created. It represents our need for God, and only God can fill the void. To "have naught" can thus be understood as the recognition that we are voids, surrounded by gravity. We depend utterly on God to plant the seed of love in the void. That seed, as it grows, is what gives us a desire for God or a love for God, so that Christ can become our treasure. Only so can we receive Christ's love and thereby become a temple in which God's love may dwell.

This brings us to the last poem of the collection, "Love," which contains the final resolution concerning the appropriate response to Christ's passion:

> Love bade me welcome: yet my soul drew back,
>   Guilty of dust and sin.
> But quick-ey'd Love, observing me grow slack
>   From my first entrance in,
> Drew nearer to me, sweetly questioning,
>   If I lack'd anything.
> A guest, I answer'd, worthy to be here:
>   Love said, You shall be he.
> I the unkind, ungrateful? Ah my dear,
>   I cannot look on thee.
> Love took my hand, and smiling did reply,
>   Who made the eyes but I?
> Truth Lord, but I have marr'd them: let my shame
>   Go where it doth deserve.
> And know you not, says Love, who bore the blame?
>   My dear, then I will serve.
> You must sit down, says Love, and taste my meat:
>   So I did sit and eat.

Although we are caught in the power of both death (the natural end of that which is made from dust) and damnation (the just end of sin), neither is to be our end. Love sacrifices itself to relieve us of both death and sin. What can we do or render in return for such a sacrifice? We cannot even serve him of ourselves. Rather all we can do is to receive his sacrifice, and we can receive it properly only by being utterly dependent. The pilgrimage forms us so that we are utterly dependent on his sacrifice; it so shapes us that we have "naught." Having "naught," we can receive him and be filled by him. So the only thing we can do is to obey the command, "You must sit down, says Love, and taste my meat." We must simply receive God's sacrifice.

There is a certain robust simplicity in the obedience. ("So I did sit and eat.") After the intensity of all the previous lines, the guest in effect says, "All right, you tell me to sit down and eat, so I will do as I am told." There is even a tone of lightheartedness; and indeed there should be, as the poem is an allusion to the final banquet in heaven, as found in Luke 12.37, in which there is much rejoicing. It should be noted that one receives Christ as an act of obedience. One does not presume to take the food from the table, even though one knows that one's salvation from death and damnation is Christ's sacrifice. It is because Christ commands it that one sits and eats.

Simone Weil expresses the same idea in a letter to Father Perrin:

> If I had my eternal salvation placed in front of me on this table, and if I only had to stretch out my hand to take it, I would not put out my hand so long as I had not received the order to do so. (WG 56–57)

HUMAN FULFILLMENT

T.S. Eliot pointed out in his essay "Lancelot Andrewes" that John Donne's poetry was a means of self-expression and that "he is constantly finding an object which shall be adequate to his feelings."[2] This is in marked contrast to Herbert for whom the object is above all Christ's passion, and our task is to shape ourselves, including our sensibility, to conform to it. Christian doctrine and the discipline provided by the Church's services and work are to form the sensibilities of the Christian pilgrim.

This is in deep harmony with Weil's concept of attention, as we find in the essays "Reflections on the Right Use of School Studies," "Human Personality," and in her book *The Need for Roots*. Weil distinguishes between lower and higher levels of attention. A lower kind of attention can be developed with school studies. "Attention consists of suspending our thought, leaving it detached, empty and ready to be penetrated by the object" (WG 111). It prepares us for a higher form of attention:

> So long as man submits to having his soul taken up with his own thoughts, his personal thoughts, he remains entirely subjected, even in his most secret thoughts, to the compulsion exercised by needs and to the mechanical play of forces. If he thinks otherwise, he is mistaken. But everything changes as

soon as, by virtue of a positive act of concentration, he empties
his soul so as to allow the conception of eternal wisdom to
enter into it. He then carries within himself the very conception
to which force is subjected. (NR 291)

That is to say, we are thinking in a way that is not under the sway
of gravity, and are "therefore on the same side as that which
dominates force." We are not the lord and master of creation and
all its forces, but we are children of the lord and master (NR 291;
see Gal. 4:1–7).

For Weil, as for Herbert, the ultimate truth about ourselves
is not to be found in an expression of our inherent potential. Self-
expression is not the road to self realization. It is by our conformity
to truth that we find what can give fullness to us. Their spirituality
raises our horizon concerning what human fullness is by showing
that to be realizing our inherent potential is to be subject to gravity,
and so to be cut off from God. Rather we are to become open to
what is from above; and that openness is made possible by conforming
ourselves to what is outside ourselves.

TRUTH AND THE IMAGINATION

Simone Weil often expressed grave suspicions about the use
of our imagination. It can be so easily used to keep us from facing
unpleasant realities and thereby to keep God from entering us. But
she clearly loved creative art, which relies on the imagination, and
she considered Herbert's "Love" to be a perfect poem, a poem in
which we are to imagine Christ as addressing us at the table of his
sacrifice. The unacceptable use of the imagination can be distinguished
from a proper use by the term "fantasy." Fantasy is unacceptable
because it keeps us at the level of gravity by allowing us to keep
our egocentric perspective intact. But a proper use of the imagination
gives us access to truth which otherwise is inaccessible.

Consider Herbert's poem "The Sacrifice," in which we are to
imagine that Christ, as he hangs from the cross, is addressing us.
We are to perceive his grief and to realize that his sacrifice sets
the problem of the Christian life—namely, what can we render to
God for his love. In the poem "Love," because Christ himself
addresses us, we are able to experience God's love. This is a proper
use of the imagination, because our egocentrism is pierced and we
are no longer motivated simply by our gravity but also by grace,
which has entered us.

Broadly speaking, although experience has become the touchstone for truth-claims in modern history, the imagination, which is itself a source of experience, has been barred as a source of truth. But experiences, such as these poems awaken, give us reason to believe that the imagination may give us access to truth. To see this we first must distinguish several senses of experience.

1. Experience can mean "sense-experience" or experiences available through the sense organs, such as when we report, "I see a car." This view of experience has dominated empirical philosophy in the modern period. If our understanding of experience is limited to sense-experience, then traditional Christianity, as well as much of traditional philosophy, ethics, and aesthetics, is likely to be excluded from serious consideration, as giving us access to truth.

2. Experience can also mean "high moments" of intensity. Examples of this kind of experience can be found in the ecstasy of mystics, such as Plotinus or Wordsworth. William James's *Varieties of Religious Experience* is the best-known collection of "high moments." Such experiences may not involve any of our sense-organs; Simone Weil's experience of Christ coming to possess her soul did not.

3. We can mean by experience those things that are needed for us to acquire wisdom. Wisdom is not associated with youth, because a person has to have lived long enough to have made some mistakes, and from such experiences, a person may acquire wisdom. At least one may, if one has the courage to admit having made mistakes. Samuel Johnson is perhaps the best-known modern moralist whose reflections on life's experiences continue to be cited. But Socrates, Sophocles, and Aeschylus, as well as sacred scriptures, are full of wisdom based on experience in the sense of life's experiences. Neither such wisdom nor the significance of "high moments" can be reduced to a set of sentences that contain reference to sense-experience only.

4. There are experiences of guilt or shame. For example, consider the following train of thought: "I can be in the company of people who are much more clever or accomplished than I. They do not make me feel ashamed, because I have learned that I do not have to have the greatest intellect to be comfortable with myself. I am not ashamed to be in the presence of great wealth either, because I have learned that fullness of life is not to be found through great possessions. People who have power over me can make me afraid, but they do not make me feel ashamed, because I know that the unjust use of power is immoral. But if someone is able to portray Christ, as the Gospel writers and as some preachers and spiritual

writers and poets do, then I do feel ashamed of myself. I find that the person portrayed judges my life and makes me aware of its invalidity, and of my inability to trust in myself." Such an experience is made possible by the use of concepts, ideas, and convictions. Without them, the experience of such a shame is unavailable to one.

5. Poetry is a special case of the use of concepts, ideas, and comparisons to make some specific experiences are accessible to us. An awareness of the nature and significance of God's love, especially as expressed in the Incarnation, is made available to us by use of imagination. Only an awareness of the grief of God and the generosity of his love to us, who are creatures, can inform the intellect and convince the heart of the nature of its task: to be so formed as to be able to receive such love.

Kant in the *Critique of Pure Reason* said that "impressions without concepts are blind; concepts without impressions are empty." We may illustrate this important observation with the game of football. If a person does not know the rules of the game or understand the game, then he or she is at a loss when at a critical moment the ball trickles off the fingers of a receiver and the crowd groans. The groan is an emotional experience, but it occurs only because people understand the game. An emotional experience is possible only because the intellect is informed.

Kant's insight has been rediscovered in contemporary empirical philosophy. A positivist interpretation of perception as a mere reporting of sense-experience has been found to be inadequate. Every kind of experience involves the use of concepts; there is no experience that is "pure." Thus the attempt to reduce all experiences to sense-experience has been found to be misguided.

Various concepts, ideas, and images are used to portray Christ. They make experiences such as a particular sense of shame possible. Likewise it is by an imaginative use of concepts, ideas, and images that the experience of divine grief and love is made accessible to us by Herbert. The fact that poetry involves the imaginative use of concepts, ideas, and images does not ipso facto exclude what is made accessible by poetry from consideration as true. Herbert is not merely giving expression to convictions, he is inviting people to experience the reality of God's love and in that experience to attain conviction or to deepen conviction.

That is precisely what happened to Simone Weil. A poem opened her to an experience that convinced her of the reality of God. Previously, as we have seen, she had thought that the problem of

God's existence or nonexistence was insoluble. But more than this experience of a visitation of Christ was needed. "I still half refused, not my love but my intelligence"(WG 69). Full conviction came because of repeated experiences of divine visitation with the recitation of the Lord's Prayer (WG 69–72) and because she developed a particular view of the relation of beauty and truth.

In the context of a discussion of the evidential force of Christ's miracles, she writes: "The exceptional character of the acts had no other object than to draw attention. Once the attention has been drawn, there can be no other form of proof than beauty, purity, perfection" (NR 269).

She claims that miraculous acts are a sign that a person is outside the ordinary run of humanity. They have such power because they are servants of either supernatural good or supernatural evil. Weil claims that it is easy to see "by the manifest perfection of Christ, the purity of his life, the perfect beauty of his words, and the fact that he only exercised his powers in order to perform acts of compassion," that he was allied to supernatural good. We are thus bound to believe all that he said, "save where we have the right to suppose a faulty transcription; and what gives the proof its force is beauty. When the subject in question is the good [meaning supernatural good], beauty is a rigorous and positive proof; and, indeed, there can be none other. It is absolutely impossible for there to be any other" (NR 268–69).

What is it that connects beauty to truth? Weil is convinced that the entire order of the universe is necessity. She is not a determinist, because the necessity of physical nature is not the same as the necessity in human life. Even the necessity of physical nature is subject to a supernatural good. It operates as it does out of obedience to that good. We experience nature's operations on our bodies as brute force. But nature is not just brute force. It is superbly ordered:

> Brute force is not sovereign in this world. It is by nature blind and indeterminate. What is sovereign in this world? It is determinateness, limit. Eternal Wisdom imprisons this universe in a network, a web of determinations. The universe accepts passively. The brute force of matter, which appears to us sovereign, is nothing else in reality but perfect obedience. . . . That is the truth which bites at our hearts every time we are penetrated by the beauty of the world. That is the truth which bursts forth in matchless accents of joy in the beautiful and

pure parts of the Old Testament, in Greece among the Pythagoreans. (NR 285)

The reasoning seems to be that beauty and truth are connected through supernatural good. Nature is not just brute force. It is orderly. That order can be grasped by the intellect and its necessity understood (see chapter 3). Its order or necessity is beautiful, both to our intellect and our senses. It is thus true that nature operates by necessity, and that truth is experienced as the beauty of the world. Beauty is superior to brute force. We do not love brute force, but we do love the beauty of the world, which results from a world ordered in a particular way. Beauty, as a good, thus gives us access to a wisdom that is a supernatural good, because it is the source of nature's order and hence of nature's beauty.

Because beauty is the result of the way brute force is ordered into a cosmos, the intersection of beauty and pain is where truth can be found. It is where a supernatural good is made manifest through the beauty that results from the order of the cosmos, from the way brute force is ordered to yield something superior to itself. Thus we can make sense of the claim, "when the subject in question is the [supernatural] good, beauty is a rigorous and positive proof; and, indeed, there can be no other"(NR 269).

At Solesmes, while in pain and also experiencing the beauty of the plain chants, Weil experienced an intersection of beauty and pain that caused the thought of Christ's passion to enter into her permanently. It was while she was at Solesmes that the supernatural power of the Eucharist became first evident to her from the angelic radiance of an English Catholic after going to communion. Here again we have the intersection of pain and beauty: Christ's pain and the communicant's radiance. Pain and beauty mediate an awareness of a supernatural good.

Herbert's poem "Love" is an intersection of beauty and suffering. It was while reciting it in wretched pain that Weil was visited by a supernatural good. That presence won her love. It only half-convinced her intellect. It took more visitations and a structure of thought concerning nature's necessity and nature's beauty before she became fully convinced. One experience, even one as powerful as she had, was not sufficient. It had to be connected to other levels of experience and reasoning to give full conviction. Nonetheless, it was a poem using the imagination that enabled Weil to break through to a domain above the intellect. That experience gave her the incentive and the ability to interpret Plato as a mystic, to see the *Iliad* as bathed in Christian light (WG 70), and thus to assemble material to develop an epistemology that related beauty, truth, pain, and supernatural good, and thus to achieve full conviction. She then can write such things as "the true mysteries of the Faith are themselves absurd, but their absurdity is such as to illumine the mind and cause it to produce in abundance truths which are clear to the intelligence" (NR 279).

PART IV
Persons and Communities

9. OF TENNIS,
PERSONS, AND POLITICS

IN THE FINAL ENTRY to her London notebooks, Simone Weil writes simply: "The most important part of teaching = to teach what it is to *know* (in the scientific sense). Nurses." (FLN 364).[1] Perhaps that entry aptly sums up the life of Simone Weil, but if it does, we struggle to know, in any sense, what exactly she meant by it. Fortunately we are given a clue only five entries earlier. There Weil writes: "Philosophy (including problems of cognition, etc.) is *exclusively* an affair of action and practice. That is why it is so difficult to write about it. Difficult in the same way as a treatise on tennis or running, but much more so"(FLN 362). The light that this latter passage sheds on the former thus initially seems to be this: that knowing, that philosophy, is difficult to write about and teach because at its roots it is something that is more than simply saying what the case is; it is fundamentally an activity of the whole person that involves what Michael Polanyi has called a "tacit dimension." Thus just as we cannot simply tell a child how to ride a bike, or to play tennis, and expect them to go out and do it—even if everything we tell them is quite true and unambiguous—so too Weil is claiming we cannot just tell people what philosophy is, or what knowing is, and expect them to know, in the deepest sense. Philosophy may use formulae, but its formulae will always be slightly misleading, because they may cause us to think knowing is something other than a doing.

If philosophy and knowing is an affair of action and practice, like tennis, we can easily see why it is difficult to write about it. The fixed written word simply cannot capture knowing; as Plato says in the *Seventh Letter*: "no intelligent man will ever be so bold as to put into language those things which his reason has contemplated, especially not into a form that is unalterable—which must be the case with what is expressed in written symbols."[2] The difficulty of adequately saying what we know so that others may understand is, indeed, a profoundly difficult task for teaching. However, if knowing is *exclusively* an affair of action and practice, there is another even deeper difficulty, for in this case every act of real knowing becomes also a matter of self knowledge. Knowing cannot on this account simply be a matter of saying what the case is, independent of the knower, it is an activity of the knower and her self-engagement with the known. As Andrew Louth suggests in another context: "Understanding is an exploration of the dimensions of human finitude."[3]

To see this truth about knowing, as we think Weil certainly did, is to see not only a fact about knowing, but something radically important about the human person who knows. It is therefore in light of her suggestion that philosophy and knowing is an affair of action and practice that we shall here try to uncover some key elements of Weil's understanding of the human person and, relatedly, Weil's own distinctive political philosophy.

Rather than beginning with Weil herself, however, let us begin by examining another philosophical tennis metaphor. Its intent is quite the opposite of Weil's, but the comparison should in the end help us to understand Weil's point better. In *Leviathan* Thomas Hobbes makes this claim: "The skill of making and maintaining commonwealths consists in certain rules, as do arithmetic and geometry, not, as tennis-play, on practice only; which rules neither poor men have the leisure, nor men that have had the leisure have hitherto had the curiosity or the method to find out."[4]

What Hobbes means here is rather straightforward, and helpfully so, since it summarizes his view of philosophy quite well. It is also quite contrary to Weil's view. For Hobbes, the task of making commonwealths—the political philosopher's task—is that of discovering certain rules, especially rules and principles for understanding human nature, and then constructing commonwealths according to them so that the ends proper to human nature may be fostered, which ends also appear to be a matter of rules. For Hobbes there is little question that such rules and principles actually exist and can be spelled out; after all that is the whole point of Part I of *Leviathan*, which traces the causal chains of human behavior, and which dictates in Part II the necessity of an absolute sovereign. That human practice has constructed different sorts of commonwealths on the basis of experience and practice, Hobbes does not doubt. What he does doubt is that those commonwealths are very good, for, he reasons, they cannot be wellfounded. Even such commonwealths that have been long-lived, he regards as no valid counter-example. He argues:

> But, howsoever, an argument from the practice of men that have not sifted to the bottom, and with exact reason weighed the causes and nature of commonwealths, and suffer daily those miseries that proceed from the ignorance thereof, is invalid. For though in all places of the world men should lay the foundation of their houses on the sand, it could not thence be inferred that so it ought to be."[5]

It is for this reason that philosophy cannot be like tennis. Practice and experience may, indeed, hit upon a happy solution in areas such as politics. Practice and experience, however, can never serve as a sure foundation on which to build our associations, for they involve no real knowledge of what holds those associations together. Their success is thus a bit of an accident; even when successful, there is nothing in them that can guarantee their permanence. Only a foundation of deductive reason can do that.

Hobbes's view of philosophy and truth implied herein is not an unusual one, either in his time or our own. Truth is to be spelled out exactly and more or less certainly, and the more exactly and certainly, the better. Anything else we have little or no reason to believe. So we can see why for Hobbes philosophy is *not* like tennis, which can be known only by practice.

Clearly Hobbes and Weil are at odds in their conception of what constitutes truth and philosophy. But in order to understand Weil better, let us look closely at what sort of difference it makes to see philosophy as being essentially a matter of action and practice, of being like tennis.

Why Hobbes thinks philosophy is not like tennis has already been briefly noted. But let us take Weil's position and see what is at stake if philosophy *is* like tennis. Let us assume here for a moment that she is right and Hobbes is wrong, and think about what Hobbes is actually doing. This is to say, let us not so much dismiss Hobbes as try to understand what Hobbes as a philosopher is doing if philosophy is a matter of practice. What we are asking is "How is what Hobbes says to be understood, including his claims of being objectively and deductively neutral, if what he is doing involves practice and not just deduction?"

In the first place this obviously involves at least seeing that what Hobbes writes *is* the result not of pure deduction but practice. For example, it is the result of Hobbes' study of other philosophers, such as Descartes, and it is the result of his own political experience in seventeenth-century England. It is, like a treatise on tennis, the result of having played the game. But assuming that Hobbes really is an original philosopher, what Hobbes writes is also the result of a distinctive way of playing the game. In this sense its originality is more than just a report on something that nobody else had seen before, for what is reported has imbedded in it a distinctive approach to the problems he discusses; it is, in an important sense, itself a distinctive practice. Thus like a good treatise on tennis, it is not simply a report on how the game is played, it teaches us how to play it better. Or to put it another way and to continue the tennis metaphor, it is a way of serving, of setting the ball in play, which ball will be returned and hit back in a characteristic way. In short, knowing, philosophizing, is the ability to serve and return; it is not really the theory itself; or at least the theory has to be understood as itself a practice, a practice of articulating and approaching a certain set of problems.[6] Knowledge is not a thing in the mind; it is the mind's activity.[7]

This much might be said about any philosopher. But with respect to Hobbes specifically, and to the tradition of liberal political philosophy that he spawned and which continues in Locke and more recently John Rawls and Robert Nozick more generally, some important additional things can also be said. What can be said has to do with how Hobbes, Locke, and the liberal tradition views persons and their political associations. Now, this specific tradition in the philosophy of politics is, in one sense, no different than many others. As C.B. MacPherson writes in an introduction to an edition of Locke's *Second Treatise of Government*:

"Every political theory which sets out to justify or advocate a particular system of government, or a limited or unlimited degree of obligation of the citizen to the state, must rest on an explicit or implicit theory of human nature. The theories must show, or assume, that the human beings who will have to submit to and operate the desired system do need and are capable of running it."[8]

This is nowhere quite so obvious as in Hobbes and Locke where a theory of human nature is spelled out explicitly to ground their political philosophy. But if Hobbes and Locke are not unusual in providing a theory of human nature to underwrite their political philosophy, what is distinctive about them is the specific theory of human nature that they give.

Much can be said about the theory of human nature and consequent view of human political associations that is broadly established in this tradition. MacPherson himself called it "the political theory of possessive individualism."[9] More recently Robert Bellah and colleagues have decried it for having caused an excessive individualism in modern political life that keeps us from even seeing the great degree to which we rely on various institutions around us for both life and identity.[10] Charles Taylor finds in it "a growing ideal of a human agent who is able to remake himself by methodical and disciplined action."[11]

Each of these critics has found some deep problems with the liberal tradition in political philosophy that dominates theory of both the left and right. Most of those problems have to do with the view of human beings on which it rests. We do not intend to add much to their insights here. What we do want to investigate is what this theory of the human person—and political associations—involves if philosophy is a matter of action and practice, if it is not just a descriptive affair that portrays results, but is itself an active way of finding out and thinking through how to be human.

Of all who have commented on the liberal Enlightenment tradition's understanding of the human person, it is perhaps Taylor who has understood best this problem. After noting the sort of ideal that evolves in Hobbes and Locke et al., he goes on to note: "What this [ideal] calls for is the ability to take an instrumental stance to one's given properties, desires, inclinations, tendencies, habits of thought and feeling, so that they can be *worked on*, doing away with some and strengthening others, until one meets the desired specifications."[12] Put into the sort of terms we have been using, this is to say, the theory of the self produced in Hobbes and

Locke is actually a newly developed practice, a newly developed action for approaching persons.

This practice of approaching persons has its value, including moral value. Despite the various valid criticisms by many contemporary thinkers of the view of persons developed in the Enlightenment, this view does allow us to look at ourselves in such a way that we can treat ourselves—and persons in general—with a certain degree of moral objectivity. Despite the very real problems that the view has caused in other areas, it can create a type of knowing that has a certain moral value, which even Weil has recognized. As she notes: "No 'I' in numbers except as a cause of error" (NB 193), meaning that this ability to treat ourselves and others "objectively" is at least an ability not to overvalue ourselves.

However, there is a negative side to this as well, for if this ability to distance ourselves from ourselves has some positive value, it also has as a practice the unfortunate tendency to hide from itself the fact that it is a practice. By attempting to describe what is, *simpliciter*, it forgets that describing is simply one practice among others of approaching ourselves and the world. It thus hides that there is human practice and action even in neutral description. This is dangerous for several reasons: by forgetting that this is an activity of knowing, we easily fall into the error of "naive platonism,"— that is, the belief that there simply is an answer "out there" and that all we have to do is describe it, and that any fool with the right method can describe it. So we forget that we, the describers, are active beings in search of knowledge for some valuable reason. We forget that what we know and what we can know depends upon how we approach what we want to know. In such forgetting, it becomes all too easy to believe that what we have legitimately discovered by our objectivity, is, in fact, *purely, simply and totally objective,*—that is, what is the case. And when we do forget in this way, if there is anything else to know, we do not have left any habitual practice of knowing it. We also by practice habituate ourselves to think, for example, that persons are the way we have described them. We develop a habit of radical reflexivity that keeps us continually at a distance from ourselves. In the end, then, if we keep telling ourselves that we are that way, we soon lose the ability to see ourselves any other way.

At this point it is well to remember that all we have said is based on the assumption that Weil is right and that philosophy is an affair of action and practice. It shall be left to the reader to decide between Weil and Hobbes. But at least we are now in a position to see how what Weil says about human persons and political associations is distinctive and unlike the tradition begun in Hobbes.

––––––––––––––

Earlier C.B. MacPherson was quoted to the effect that every political philosophy must rest, explicitly or implicitly, upon a theory of human persons. Not only is this true, and obviously so, of Hobbes and Locke, it is true of Weil as well. In what follows we hope to make clear some of the connection between Weil's understanding of the human person and her political thought.

Unfortunately the details will have to remain quite sketchy, but perhaps that is just as well for what needs to be stressed is less the details than the point that Weil's understanding of persons, and thus the relation between that understanding and her political philosophy, needs to be read in the light of her understanding of what philosophy is. This is to say, we need to see that the difference in understanding between what Weil takes the human person to be and Hobbes takes it to be, is not just a matter of specific details, but a difference in the very way either approaches human persons. For Weil, any theory of human persons is a matter of having dealt with them, but it is not just the report of that dealing; it is also self-consciously a dealing and action, which dealing invites further dealing and action. The difference then that exists between Weil and Hobbes on what philosophy is also becomes a difference between Weil and the standard options of liberal theory of both persons and politics.

We must be careful, however, not to think that such a view precludes the sort of "objective" study and theory that Hobbes undertakes. Dealing with persons can—and ought—to give this sort of reading of them, and clearly Weil herself thought so. Even in an essay as late as "Is There a Marxist Doctrine?," she argues for a quasi-materialist position that seems as mechanistic as Hobbes'. Praising Marx for having come up with the idea of nonphysical matter, she goes on to claim that in the moral order always "there is something analogous to matter properly so-called." The result is that while moral phenomena are not subject to physical necessity, they are nevertheless subject to necessity. She argues: "They are exposed to the repercussion of physical phenomena, but it is a specific repercussion, in conformity with the specific laws of that necessity to which they are subject. Everything that is real is subject to necessity. . . . The relation between cause and effect is as rigorously determined in this field as it is in that of gravity. Only it is harder to know"(OL 178). In this sense Weil clearly seems committed to a position that maintains that there is something to know objectively about human beings. If philosophy is difficult to write, Weil still thinks it can and ought to be written.

But if philosophy can be written this way, by seeing it as a matter of action and practice, it needs to be written in such a way that the writing can be seen to be integrally linked to that action and practice and linked in at least two ways. First it must be linked in such a way that the writer becomes aware that he is not simply reporting on what is, but that he is also reading humanity through his actions. The failure to do so is a weakness of the liberal Enlightenment tradition; it is also a weakness for which Weil criticizes Marx and the Marxists. On the other hand, to be aware of that limitation is to recognize and strive in any limited act of understanding for a greater understanding. It is to make any act of limited knowing into a *metaxu*.[13] Second, it must be linked in such a way that, like a treatise on tennis, the reader becomes capable of reading humanity fully, which surely means understanding humans as active beings. It ought to be a *metaxu* for the reader, too.

Seeing philosophy this way greatly affects how one reads both Weil's political philosophy and philosophy of persons. For the finished product—for example, what is found in *The Need for Roots*—on this view is not a deduction of the optimum political society from a theory of human beings, but an attempt to understand them, which understanding involves caring for them. That is particularly important to recognize, for it goes a long way toward explaining why Weil does not fit into any standard classification of political options. If the point of standard political classifications is to classify the normal options for producing a society of persons understood in strictly objective terms, and Weil does not see persons in that reductionistic way, then obviously she is not going to fit into any of the standard classifications. When T.S. Eliot calls Weil one who is "more truly a lover of order and hierarchy than most of those who call themselves Conservative, and more truly a lover of the people that most of those who call themselves socialist"(NR viii), a paradox appears only to those who understand political philosophy in the standard way.

There is another way of putting this difference between Weil's approach and that of classical liberalism, which will also bring us closer to saying something specific about Weil's theory of persons.

In discussing the notion of equilibrium in the essay "Reflections Concerning the Causes of Liberty and Social Oppression" Peter Winch notes that at this early period (1934) of Weil's thinking that "the whole emphasis in her account of freedom . . . is that it is to be found in a direct confrontation between the individual and nature: *without* the intervention of other human beings. . . . The point is not that she just *happens* to have provided no account of a social background against which this talk . . . would make sense; it is rather that she is trying to *construct* an account of what a community would look like in which there was room for the dignity of individuals."[14]

Winch's complaint is that at this point Weil has failed to see the essential social nature of human beings in her talk about them. A bit like Hobbes and Locke and the whole liberal tradition, she has first described an isolated human person and then tried to construct a social milieu for the indivdual in which the individual can thrive. Winch's point is that this is at least misleading. Human beings as active beings are social through and through. There is no constructing that does not imbed within it a whole set of meanings dependent upon prior social practice and human activity. But to see this weakness in Weil's earlier political thought is also to make the point, as Winch does, that in time Weil came to see that this is a problem. And part of the point we are making is that it is that sort of insight that underlies her claim that philosophy is exclusively a matter of action and practice. For, in the end, that claim entails for Weil the essential heart of her theory of persons and their political associations. To know, to be human, is to be engaged in a specifically human activity, which is at least to be related by a whole set of socially instituted actions to other human beings.

We can now better see what Weil was trying to do in her theory of human persons and political associations. The project can no longer be seen as one of trying to create ideal political situations that are objectively fair and fitted to human "nature," but of trying to make people fair and just who are already socially related. The point is to get *them* to see that their societies are not artificial constructs, but organically related to the very beings who think them and inhabit them (and even "inhabit them" is a very bad way of putting it.) A good part of the problem is to get them to see their very knowledge of themselves as their own activity. That is the connection, we suspect, between what appear to be the two very different thoughts in Weil's last notebook entry, the problem of teaching what it is to know in the scientific sense and her nursing project.

In the interest of finally saying something specific about Weil's understanding of persons and its relation to her political thought, we should like to make some short concluding observations about two prime texts that deal with Weil's theory of persons and her political philosophy—namely, the essay "Human Personality," and *The Need for Roots*.

"Human Personality" is, of course, a prime locus for Weil's theory of persons. But what we want to suggest, given what has been said above, is that one needs to be careful in recognizing that Weil's understanding of theories is going to affect what her theory of persons could even be. If one is not careful, it is very easy to read "Human Personality" as a sort of mystical, but perhaps naively dualistic, understanding of persons. There is, on this view, a social part of the persons governed by necessity, which part Weil criticizes Personalism for celebrating, and there is an "impersonal" part, that which is sacred in human beings. The evidence for the impersonal part is hard to come by and seen only indirectly in the human desire for good, which cannot be satisfied by any finite thing. To respect humans truly is to respect this part. All this Weil herself indeed says quite plainly. But there is a problem in what exactly she is talking about, a problem that centers around how we are to take this talk of "parts." Given what we have already said about knowledge as activity, this talk of "parts" can be extremely misleading if by it one thinks that the various parts, but especially the impersonal one, are just "there" to be described. It is also misleading to think that respect can also be described in any definite sense as the logically and morally appropriate response to the "sacred" part of human beings.

Just how misleading that talk can be is seen by noting another key feature of the essay—that is, Weil's criticism of Personalism. That critique is directed specifically against Jacques Maritain.[15] Why that historical fact is particularly interesting is that Maritain's own moral philosophy is pretty much similar to a reading of "Human Personality" that does take the talk of "parts" literally, at least in that both posit an essential inner person and see morality as a matter of prescribing rules or principles (rights in the case of Maritain) by which the person can be respected. Philosophically, Weil's critique, if it were simply a matter of criticizing Maritain on details, such as the degree of an inner/outer dualism, would in the end not amount to much. The critique is important, though, because it is not a matter of details at all, but of a radically different way of viewing human persons in the first place.

This can be seen by noting just why Weil criticizes Maritain's Personalism. It and the notion of human rights, which is central to it, simply does not do enough for persons. It fails to see the person behind the personality, or, better put in Weil's terms, the "impersonal" behind the personal. Why? Because it fails in *attention*, which, as is quite clear in all Weil's writings, is not and cannot be reduced to a method. Attention is not something describable in the third person, but is a first-person activity. Attention is not an activity you can easily tell somebody how to do and expect them to do it. It is much less accessible to this kind of telling than telling somebody how to ride a bicycle is. For attention is primarily, at least for Weil, a certain moral stance to others that involves the one who is paying attention.

The conclusion to be drawn from this is that, since it is attention that discerns the so-called inner person, the impersonal is itself not describable in third person terms and may perhaps even be said not to exist in those terms. Or perhaps, put in less extravagant terms, third-person descriptions always fail to capture the sort of knowledge involved in attention. Although Weil talks about an impersonal part of the soul, which is a bare and deep desire for the good, a sort of center around which the person is formed, to talk that way is less a matter of description than it is an attempt to get the reader to see the sacredness of each human being for him or herself, and to see that sacredness is not something that can even meaningfully be described objectively and neutrally. (We would have every reason to doubt the word of one who, yawning, said he had just seen God.)

It is our seeing, our engagement with another, that is crucial to knowing that they are somehow sacred. This seeing, however, is not the unveiling of a psychic incubus. It is a moral activity and moral knowing we perform. In this sense attention does not so much see by nonnatural means a "something" that is there at the center of the human person, but *is a moral activity that creates* the very human person by actively responding to his or her desire for good. In an important sense therefore the human person is the sum of attention paid to her or him by God and other persons, and what a society is, is essential context for the creation—or annihilation—of persons.

Conversely we can therefore also note that not only is the human person created by the active attention of others, he or she by paying attention is a creator of others. But that is also to say something important about ourselves, for if we are creators of others by paying attention to them, we also create ourselves in that act. Not self-creators so much in the sense that, say, Nelson Goodman gives to that notion, but self-creators because in paying attention one, in the moral sense, acts out of the first person and engages himself at real moral depth. So even here one does not want to say that in self-creation that one realizes something of him or herself that was there but dormant; rather, one becomes fully human by acting in a fully human way toward others—that is, by paying attention to them. One is one's activity. This is further to underline our contention made throughout this book that the notion of a "supernatural history" is crucial to understanding Weil and her case.

To see Weil's search for a theory of persons as a search for a first-person perspective on persons allows us then to make a far briefer observation about Weil's distinctive political philosophy in *The Need for Roots*. As we noted earlier, political philosophy explicitly or implicitly rests on a theory of the human person. This is obvious in the case of Hobbes, not only in that—given what he takes persons to be—his sovereign state could not be much different than he makes it out to be and have any chance of success, but also in the sense that—given how he approaches human beings—his problem really is one of constructing a state for their protection and flourishing. The state is a construction problem for Hobbes, because he has to relate isolated individuals and balance their wants and needs against each other. In the case of Weil the problem of politics is quite different, because her view of human beings is quite different. In this sense what she is trying to do in *The Need for Roots* is not a matter of construction, since humans are already related anyhow, or at least need to be if they are going to be fully human. Political philosophy is therefore much more a matter of reorienting human associations so that the sort of attention can be paid to human beings that can create them and allow them to flourish in the associations that make them what they are.

If that understanding of the human person underlies the form of Weil's political philosophy, it also gives us some important hints as to the import of some of its contents as well. A crucial example, and we shall confine ourselves to it, is her contention that the moral basis of politics is not the notion of rights, but obligations. To a certain extent it is relatively easy to see the high moral tone of this recommendation, especially when Weil pointedly notes that rights tend always to be asserted in "a tone of contention." But there is more to it than that. For surely what distinguishes politics done from the perspective of obligations from that of the perspective of rights is that obligations presuppose a moral relation to others from a first-person perspective.[16] To be human is to be in a specific active relation with others. (This is a crucial point that both Rousseau and the later Wittgenstein also saw.)

The point then of political philosophy for Weil is to make that relation apparent and central in any state, and to arrange the relations within any political and social association so that these relations may be advanced to the greatest degree possible. It is precisely for this reason why Weil felt she could cite the nurses' project as the prime example of knowing in the scientific sense. It is an activity of attention and so a very distinctive way of doing political philosophy. It is also one that Weil hoped would cause others to pay attention, and which would cause a recentering of political thought.

10. ROOTEDNESS:
CULTURE AND VALUE

SIMONE WEIL once noted that the sloganlike quality of capitalized value-words creates an effective smoke screen that keeps us from seeing what is really behind them. Each age has its own set of such words. Ours has introduced "Pluralism." Far from signifying one thing at all, "Pluralism" has at least four different meanings. It can refer:

1. to the fact that people think differently;
2. to the fact that groups differ on what they hold valuable;
3. to the idea that our differences over what is good and valuable is not always a strict matter of right or wrong, but of differing cultural histories;
4. to the liberal notion that what is good and valuable is essentially a matter of individual choice.

Because of the plurality of meanings, calls for "Pluralism" run the gamut from recommending that we be tolerant of others and humble about our own opinions to a rather dogmatic insistence that there are no goods other than those we choose, with no ultimate, universal good to choose.

Important differences are concealed by the single term. One who believed that either #3 or #4 is true would see the relation between culture and values very differently than a medieval crusader, although a crusader would have been well aware of cultural differences and could have made use of them intellectually and economically whenever his sword was sheathed. But a common difference does not entail a common meaning. While the liberal view, #4, may rest on and incorporate a recognition of #3, to believe that our values are historically and culturally contingent does not necessarily imply that what is good only extends as far as human will. Insofar as it does not, thereon hang two very different alternatives to how we view our values, our history and world, and ultimately to how we shall live.

Why are values now often regarded as culturally and historically contingent? The explanation itself is historical. Once we assumed the existence of clear and distinct ideas and believed our ideas clearly mirrored nature. The success of science seemed to prove it. However, once we began to engage in philosophy of science, once we began to reflect on what we were doing as thinkers, the older picture appeared a fantasy. Since the Enlightenment, Karl Marx has taught us about ideology, the presentation of ideas as objective when they are merely reflections of contingent social and material conditions. Wittgenstein has taught us that our words, without which we cannot say anything about anything, have their validity within a cultural context and that none are universally privileged. Thomas Kuhn has taught us that science is not, as Bacon suggested, induction from hard facts, but the result of historically contingent research paradigms.

Nowhere has all this been quite so clearly recognized as in social, political, and moral philosophy. While attempting since Kant, if not before, to find hard and fast primary moral principles, philosophers have always recognized that such principles are established on shakier ground than scientific ones. Contemporary disavowals of essentialism and epistemological foundationalism have nearly completely undermined that ground for many.

Thus moral philosophy has now tried to stress, as Bernard Williams and Martha Nussbaum have done,[1] that there is no single answer to the question: "What should I do?" It, rather, provokes a futile effort with which we have lived since Plato. It has discovered, in Charles Larmore's words, "patterns of moral complexity,"[2] declaring our seemingly transcendent values to be cultural and historical, contingent and not universal as Kant thought. Undisturbed by this turn of thought, contemporary moral philosophy has felt a certain degree of liberation and tried to teach us to enjoy the rich fruits of diversity in lieu of transcendent certainty.

Indeed, much contemporary moral philosophy has tried to teach us that commitment to unimpeachable, transcendent values is not only philosophically indefensible, but also unwise. While few philosophers would agree with Arthur Schlesinger, Jr.'s, sophomoric remarks crediting all wars to nonpluralists,[3] they have become increasingly suspicious of single principle moralities—with good reason. Not only do such moralities cause us to miss the rich diversity of moral experience, they are positively misleading. Sometimes they even create fanatics. The notion of freedom, which Enlightenment liberalism considered an absolute moral principle, is an example. Broadly construed, it is hardly absolute; instead, as Marx suggested, "freedom" is too often simply a justification for the socially strong. But that is not always recognized. Philosophies of freedom quickly become ideologies of freedom used to dominate others rather than to liberate them. As Nicholas Lash observes, what happens is that not only has appearance been confused with what is really going on, but it is assumed that what goes on, here, today ought to go on everywhere and at all times, and further that it necessarily goes on.[4] Thus appearances taken to be necessary moral principles are easily used to justify, and even create and demand, some very bad behavior.

The call to recognize values as contingent and historical has not been greeted with unmixed enthusiasm. Many defenders of absolute principles have complained that all this contingency entails moral relativism. While we may dismiss at the outset objections based on passé metaphysics and absolutisms,[5] at least two important questions need to be considered carefully. First, is there any binding quality to morals, which we believe to be contingent and related only by historical and cultural accident? Second, how, when values and morals are only accidentally related to human life, can a moral agent find or make any sort of coherent moral life, any sort of life with deep meaning?

In response to the first question, we may simply note the degree to which it is question begging. Why is it that only necessary and universal principles can bind us morally? Why, we may ask, should we assume this at all?

Ironically, the reason why it is assumed turns out to be itself historical, involving as it does a concept of the person that began in Renaissance humanism. It was then that we began to look into ourselves to find a world of meaning instead of looking outwardly toward some universal principle on a macrocosmic scale. This budding inward reliance then found full bloom in Kant, who posited an ideal inner autonomous self that chooses the good and is radically prior to all social and historical determination. Within Kant's philosophy, this concept of the self does not undermine moral commitment, for a very good reason. For Kant the transcendental subject maintains its radical freedom precisely by generating moral principles on which to act, and since Kant believed that rationality was universal and necessary, it meant that all subjects could and would, if rational, generate the same principles. This allows for a society that is a kingdom of ends and of perfect, procedural justice. When we realize, however, that there are no universal principles, a problem does arise, at least as long as we maintain the same view of the self. The self, still thought capable of unconditionally choosing its own good, yet no longer operating under a universal rationality, is thought to be cut loose from any shared values, other than a respect for the right to choose. In short, it easily becomes what Alasdair MacIntyre calls the "emotivist self,"[6] exactly the democratic man that Plato feared.

Yet what reason is there to think that we are autonomous in quite that way, *other* than our supposed ability to generate universal principles? There is little. In a masterful critique of John Rawls's attempt to reinterpret the Kantian transcendental ego and thereby to establish a rational system of pure procedural justice, Michael Sandel has argued that the problem with Kantian liberalism is precisely its improbable view of the person, and that *it*, and not a lack of universal principles, is what is damaging morally, for who we are is constituted to a very great extent by our social relations and allegiances. Sandel writes:

> But we cannot regard ourselves as independent in this way without great cost to those loyalties and convictions whose moral force consists partly in the fact that living by them is inseparable from understanding ourselves as the particular persons we are—as members of this family or community or nation or people. . . . Allegiances such as these are more than values I happen to have or aims I "espouse at any given time". . . . They allow that to some I owe more than justice requires or even permits, not by reason of agreements I have made but instead in virtue of those more or less enduring attachments and commitments which taken together partly define the person I am.[7]

If Sandel is right that our selves are, in fact, to an important degree social, then having numerous, contingent moral allegiances is neither surprising nor troublesome. We can no more avoid some degree of social solidarity and shared social values than our limbs can live on their own without being connected to the rest of our body. Thus what most liberal societies need to worry about when faced with anarchy in cultural values is not a lack of universal principles, but about having historical values, such as individualism, which have come to override all other competing values and which are more the result of economic factors[8] than metaphysical insight. So the problem involved in our fear of moral anarchy is not one of having no shared principles, but of having ones that do not allow us to flourish. As Stanley Hauerwas ironically remarks, when Western liberal society keeps telling itself that human beings are autonomous and selfish, it is no surprise that people become that way.[9]

So having contingent values per se need *not* entail cultural and moral relativism; indeed, by recognizing that values are primarily cultural products we may simply dismiss "cultural relativism" as a contradiction in terms, since any value is necessarily something that is shared. Our cultural values have, in Simone Weil's phrase, "gravity," a certain weightiness all their own, which is extremely difficult to overthrow in fact, if not in fancy.

The real problem is not having values that will give our lives weight, it is finding meaning and coherence in the values that bind us, a sort of "grace," or lightness. Socially imposed duties that bind us to others can become onerous unless we can make sense of those duties. For example, a teacher may faithfully keep correcting papers and advising students each day, that does not keep him from ennui or despair. Also, not all our duties cohere nor are they commensurate. The histories that have brought Western culture to where it is today and that impinge on us, do not form a seamless garment. On the contrary, they often present us, their heirs, with competing and incommensurate demands. How then do we put a meaningful moral life together?

One of the best Liberal attempts at an answer without recourse to absolute principles comes from Richard Rorty. Arguing that we need to accept the contingency of ourselves and our languages, he has suggested that culturally we should employ a nominalist and historicist rhetoric, instead of the rhetoric of absolute philosophical principles. This nominalist rhetoric, he argues, should help us understand that what binds cultures together are "common vocabularies and common hopes," with the former dependent on the latter "in the sense that the principal functions of the vocabularies is to tell stories about future outcomes which compensate for present sacrifices."[10] We need to be aware that our values are not based on absolute principles, and we need culturally and personally to weave together and balance what values we do have in such a way that they present concrete alternatives and scenarios. Not that we ought to be or can be skeptical when doing so; Rorty "cannot imagine a culture which socialized its youth in such a way as to make them continually dubious about their process of socialization."[11] Rather, he suggests, that while socially bound, we ought at the same time to engage in private, ironical projects of self-creation and redescription, which cannot, because of our social nature, destroy the public vocabulary. "Ironists have to have something to have doubts about, something from which to be alienated," he notes.[12]

Rorty's use of "irony" is not, as we understand it, a call for anything like cartesian skepticism. Rather, it seems far closer to what is often called self-knowledge, if by that term we do not redevelop mistaken notions about the self. It may even be a call for wisdom in the sense that the book of Ecclesiastes used the term. Irony involves a deep personal recognition of contingency in our cultural values, a recognition that "man cannot find out what God has done from the beginning to the end"(3:11). Yet it also calls us not to doubt those values, but to imagine new uses for them. If wisdom is not absolute, "it excels folly as light excels darkness"(2:13). Far from distancing us from others, this irony is precisely what allows us to see others as people, as individuals, and not simply as examples of a category. By understanding that our categories and values are limited, our actions cease to be limited by them. In this sense, Rorty's irony can even be a principle of reformation. Deliberately antiutopian, it is the sort of thing that may save us from utopias.

To summarize the above arguments briefly, we claim that the recognition that our values are cultural products, plural in form and radically historical, does not entail, or even imply, moral anarchy or relativism between persons in a culture. The very fact that we are historical, socially conditioned beings, and not ahistorical egos, that we speak a common language already infused thoroughly with values, argues that what values we have are no less binding on us for being cultural than they would be if they were thought to come from God himself. Furthermore, such recognition may even be morally good for us to the degree that it keeps us form absolutizing the values peculiar to our own history and thus making us insensitive to others. It keeps us from absolutizing ourselves. In this sense, it even allows for a certain degree of moral change, or dare we say, moral improvement? But, we must ask, does it involve denial of an overarching good?

———————

Surprising as it may be to do so, we want now to argue that Simone Weil in her last writings advanced similar "pluralistic" views, at least insofar as not only did she argue that cultural values are historical, but that they ought to be positively valued as such.

It is, of course, surprising to say this, given Simone Weil's own harsh criticism of social institutions as the "Great Beast" of Plato or as belonging to the Prince of this World. It is equally surprising considering how often she makes remarks to the effect that true morality has always been the same everywhere and at all times; that divergences from that morality are perversions or simply false. However, I shall argue, that if we take her latest writings, those composed in London during 1943 shortly before her death, we shall find a far more nuanced view than her dogmatic, undialectical words would suggest. These writings are not piecemeal observations, but part of a much larger synthesis she was making of her religious and social ideas, a synthesis of which she was conscious and to which she refers in one of her last letters to her parents "as a deposit of pure gold . . . indivisible . . . [and] more compact" (SL 196).[13]

We shall contend that while Weil did indeed continue to talk of the Great Beast, and inveigh against what might be called "moralities of gravity," she began to discover that the necessity, the gravity, under which social life operates is not antithetical to an absolute good but a *metaxu* to transmit that good. She recognized that the values we hold are initially a function of our culture, and we as social and material beings do not exist outside culture. As such they are contingent. But if we can get the right sort of perspective on cultural values and learn how to balance them and make them cohere, they may point to something more ultimate. For Weil the solution hinges on seeing our history as a matter of being rooted.

To a degree there are similarities here with Rorty's liberal humanist position. There is also a decided alternative to that position. For within these late writings she also insists that the point of balance around which cultural values needs to be centered is divine and supernatural, and not simply the product of human imagination. But in saying so, she is not interested in this supernatural center to justify cultural values as such; rather she offers it as an alternative to a humanistic vision that makes us rely purely on our own imaginative, rational and historical resources, which taken alone add only further chapters to a genealogy of power. Her alternative is one of hope in a world that can genuinely be tragic.

In order to present Weil's position, we shall proceed by partially reconstructing her writings from the London period. Three of the most important ones, "Human Personality," *The Need for Roots*, and the misleadingly titled "Draft for a Statement of Human Obligations" can be put in just that order. This order, we argue, reflects a development of her most mature thought on culture and values, as she moves from a critique of cultural values in "Human Personality," which sets up the problem in a way with which she is satisfied through her insights in *The Need For Roots* to her succinct spelling out of her answer in the "Draft."

On the proposed reading, "Human Personality" is the earliest of these essays. On the surface it is also here where there is the most evidence *against* the claim that Weil smiled upon the idea of historically contingent social values. It is this essay that claims "the collectivity is not only alien to the sacred, but deludes us with a false imitation of it" (SE 14). It also contains her attack on Personalism as she claims that personality is nothing but a social creation that entitles us to no natural rights. This, along with her seemingly sarcastic remarks about important cultural values such as rights, personality, equality, and democracy as being mediocre and belonging to a realm of "middle values," lends supposed evidence to the position that Weil was on a precipice overlooking a manichaean political acosmism, if not over it. Her tone, if not her language, seems an outright attack on "moralities of gravity" as if there were an either/or decision to be made between them and "moralities of grace."

The tone of voice, however, hides the very positive achievements of this essay. Yet that tone is necessary because the first achievement of the essay is Weil's reaching a point of great personal clarity on where she differs from and disagrees with the assumptions of mainline liberal and humanist political philosophy, the particular object of her criticism. Once this is clear her project will not be confused with another's, once she has washed the terms clean, she is able to use them in a new and far more positive way.

Let us first consider the specific, named object of Weil's attack, the movement known as Personalism. If unaware of what exactly this movement involved, based on Weil's portrait of it, we might assume it to be a movement that celebrated individualism and egotism. This is far from the case. In many ways Personalism represented simply a focused liberal view of the person. It stressed that persons are not only individuals, but possess both an intrinsic dignity and basic rights that are best respected in a free and responsible democratic society. While Personalism is normally associated with Emmanuel Mounier, it seems evident that Weil had Jacques Maritain in mind.[14] For Maritain personality is a "metaphysical centre," referring "to the highest and deepest dimensions of our being." Personality is what enables "one freely to perfect and freely to give this substance."[15] It is "interiority to oneself." Personality is also the bearer of inalienable rights, which Maritain believed were best respected in a democratic society where each individual is duly respected.

How could Weil possibly object to this highly moral position? There are two reasons. First, partly by virtue of her early studies of Marx, she simply did not believe that there was a metaphysical self or that there are universal and inalienable rights. Personality for her is but a function of what she calls "social matter," analogous to physical matter, operating with its own quasi-mechanical laws. As she argues in another of her last essays, "Is There a Marxist Doctrine?," not only is there this social matter, but also "psychological matter," and that "under all the phenomena of a moral order, whether collective or individual, there is something analogous to matter properly so-called" (OL 177-78). Thus for Weil the philosophical problem with Personalism specifically, and classical Liberalism more generally, is that it fails to see that its notion of the essentially free inner person and the inalienable rights he or she supposedly enjoys are but historically and socially contingent outworkings of social forces that have been reified. It is an ideology.

Weil's second reason for objecting to Personalism is deeper. Not only is Personalism philosophically uncritical, it also fails to do what it sets out to do—to protect the dignity of human beings. By locating human dignity in a metaphysical inner core, believing that their analysis is universally and necessarily applicable, the Personalists fail to see the very real possibility that human beings can be crushed and destroyed. They thus fail to see the real nature and depth of human suffering, convincing themselves that destruction cannot really happen; it is a metaphysical impossibility. Weil, however, having discovered "affliction" in the factories several years before, knew differently. Human beings can be destroyed. As she put it in the essay on the *Iliad*:

> [Might] when exercised to the full . . . makes a thing of man in the most literal sense, for it makes him a corpse. . . . [But] from the power to transform him into a thing by killing him there proceeds another power, and much more prodigious, that which makes a thing of him while he still lives. (IC 24,26)[16]

By mislocating it, Personalism and liberalism thus fail to understand what is really sacred about a human being, and thus ultimately fail to allow for a really deep sense of justice in dealing with other human beings. Borrowing the phrase "pulling one's self up by one's own bootstraps," one can see what has gone wrong. Believing that there is always an essential person inside, liberalism thus believes that there is always somebody inside who can do the pulling up, who can overcome circumstances, no matter how bad they are. Weil, however, tries to get us to see that there may be nobody left inside at all.[17]

This view is often troubling to anybody who wants to be uncompromising in her respect for persons. How can we respect one who is no person at all? This obviously troubled Weil for, she asks, if we are but a concatenation and wielders of social forces, what makes us sacred and the object of moral respect?

The answer she gives is that it is simply nothing more than our inchoate striving after good. Minimal in form, that is a supremely important answer. One does not respect others because of something they are or have, which, after all, may be quite accidental. Rather, true respect means respecting them as a whole, and for whatever keeps them whole. Their attempt, their need to unify life, is, for Weil, exactly what this inchoate striving after good is. To be cruel to a person in any way thwarts that striving, for he would receive evil when he hoped for good. What then damages the people we hurt is rarely the specific injury but the thwarting of their aspiration for a whole life, body and soul.

In traditional philosophical terms, Weil's location of the sacredness of a human being owes little to either metaphysics or essentialist thinking. Instead it rests in a primitive human hope. If Weil then calls this sacredness "impersonal," it is not because she wants it to be abstract; it is because she wants it to be less abstract. And what is abstraction but what the Personalists have done in emphasizing a single, albeit important, feature of the human person, placing it beyond the play of contingent forces, the realm of the personal?

But why is liberalism, particularly in its notion of rights, inadequate for recognizing that hope and dealing with it? For Weil, the answer simply is that that aspiration is for a good that is in Plato's words, "perfect, adequate and desirable."[18] And the reason she thinks that the aspiration is so high is precisely because notions such as inalienable rights, crucial to the Personalist picture of the person, fail to be of much help when dealing with the afflicted. Through numerous observations made in the factory and in watching court cases being tried in Marseilles, she realized that there was something profoundly unsatisfactory in the way that the poor and disenfrachised left these institutions. Pure procedural justice, even when followed scrupulously, simply was not enough. Their suffering simply was not being heard, even though they had had their day in court. Something was continually being left unsaid. What was left unsaid, was, in fact unsayable. What is spoken, on the other hand, in procedural justice are the words that make up social personality. Thus she concluded that even the notion of rights, supposedly eternal and universal, is a matter of the contingent play of social forces, incapable of satisfying our deepest hopes. It is not hard, then, to conclude, as she did, that a democracy, even one where procedural justice is never perverted, also does not enjoy a necessary and unassailable status.

The essay "Human Personality" is, to be sure, a critique of collectivities and the false absoluteness they give to a supposed inner person. But on the reading we have given it, its focus is not really collectivities as such; the essay is most fundamentally a highly pointed and focused criticism of certain notions of persons and moral principles that can make collectivities oppressive. Even liberalism simply does not do enough for people, nor, for that matter, does it let us do enough because it keeps us from seeing a much deeper problem of justice.

This critique of liberal doctrine has an important positive side, though. It allows Weil to make a crucial distinction between two senses of justice. First there is a social conception of justice embodied in the notion of rights, making it a contingent, historical matter. But there is also a second, more vital sense of justice to which we ought to pay closer attention if we are ever going to do anything for those who do not share, for whatever reason, in the distribution of social power. That is, she says, a "supernatural" sense of justice. This justice operates when an individual hears something more than he has been culturally conditioned to hear, when he hears the silent word of affliction that the language of rights cannot speak.

The distinction, however, appears to leave Weil with exactly the sort of problem we suggested above that she might have. Namely, it appears that societies and cultures are irredeemably trapped in the realm of necessity, unable by their very collective nature, to express and appreciate what is essentially only heard by individuals. They appear to be all gravity, and no grace. This distinction, important as it is, seems to undermine radically the importance of social and cultural activity. To be sure, Weil says, the words that express collective, cultural values are "valid in their own region, which is that of ordinary institutions" (SE 33). Still, they are quite distant from what Weil is calling "real justice." That, at least, would be the impression with which we are left, were it not for some hints that she leaves at the end of the essay, hints that she later will develop in such a way as to reorient cultural values.

The first hint comes in her suggestion that there are certain words such as God, truth, justice, love, and good, which have a power in themselves to illumine and lift the soul toward that Good, a power realized when we "do not try to make them fit any conception . . . [for] what they express is beyond our conception" (SE 33). What exactly could Weil mean here? That certain words, like sacraments, confer grace *ex opere operantis*?

What is meant by this suggestion is obscure but not particularly mysterious or occult. Weil simply means that in order to break out of our linguistic and cultural moral cocoons, we need some kind of public expression of the fact that we are in such cocoons. People need to be made aware of the limited nature of their cultural morality, at least so that they might become aware of another sort of morality. At this point it seems that Weil had in mind that these "big" words would function in the public realm not so much as real linguistic operators than as icons whose purpose is to remind us of the less than absolute nature of our public morality and to draw our attention morally upward. They do not negate the force of cultural conventions and morality, nor condemn them, they simply put them in perspective. These words indicate an object of striving that words such as "rights" and "personality" otherwise terminate too quickly.

Weil's suggestion bears a certain analogy to Rorty's use of "irony" insofar as both writers, while believing that reason is inescapably public, also want to find a way to appreciate and go beyond any sort of moral conceptual determinism and its illusory claims to absoluteness. If Weil is not exactly calling for a nominalist rhetoric, she is at least looking for a way to use language that will demystify most moral terms by standing them against some real absolutes.

Weil and Rorty differ, though, on two important points. The first is that Rorty's irony is formally aimless, aimless in the sense that the individual alone remains in control of his choice. Thus his irony remains wedded to certain liberal notions (such as pluralism #4) as he freely admits. Weil, though, thinks there is an aim. Yet she is wise enough not to place its domain unwittingly back in the public realm.

The second difference is that Weil thinks that there can be a public expression of this contingency other than a "historicist rhetoric" and that there can be a public expression that will help serve as a positive reorientation of cultural values vis-à-vis supernatural justice. Hardly believing that cultural values are essentially opposed to justice, she thinks that if they are oriented correctly, if they are balanced around a supernatural center, and inspiration, they can serve a higher purpose.

The views laid out in "Human Personality" are not without their difficulties. While refusing to fit words such as "God," "good," "justice" and the like, to limited conceptions might give a better perspective on our other value words, one may very well ask whether it is possible to avoid giving them a limited conception. The temptation seems almost irresistible. For example, few thinkers have ever had such a deep sense of the transcendence of God as Augustine. Think how in the *Confessions* he found God nowhere in the mountains, the air, nowhere but in his own breast. Yet he was quite willing not long afterward to identify the bloody suppression of the Donatists with God's will. It was not until the *City of God* that he truly realized his inconsistency.[19]

Weil was not unaware of the problem as an examination of the writings following "Human Personality" will show. It is in those writings that she tries to find a way in which the transcendent nature of "God," "truth," and "good" are not degraded but can nevertheless be thought by limited, historical human beings.

The writing known as "A Draft for a Statement of Human Obligations" is an important case in point. In fact, if its original intended usage is kept in mind, its very existence and Weil's constant reworking of it indicate the degree to which she believed that there needed to be a public profession of ultimate, supernatural justice so that the word would not be just left hanging. That intended usage was as a "proposed examination of Resistance groups,"[20] a sort of public credo, undoubtedly meant to replace Enlightenment slogans such as *Liberté, Egalité, Fraternité,* and even Maritain's preferred "International Declaration of the Rights of Man."

The intended replacement is canny. Despite sounding dogmatically descriptive, closer examination shows that it is no *Quicunque vult.* . . . Its initial central features are, to be sure, seemingly descriptive, including a profession that there is a reality outside the world, which is the sole realm of good; that this good corresponds to the human longing for absolute good, and that it is only through individual persons that this good "descends and comes among men" (SE 219). On the face of things, it seems that she says little more than she did in "Human Personality." It may even appear that her position is inconsistent insofar as a public profession of good with specifications is an attempt to make "good" fit some conceptuality.

A fragment from the London period outlines her motives for proposing such a credo and clarifies her project. She writes:

> *Sketch of the foundation of a doctrine (chiefly for the use of study groups in France):* A doctrine is quite insufficient, but it is indispensable to have one, if only to avoid being deceived by false doctrines. The sight of the pole star never tells the fisherman where he ought to go, but he will never make his way in the night unless he knows how to recognize it. (EL 151)

This credo was, therefore, never meant as a metaphysical description or explanation; it was meant to give orientation—a pole star for navigation. She adds, "for when a man wants something that he cannot name, one can easily make him believe that he wants some other thing, and turn the treasure of his energy away toward something indifferent or evil" (EL 151).

But how does one avoid vacuity while still trying to give orientation? First, as part of giving this orientation, Weil notes, it is necessary to clear away inadequate doctrines. That is, we have suggested, part of the aim of "Human Personality." Second, in order not to be misunderstood, she adds to this doctrine in the "Draft" the intended *effects* of this credo—namely, that the recognition of this supernatural good carries an obligation to act on it, to bring its light into play in the natural world and that a society is good or evil, is a legitimate society, in proportion both to the degree that there is within it a consent to this good and to the degree of the "distribution of power between those who consent and those who refuse" (SE 222). She also states that to be just, a state must ensure that "all forms of power are entrusted, as far as possible, to men who effectively consent to be bound by the obligation to all human beings . . . and who understand the obligation" (SE 223).

What does it mean to make a profession like this? To say that it involves subscription to a systematic and descriptive utopian orthodoxy would be a wooden reading, indeed, especially since she has explicitly called it simply a "pole star," and has said that simple "belief" or subscription is not enough. Rather, the profession has illocutionary force,[21] above all making action primary. It is in this way that supernatural justice is not simply an empty phrase, but a definite way of acting. It is a commitment to playing out that justice in life of the one making the profession. Indeed, she concludes the "Draft" with these words: "assent to this Statement implies a continual effort to bring such institutions and morals into existence as rapidly as possible" (SE 227). These additions, therefore, suggest that Simone Weil's supernatural justice must be played out socially and that she hardly believed that the social world is entirely alien to justice.

Therefore whereas "Human Personality" sought to distinguish the social world and that of transcendent good, and social justice and supernatural justice, the "Draft" assumes a link between the two, a link in human action. It is in this link between the necessary and the good established through the consent and action of individuals that Weil wants to find the balancing point around which cultural values can be centered, reformed, and thus used as means of contact with a higher sense of justice.

It is fairly clear, if we again consider the full range of Weil's London writings, that she was intensely interested in this problem of links and balances, particularly in light of the fact that a war, a struggle of natural forces, was going on. Not only was she interested in raising the question of what kind of justice it was for which the Allies were fighting,[22] she was also interested in seeing how cultures and nations, by the way they actively orient themselves to the Good, are essentially religious and can be critiqued as such.[23] They may, for example, with what she calls "only an infinitely small difference" in their values at the strictly verbal level either be idolatrous by putting those values in service of something finite, such as national sovereignty and prestige, or be mediators of the Good. A similar concern for the individual's consent to the Good also leads her to call both for a repression of political parties, which she thinks coerce souls by propaganda, and for an end to colonialism. Until such things occur she believed that society could not be renewed, and higher justice incarnated in it since the violence of propaganda and the hegemony of the national state over the lives of its citizens effectively denies and dissolves the essential link to the Good, no matter what they claim they believe.

It is this link above all with which Weil is concerned in these last writings. She did not want to revise and undo a culture's values, but she did want to reorient them so that they provide and make apparent that link. Thus the word "culture" for Weil carries the sense of the verb "to culture," for she envisions culture as a vital medium in which human beings grow and which nourishes them.[24] Weil's concern then is not to replace culture as if it were faulty because it did not have full-grown plants, but of making sure it is nourishing.

Yet this still is quite abstract. What possible means exist to do all this? What are the resources and how are they tapped? For Weil, what is required is a way by which a culture, which through its history is rooted in something more ultimate than itself, can provide nourishment for the people who comprise it.

It is in the beginning of *The Need for Roots*, when she discusses the relation of rights and obligations and the "needs of the soul," that she discovers and specifies this link. It is here that she finds the key to answer the sorts of questions with which she was left at the end of "Human Personality." Here we find the transition to the subtle formulations of the "Draft," allowing them to be read in the way we have suggested.

Those questions left by "Human Personality" were, we may recall, how natural justice, exemplified by the notion of rights, can be reconciled and linked with supernatural justice, exemplified by the eternal obligation to respect what is sacred in human beings. The problem is that rights belong within the entirely contingent realm of necessity, and are not, *pace* the "men of 1789," either universal or necessary features of moral thinking. Since they are also rooted in social power, not only do they provoke and justify moral contentiousness, they are incapable of teaching us how to hear or deal with powerlessness. Thus there is a problem, not because the notion of rights is worthless, but because the supernatural justice that can hear and respond to the hurt of the afflicted itself cannot be so neatly defined in such concrete terms. Its seeming resistance to concretion would make it appear impossible to institute within the concrete world.

The solution proposed in *The Need for Roots* comes in its opening pages, where Weil gives a distinctive analysis of rights, at once denying them absolute status, since they are cultural products and yet at the same time making them a link to supernatural justice. She does this by proposing that we, indeed, see rights as specific cultural values, but as having a legitimacy—that is, a fundamental concern for the person—that ultimately derives from supernatural justice via an obligation each human being has toward others. Rights are then simply the specific historical and cultural specifications of this obligation, which actualize it but never exhaust it. Thus rights (but not obligations) are mutable in changing historical circumstances. But even if rights are thus historically contingent, when they are the result of obligation meeting need, they are also historical witnesses to specific acts of recognition of the sacredness of human beings, to the descent of good "among men."

The point of this proposal is to solve the problem of respecting the sacredness of human beings when that sacredness does not rest in any one thing, including personality, and when we cannot concretely pay supernatural respect to persons without trying to make the universal reside completely in a contingent act directed toward a contingent self. Therefore taking up a suggestion made in "Human Personality," Weil proposes that since what is sacred in a person, her concern for ultimate good, is affected by what happens to her in the world of concreteness, we can at least respect her indirectly by dealing with what Weil calls the "needs of the soul."[25] These needs, analogous to bodily needs, if not met, would cause her to despair of good. It is by paying attention to these needs that we can, and indeed must, concretize our obligations in such ways that aspiration for good continues to live in her.

How this solves the problem left behind by "Human Personality" is that by dealing with the "needs of the soul" one does not leave "God," "truth," and "justice" as empty conceptions. They have meaning in how we recognize and treat others. But such words also can never become conceptually determinate for they indicate a "something more" that we can never exactly capture conceptually.

Simone Weil thus gives a way of approaching morality that is distinct from the classical liberalism of universal and inalienable rights. For Weil, rights do involve morality, but they neither define nor limit it. Like personality itself, which rights has traditionally protected, rights must be understood in the context of a larger whole and have validity only within it. It is important to understand here that by claiming that each specific right owes its real moral force to an eternal obligation Weil is *not* trying to legitimate each contingent right directly at all. Neither obligations nor rights can be thought of as principles, and there is no sort of calculus for each possible circumstance that entails a specific right by deriving it from the eternal obligation for respect. Weil's approach is far more organic, and far more "personal." The importance of recognizing obligations is to give a historical moral sense that balances specific rights as a whole within a society.

An example will help to see the distinction. For Simone Weil a democratic society may feed or even satiate a person's need to believe herself an equal to others, yet still fail to really provide respect for her. For example, it may ignore a concomitant need for a hierarchy of values and purposes that she can respect. The better society balances the two. Within a morality of principles, however, any right to equality tends to be absolute, regardless of what else is the case. Even on Rawls's nuanced view, which allows for the tailoring of equality in the original position, there is no tailoring of it afterward for historical contingencies. The principles are absolute, even if they contain an empirical twist. What is key for Weil, on the other hand, is the eternal obligation we have to the whole person, which insists that not only must any right be tailored continually, it must be tailored within a specific cultural whole. It is, of course, precisely for this reason that she declares the need for order—that is to say, "a texture of social relationships such that no one is compelled to violate imperative obligations in order to carry out other ones" (NR 10), as the first of the soul's needs, the one most nearly touching on the soul's eternal destiny.

It is clear that Weil has broken with a Kantian rationalism that seeks to extend the reign of law over the whole world. Her claim is that individual cultures should continue their own traditions and remain bound to them since both cultural and personal identity is bound up inextricably within that unique history. What needs changing in any culture, then, is rarely institutional forms, but how those forms are balanced against each other by relation to a center, a center represented by the notion of supernatural obligation. We need to worry less about actual institutions than how they work as a whole upon individuals.

Not surprisingly, Weil's attempt to find meaning for supernatural justice in a world of gravity has attracted liberal criticism as being ultimately apolitical. Mary Deitz has sought to show:

> Just how bereft of political possibility—of action (individual or collective), social transformation, emancipation, even the mere betterment of everyday life—her mysticism is. . . . Her mysticism grants no value or meaning to either individual autonomy or collective political action.[26]

With more self-awareness of his own liberalism, Michael Ignatieff has argued that:

> [Simone Weil] didn't like rights because they were specific, precise, and enforceable by law, and as such truncated the full compass of the human good. . . . But surely it is an illusion, a dangerous illusion, to suppose that a politics can be based on supposedly indubitable facts of human nature. The human good is conflictual; moral conflict is real, and a regular feature of the social world; people disagree about what people need. That is where politics comes in. The language of rights represents the extent of our agreement about human ends. . . . To denounce the language of rights as Weil did . . . it is . . . also to deny politics its vocation, which is the adjudication of irreconcilable conflict between competing ends. . . . In denying that human ends were in conflict, Weil was wishing away politics altogether.[27]

The point appears to be well taken. But one may well ask what exactly is meant by talking about "irreconcilable conflict between human ends"? For while contemporary social life may show conflict (pluralisms 1–3) too often that fact of social life slides over into a theory about ends (pluralism #4). For example, Charles Larmore in his *Patterns of Moral Complexity*, after lucidly arguing for a liberal ideal of political neutrality toward differing ideals of the good life, goes on to state: "Thus, if we detach morality from religion, we must reckon with a fundamental *heterogeneity* of morality. . . . The *ultimate* sources of moral value are not one but many."[28] A fact of social life has just become a theological dogma.

If Weil does not worry about individual autonomy or collective political action, it is precisely because there is an issue deeper than the continuation of present politics, an issue on which she thinks thinking has gone wrong in Western moral and political philosophy. It is because we have seen individuals as ahistorical and autonomous, capable of and entitled to decide on issues of good, that the purely procedural justice necessary for collective action becomes the sole issue of justice. For the same reason, modern Western culture shows a certain hatred of the past, which in turn makes collective action necessary to establish a just society in the future. Weil, however, is not interested in defining a single just political form, as Marx *and* liberals do; she does not even believe there is such a thing. She is less interested in changing what we are doing than in changing the way we do it. Otherwise, to force change is to remain within the realm of necessity.

Thus Weil's political and cultural philosophy tries to find hope by discovering a way that the limited world of necessity might have meaning, and it does so by trying to reduce human alienation from the natural order by relating that order to the deepest human aspirations.

This is nowhere seen quite as clearly as in the longest part of *The Need for Roots* where Weil unravels the metaphor of rootedness. What is at stake in that metaphor is no less than the belief that human beings, subject to material and historical conditions, must be able to find some way to use those conditions to recognize supernatural good and the obligations to people that that recognition implies. For Weil, it is the idea of roots that finally bridges the cleavage between the limited values of social necessity and the undefinable values of supernatural justice.

What is ultimately implied in the idea of humans having a natural need of the soul for roots is that it is by the natural need of feeling a part of a larger historical social whole one may come to finally identify with the center around which all necessity is balanced. Despite her oft expressed reservations about particular natural loves, I do think that Weil, like Plato in the *Phaedrus*, recognized that love and justice begin, not impersonally and universally, but within particular communities and with particular people. The problem then is how to metamorphosize this particular love born out of natural need for others into one of universal concern, both for all people and for the whole of the particular persons whom one loves, even when they have unattractive aspects.[29]

There is an important sense in which the historical communities in which we find ourselves play a role analogous to natural love. We are originally bound to them by very natural reasons; if not by personal preference, then at least by virtue of the fact that they give us our sense of personal and moral identity. They do so not simply by molding us, but because they are that with which we identify and thus individuate ourselves. As John Dewey argued, "Stability of individuality is dependent upon stable objects to which allegiance firmly attaches itself. . . . Assured and integrated individuality is the product of social relationships and publicly acknowledged functions."[30] Thus communities are not imperious creators of our persons, but creators because they allow us our ability for self creation—or decreation.

Where, of course, our relation to historical communities is disanalogous to personal loves for Simone Weil is that communities are simply not persons. But if they proceed by an inexorable gravity, nevertheless, their parts can at least be organized around a supernatural center. They are not that center, and that above all has to be recognized. But they can witness to the center and can be so organized by men and women who do recognize it. If as natural they cannot force consent to a center or make anyone recognize it against their consent, they can at least dispose persons to recognize that center. In this sense, while they provide us with limited values, which naturally bind us, they, if read properly, may allow us to understand the fulcrum on which those values are balanced. They allow us to see beyond their limited nature, to invite us to criticize them as limited, and they can therefore become transparent.

It is on this line of reasoning that a peculiar idea that Weil had about cultures beginning in an original divine revelation, and which she was developing at the some time she was writing *The Need for Roots* begins to make some sense. It is the idea that cultural and social activity, while certainly the outworking of nature and necessity, is actually the historical response to whatever value a culture holds as ultimate; ultimate not simply in conception but in act.[31] Thus limited cultural values can actually serve a nonnatural purpose by being a response to that revelation, which in its cultural forms invites further response. Cultures become in this sense, she says, "the formation of attention"(EL 160).

We can now see quite clearly what exactly the idea of rootedness itself is meant to convey. It is not simply by having "roots" in the most general sense in a community that we are nourished, but by that community itself having roots that draw upon the supernatural.[32]

So Weil is far from dismissing cultural values, the values of the middle realm, as having no worth. They have great importance insofar as they can be related to something more fixed. So said, we can also understand why Weil spends so little time trying to emphasize politics, as Deitz would have her do, as the result of human action and creation.[33] As creatures of necessity we inevitably do act and create; but that is not what is problematic for Weil. It is how we see and describe our activities as related to some higher purpose.

Not to see this is to seriously misread fully the last 90 percent of *The Need for Roots.* For, in the sections on how France came to be uprooted and how it might reroot itself, Weil is concerned above all with showing how the center became perverted in French history, thus altering the moral and spiritual balance of activity. What that history of uprootedness is meant to show is that the state itself gradually became the center of all obligation, commanding all affection and duty. This is what allows her to claim that not only is the state a perverse center, because it is finite itself and the wielder of finite forces, but also that it maintains itself as the center at the cost of failing to allow its citizens recognition of values other than those that brought it into power. For example, in her discussion of false greatness, Weil not only criticizes an unfortunate conception of greatness as being responsible for the rise of truly evil people such as Hitler, but also argues that we have little defense against similar future excesses as long as our actions are motivated by the same idea of greatness that inspired him. The center in this sense, whatever it is, affects the outcome of all our actions; until it is located in what is truly good, our actions will tend to our own moral destruction.

Therefore the goal of rootedness is much less a matter of changing our specific, cultural values—that may be asking the leopard to change his spots—as it is a matter of changing how we read those values and orient them. The point, for example, of her criticism of modern science is not to get rid of science, but to look at it differently, especially in its relation to an ultimate goal for which we hope. Or, similarly, in suggesting that labor ought to be the spiritual center of any culture, the point is not to send everybody back to work on a farm for reeducation; it is to put something other than the foolish Marxist and liberal hope for freedom from necessity at the center. Our actions so understood cannot help but change according to what Martin Andic has called, a sort of "spiritual mechanics."[34]

In an earlier section of this essay we suggested that Simone Weil's position bears certain similarities to Richard Rorty's insofar as both admit cultural values as binding upon us, not for metaphysical, foundationalist reasons, but purely and simply for social ones, while at the same time seeking a way to add some sort of insight into their limited nature, which allows us to redescribe them in such a way that we can find a deeper, more personal morality. By such a means both Rorty and Weil go beyond classical Enlightenment Liberalism. But here, of course, the similarity ends. Rorty obviously is not interested in finding a supernatural center to contingent social values, other than perhaps as an outmoded way of talking about how to make personal sense of them. Weil, on the other hand, quite clearly wants to call this center supernatural. Rorty's "irony" is indeed a long way from Weil's "consent to a reality outside time and space," even if both tend to be related in similar formal aspects to cultural values.

What exactly is the difference? It can be seen in a question Peter Winch raises about Weil's use of the supernatural. Noting accurately that she does use the term as a way of countering an all too common morality of shallow concern for others, he asks, nevertheless, what real sense there is to the term since:

> Our reactions to beauty, and to each other, are as much a part of human nature as our other reactions. Even if it could be shown that these reactions are comparatively rare in relation to other opposing reactions, we should be a long way from considering them as supernatural.[35]

But the point is not to give the supernatural as an explanation for morality; rather, Winch continues:

> I believe the point of this sort of language is to provide a way of expressing the connections between various attitudes, interests, strivings, aspirations, which are all part of our "natural history." It is only because they are part of our natural history that we have any chance of making sense of the notion of the "supernatural."[36]

What Winch is subtly pointing out is that philosophically Weil's "supernaturalism" is not an explanation intended to defeat "naturalism," but speaks more of a type of life to be lived. In this sense, there is a similarity with Rorty to the degree that both are looking for something that makes a difference to our natural history and is locatable in it. Both are hoping to find a way to achieve the rare, beautiful moral action.

We think that Winch's analysis is essentially correct on this issue, and that Weil recognized the problems of a purely analytic approach in her later writings. As she notes, if words such as "God," "just," "good," and "love" are to be effective, they have to operate within the public sphere and have to be linked to our history. Imbedded within this history, their real function is to provide and show an alternative to an all too dreary and mediocre moral vision. But that does not mean that the difference between her and Rorty is simply one of terms. There is still a substantial difference implied in that term "supernatural."

Where that difference lies is in the hope it implies. The issue at stake is one that is raised by Simone Weil in the essay "East and West: Thoughts on the Colonial Problem" (in SE). Arguing that natives in French colonies need to be rooted in their own cultural traditions, she raises the question of why it is important for any group to maintain its past. The reason has to do with the question of whether or not we are self-sufficient in the world. If we are not and cannot gain a sufficient perspective on the world to live by building rational systems from ground zero out of our native capacities, then our cultures and the treasures of the past they embody become an essential means of help. They above all give us the alternatives we need when present imagination fails. Thus far she is perhaps not very different than Rorty other than in laying greater emphasis on the need for a tradition. Her question about self-reliance, though, can be taken at a deeper level as well, a level at which she is asking whether or not human capacities are sufficient for life that hopes for good.

The issue can be enjoined by comparing Rorty's treatment of George Orwell's *1984* with Weil's analysis of what she called affliction. In discussing O'Brien's treatment of Winston, Rorty notes that what Orwell has shown us about cruelty is not so much that O'Brien can force Winston to admit that 2+2=5, but that he puts Winston in a position where he actually wants Julia, whom be loves, to be tortured instead of himself. The result? Winston cannot any longer weave a coherent story about himself as a moral agent. He can no longer identify with himself.

(T)he belief that he once wanted them to *do it* to Julia is not one he can weave a story around. That was why O'Brien saved the rats for the best part, the part in which Winston had to watch himself go to pieces and simultaneously know that he could never pick up those pieces again.[37]

Simone Weil, in a similar way, after her factory experience notes that one of the chief characteristics of affliction is not just having to operate in an irrational system, but that in time the agent becomes both alienated from the larger world and directs that alienation toward herself. She finds nothing to love, and nothing in herself with which to love. Winston in this regard may be a prime example of what Simone Weil means by affliction.

In such cases what are the human alternatives? Rorty, since he is considering Orwell's value as a writer, does not really address the question other than arguing that Orwell by imagining O'Brien's awesome cruelty and its effect on Winston, shows us something about the nature of cruelty and thus teaches us to avoid it. But what of someone who is genuinely in this position? Of someone who, in Nussbaum's sense of tragedy, has to choose between incompatible values, knowing that his choice will destroy him? If he cannot escape, in any sense, total and utter personal destruction, not only is his outcome tragic, the universe itself will be read as tragic.

Weil, on the other hand, while fully admitting the existence of tragedy, of lives destroyed, by virtue of her supernaturalism suggests that the loss need not be ultimate and that one may hope even in such circumstances.[38] For her, what "supernatural" means, we suggest, is seen in our reading possibility in impossibility, in reading love and goodness behind every event. It is a life of hope.

Simone Weil, unlike orthodox Christian theologians, of course does not place that hope in a realm of future rewards. And for that reason what her supernaturalism amounts to is a bare, undefinable hope, a faith, in a goodness that transcends the human attempt to imagine—and limit—goodness and the human capacity to despair.

That hope is, as Weil suggests, something undefinable, for in the words of the Letter to the Hebrews, it itself is the evidence. But there is also an entire "cloud of witnesses," an entire history, that makes it plausible. To be rooted in that story makes, as Weil says, only an infinitely small difference. But it may be a difference around which we can balance all other values and a difference that keeps us from lying to ourselves and falling back into a false absolutism. Thus if there is no proof for choosing her supernatural vision to a humanistic one, there is at least a choice and a real alternative.

PART V
Epilogue

11. FROM WORDS TO THE WORD: WEILIAN RESOURCES FOR A NEW CHRISTIAN HUMANISM

WE HAVE THROUGHOUT the course of this book sought to address ourselves to certain crucial elements in Weil's thought—necessity, the supernatural, love and friendship, the underpinnings of her social and political philosophy. We have also sought to relate Weil more thoroughly to important issues and thinkers in contemporary philosophy than has usually been the case.

Much ground has therefore been covered and it would be well to try to summarize it. That may be well nigh impossible, though, and even to attempt it may be to misunderstand Weil's own ways of thinking, in any case. Nevertheless, it may be helpful to make another final run at what we have discussed and to integrate it in some way. Such an effort, of course, runs the risk of showing less insight than has been gleaned from considering the specific elements that go into it. But even if it is, it can be helpful in showing that these various elements can go together in more than one way. *That*, we think, is true to the thought of Weil and in order to highlight that aspect of her thought, we shall consider what we call Weil's "Christian Humanism," especially in relation to questions of education. The usefulness of the term may be easily disputed; hopefully, though, it will highlight the breadth and comprehensiveness of Weil's philosophical and theological vision, and its very concrete direction.

There is a rather amazing story told of a young math student in a large Midwestern university. This young lady had throughout the semester been nothing more than a C student. What brought her to the attention of her preceptor was her complaint that that was all she was getting, despite the fact that she was spending an inordinate amount of time studying. Upon investigation the preceptor discovered the root of her problem: at the beginning of the semester when the class was correcting its first exercises, the answer to the first problem was $x = 1/14$. This student, apparently unaware that x is a variable, had assumed from that time forward that x is always equal to 1/14 and prepared all her work accordingly.

Aside from demonstrating what must have been the extraordinary gifts of this young woman which enabled her to pull a consistent C despite her systematic error, this story illustrates a fundamentally important lesson for all students. It shows the need to be aware that the x's we use everyday—that is, our words—have more than one meaning. The phenomenon is common; anybody who teaches can easily point to examples of students who have fallen into ambiguity, equivocation, and outright error in a paper or discussion simply because they have not paid attention to the fact that words are used in many different ways.

It is not only students, however, who have this problem. Adults have it as well. The confusion that comes from them is often just as weird as that of students, but with far more unfortunate results. One word where confusion very much abounds is the word *humanism*, a word that is extremely important to how we understand education, but which has been an educational battleground for a number of years, even at schools whose form of education is professedly humanistic. The confusion is twofold: first, the definition of the word *humanism*; second, the confusion that belongs to the practice of humanism, a confusion involving the very way in which words are to be taken.

The first sort of confusion that surrounds the word *humanism* is the rather simple one of definition. It is a matter of becoming clear on that to which we are referring. One of our colleagues, an English professor, gave us a very clear example that bears repeating.

In a discussion with the pastor of his church, this colleague maintained that Luther was a humanist; the pastor adamantly refused the designation. The dispute was one of definition. The professor was right; historically Luther was a humanist insofar as he partook of the humanism of the Renaissance, which rejected the absolutist, scientific formulaes of Scholastic theology. This sort of humanism had found Scholastic logic sterile and turned its scholarly attentions to the humanities of language and history—to texts and away from syllogisms. The pastor disputed this, not because Luther's involvement in the Renaissance was somewhat minor compared to, say, Calvin. Rather, the pastor, apparently unaware of this sort of humanism, instead had in mind the philosophy of humanism, sometimes referred to as secular humanism, which holds humanity as the center and source of all values, something that Luther clearly did not believe.

It is worthwhile knowing that *humanism* is used in these two senses. We would spare ourselves a lot of arguing if we recognized the fact. However, confusion over the reference is not the only problem concerning humanism. It was pointed out to our friend when he related this discussion that definitional clarity on the issue probably would not have helped anyhow; the pastor probably would not have been convinced even if he had been given a definition of classical humanism. For this pastor came from a branch of Lutheranism that, one hundred years after Luther's death, had turned its back on the humanism of the Renaissance and had invented its own scholasticism and absolutism. For Protestant scholasticism the text was in no sense ambiguous, needing careful historical and linguistic study; or rather, if ambiguous at all, it was susceptible to method. What was to be uncovered was something clear and unequivocal, providing universal premises for contemporary syllogistic manipulation.

Now really important issues are raised, issues that go beyond the definition of the word *humanism*. These are issues of the role we expect words to play, how we use them to determine reality for us, and whether there is an ultimate reality or not. These issues then lead to crucial questions about the possibility of a Christian humanism and subsequently to issues of how we educate in Christianity. They are therefore issues that go beyond the mere history of Protestant scholasticism.

The views involved in the discussion can be broadly divided into two camps. On the one hand there is the antihumanist position, which may also be called absolutist. Hardly confined to theological dogmatists, it also includes scientific positivism, Liberal rationalism, and epistemological foundationalism. It takes our words to mirror reality rather directly, or at least allows that once the proper method is applied, reality can be uncovered. For this camp words are not entirely ambiguous and can express absolute certainty. On the other hand there is the self-styled humanist position, which may be called relativist, at least broadly considered.It involves, in the words of William James, "the doctrine that to an unascertainable extent our truths are man-made products. "[1] This position takes our words, including both our biblical and scientific words, as essentially ambiguous, reflecting the ambiguous nature of or lives and reality itself. Each side raises important questions; unfortunately neither side hears the other very well. But, furthermore as we will presently suggest, both rely on an unfortunate view of humanism, presenting a truncated view of human nature.

In intellectual circles the humanists clearly dominate at present. They deserve to, for they convincingly point to the degree to which truth, even scientific truth and not just the truth of humanly produced texts, is a matter of our history. They rightly observe that we do not get black and white answers in matters important to life, not even in religion or science. They carefully point out that not only have human beings been subject to their own historical context and had a hand in producing our authoritative texts, but also that the interpretation of texts is part of a history of interpretation. Similarly the seeming certitudes of science depend upon historically conditioned theories and are continually revised: Ptolemy by Copernicus, Copernicus by Kepler, Newton by Einstein. In sum, they argue that what we know is a web of objectivity and subjectivity that we cannot disentangle, which has its own history.

While humanists need not go so far, it is not difficult to conclude that because we are that history, and have no means of getting beyond it, "man is nothing else but what he makes of himself," as Sartre declared.[2] This conclusion of its atheistic wing is a philosophy of humanism, is secular humanism, in the sense that humans are the center of value, for where else can we derive values? We have no access to anything else.

That even many self-claimed humanists balk at this conclusion is evident by their tendency to smuggle something more certain into their lives. Rarely is the contraband overtly religious, since a simple reliance on science, a continual returning to technical solutions, will suffice. We can easily see that if on the one hand a historical view convinces us that absolutist positions are easily defeated, on the other hand history also shows us that the tragic view of life engendered by a wide open humanism is not easy to maintain. For every attempt to maintain a wide open humanist position there has also been a counter-attempt to become more certain—Plato follows Heraclitus, Descartes follows Montaigne, and Protestant scholasticism (and Tridentine Catholicism) follows classical humanism. Values, if taken seriously, cannot be regarded as merely relative; otherwise they would not be values but mere practical hypotheses.

It is in the face of these considerations that the absolutist camp which worries about the philosophy of humanism, about secular humanism, asks an important question. It asks whether or not we can rely only on our own created values and history to discern value. We cannot ignore that question, for it asks whether we are self-sufficient or not, able to provide for ourselves by ourselves. The history of the twentieth century suggests that perhaps we need to rely on some deeper inspiration than we have been able to provide for ourselves, since that history is hardly one of an inexorably ascending moral spiral. If we cannot sufficiently provide for ourselves, if we need inspiration, then we cannot continuously delight in ambiguity. The book of Ecclesiastes was not wrong when it claimed that "of the making of many books there is no end, and much study is a weariness of the flesh" (12.12). There are indeed ambiguous words, but not when speaking of the Word. We cannot afford ambiguity there.

Do these two positions then leave us with an insoluble dilemma, which, in attempts to ease the discomfort of sitting on either of its horns, forces us to oscillate perpetually between them?

Simone Weil once wrote an essay that suggests a possible way of construing how we use words that would break both horns of this dilemma. It is one of those exercises of hers in historical analysis that is often historically suspect but is, nevertheless, at least a penetrating parable that contains a great deal of truth. It is also an appropriate parable, if that, since it deals with the historical roots of humanism.

The essay "The Romanesque Renaissance" (French—"En quoi consiste l'inspiration occitanienne?") was written during World War II, a point at which the Western mind was facing the destruction of one of its pet beliefs—the belief in inevitable progress. Weil observed that in this situation there seemed to be a turning to the past for inspiration, a turning she thought was salutary. For too long the West had lived with the idea of progress. It is an idea she claimed that is bankrupt and always has been, for although we might dream of better things to come in the future, the future of which we dream contains nothing more than what we presently are capable of—"the future is empty and is filled by our imagination. Our imagination can only picture a perfection on our scale" (SE 44). The virtue of studying the past to find inspiration, however, at least offers "a partially completed discrimination. . . . Our attachments and our passions do not so thickly obscure our discrimination of the eternal in the past as in the present" (SE 44–45).

For these reasons she therefore proposed a study—in order to find inspiration—of Languedoc, an area of southern France, which flourished with its own distinctive culture until its brutal suppression by the Inquisition in the twelfth century. For those who have read Weil at all, the choice of Languedoc as a suitable source of inspiration hardly seems surprising. It was in Languedoc that a neognostic group, the Cathars, flourished. Her choice only seems to confirm our suspicions of her own gnostic leanings.

Weil certainly praises the Cathars, especially for their sense of purity in matters of love. Yet despite the praise of the Cathars, the essay as well as a companion one, "A Medieval Epic Poem," is not actually about the Cathars. It is about the culture of Languedoc, which contained *both* Cathars and Catholics. It was their coexistence that Weil found admirable, for it bespoke a deep underlying sense of balance within the culture as a whole. If each side tended toward excess—for example, the Cathars toward freedom of theological expression and the Catholics toward dogmatism—nonetheless the two balanced each other against a center that neither side could possess by themselves. It was a deliberate balance, not an accidental one, for each side saw the other as essential to the life of the country as a whole, a life in which both sides participated.

The depths of this balance were especially evident, Weil noted, when the Cathars were suppressed, for the Catholic prince of the country came to their aid against the powers of the Inquisition. The balance of the culture, however, went further than the harmony of Catholics and Cathars. It was also represented in their architecture, particularly the architecture of the Romanesque. This architecture, she claims, is based on the idea of balancing forces and is quite unlike the totalitarian spirituality she discerned in the later Gothic era.

The key to this culture she then found to lay in its sense of balance, a sense that sought to harmonize opposing forces. The people of Languedoc recognized that they were not gods who command force at will, nor did they suffer from the illusion that right is always on the side of might. They therefore sought to make their way in the world differently, by mutual consent and balance. This refusal of force as anything to be admired penetrated both their architecture and art, as well as their social relations and spirituality. Mutual consent and balance refuse to accept dominating force in things human and divine.

Weil did not think the people of Languedoc invented this idea. Rather, she thought that it was a direct appropriation of the Greek genius, thus making the culture of Languedoc the first renaissance of classical ideas. In fact, she even goes so far as to say this was the true renaissance, having understood far more deeply and with greater vision what that Greek genius really was and meant. The later one, the one that we normally call the Renaissance, she thought was a false revival of the Greek spirit.

Why would anyone call either of these two periods either true or false? If renaissance means a rebirth of classical learning, both are simply that. In fact, there are even more than two. The reason, however, for Weil lay in what she thought each had appropriated from classical learning. The Romanesque renaissance had appropriated the real spirit of classical learning; the later one inherited only the trappings of that learning in a disastrous misunderstanding of what they were to be used for.

The central inspiration of the ancient Greeks, Weil argued, the inspiration that gave the idea of balance, was their understanding of "the infinite distance between God and human beings" (SE 46). Haunted by this distance, she says, the Greeks sought to bridge it, to move closer to God. Their entire culture was a search for these bridges; in the end, their culture itself, human product that it was, was meant to be a bridge. Let us not forget here that bridges depend on the balance of opposing forces, not to their mutual destruction but to create a positive force.

It was this understanding of a culture as a bridge that Languedoc inherited from the Greeks. The later renaissance did not. Instead, Weil claims, they merely inherited the bridges—the literature, art, and sciences. While it clearly understood the humanly made qualities of these bridges, it however misunderstood their function as means of crossing to the other side; thus it took these bridges "for permanent habitations" (SE 47). This, Weil suggested, produced the philosophy of humanism, for rather than seeing us as beings in transition, it took our ambiguous and historical nature, and our glorious creations, of which there are many, to be something permanent, a notion as easily compatible with the absolutism of rationalism or the pluralism of a relativism. Thus the philosophy of humanism became overarching.

Although her historical method is idiosyncratic and her pronouncements nearly oracular, Weil is right as recent studies on Renaissance humanism indicate. Far from simply adopting ancient ideals through adopting their texts and rhetoric, the Renaissance saw humanity and its relation to the world quite differently than the ancients did. The ancients saw themselves as part of a harmonious whole and patterned their lives accordingly; the Renaissance began the development of the notion of the autonomous individual who could find all the resources he needed for life within himself. The Renaissance man (and "man" is used purposely here, as this is a male ideal) is therefore primarily marked not by his ubiquitous, humane knowledge, but by his sense of self-creation. Robert Proctor succinctly puts the difference between the ancient and Renaissance ideals: "For Cicero, the individual human being is part of the whole; for Bruni, the individual becomes the whole. . . . Bruni's *studia humanitas* promise self-perfection; Cicero's *artes humanitatis* turn the soul away from the human and toward the divine."[3]

What went wrong might be put as simply as saying that the ideas that absolutism and humanism represent, far from balancing each other, became opposed alternatives and thus half-solutions between which we have to oscillate, since they are meant to be incompatible. Humanism, on the one hand, is often understood in terms of what it defines itself *against*—namely, the absolutist position that forgets the degree to which we do make the truths of our existence, and that consequently fails to see the need to balance itself with anything, since the only thing with which to be balanced is error. Yet forgetting the legitimate challenge of absolutism—that is, that the truths upon which we base our lives are too often inadequate to our deeper needs, forgetting that absolutism is at its best a search—humanism delights in what is only a promise of fulfillment. While tolerant and broadminded, it fails to be a bridge whenever the forces it balances do not produce a larger structure that can give meaning to the individual forces. Ironically, it thus sows the seeds of its own destruction by inviting an absolutist position, which promises to build that structure. We then hand ourselves over to technical thinking as the solution to our despair. When it then fails to do the job, the pluralist position returns to offer itself.

That we continually oscillate between the two positions is thus the result of posing them as alternatives to each other. Rather than seeing them as both essential to our lives, to give us direction *and* richness, they become antagonistic. Far from being solutions at all for us, they do us violence. They first violate our transitional nature by ignoring it, letting us believe that half-lives are full ones. They are also violent, because the words that we would normally use to build bridges between ourselves and others and between ourselves and God are now used to build unassailable positions. In an essay entitled "The Power of Words," Weil notes that people continually struggle over such things as "democracy," "freedom," "communism," and the like (and we might add "humanism"), forgetting that these are words that signify means and not ends. Yet people fight as if they were ultimate and they use these words to stir themselves to pay the ultimate price. Why? They have either forgotten the ends to which these words are the ambiguous means, or have confused ambiguous words with an ultimate Word. But in either case they seem to feel no need to keep in sight the fact that we are beings whose lives really are ambiguous, because we are in transition and that we need direction.

———————

Despite a long and distinguished history, the term "Christian humanism" to many contemporary thinkers seems a blatant contradiction in terms, for it tries to blend what is regarded as Christian absolutism with the relativism of contemporary humanism. That sort of contradiction does not apply to all forms of what is called "Christian humanism." It does not, for example, apply to its original sense, the one, say, Erasmus gave it, nor to the one where it is made to appear to be a Christian polar alternative to secular humanism.[4] It does somewhat apply here for we do mean it to be taken as an oxymoron where the two terms are set in opposition to each other in order to highlight the distinctive nature of what we are after—a balance of humanistic and absolute elements, of words and an ultimate Word. For on the one hand, Christian humanism is not a philosophy of humanism, for it does not recognize humans as the center of value. Neither is it, since it is humanism, absolutist. Rather it recognizes our ambiguous, historical nature. But it also recognizes that through all the ambiguity, we have an end that is only ambiguous in the way we perceive it now. It is a position that at its root seeks the bridges that can be built, and have been built, between ourselves, and between ourselves and God. It seeks through the ambiguity of words to find the Word; this is its key.

Rather than explaining what it means to use the ambiguity of words to find the Word immediately, though, it may help first to illustrate it. We will do so by the words of the book of *Job*, for Job shows in his individual experience what Languedoc exhibits on a cultural level—that is, a balance between ambiguous human nature and ultimacy. We also do so because, the story itself aside, the illustration indicates how the human words of scripture may lead to an ultimate Word.

The story of Job is well known. It is the story of a righteous man who suffers for no apparent reason, and who loudly protests that he wants to present his case before God. Yet he knows this is impossible and that he is therefore left with the grossest sort of ambiguity at the center of his life. His only comfort comes from three friends who seem to have all the answers; who tell him that since he is suffering, he must have sinned. Q.E.D.

Because it is a story of suffering, the book of *Job* has always been regarded one of the most imaginatively powerful in scripture. Yet because of its ending, it has always seemed somewhat disappointing. Job is asking good questions, yet when God finally gets around to answering Job, we are not so sure that Job gets an answer at all. Instead, it seems that God has merely bullied Job into submission by pointing out what Job seemingly knew already—that God is big enough to create the world and that Job is not capable of beginning to understand the "why?" of it at all. When Job then simply responds by repenting in sackcloth and ashes, it seems he is beaten and has caved into authority.

When we look at Job's answer more carefully, however, it reveals something other than mere capitulation. It tells us what has really gone on between God and Job. Job tells God this: "I knew you then only by hearsay; but now, having seen you with my own eyes I retract all that I have said" (42:5). In other words, Job says that what he knew about God was only what he had been taught in school by the ever-ambiguous human word; what God's wordy answer has now given him is vision that goes beyond the ambiguity of human words. He *sees*, or perhaps, hears, for first time. On one level, to be sure, Job has not received an answer to his question; on the other hand, though, once he has seen the true beauty of God's world, he has no need to ask the question. God's answer is only intolerable to those who still want to have a "position;" who want to be "postfriend" friends.

Despite the fact, however, that Job no longer feels the need to ask his questions, we ought not to assume that his questions were irrelevant to his vision. In fact, it may have been because he felt the ambiguity of his hearsay knowledge and continually questioned it, that he finally reached vision. The three absolutist friends did not, and God roundly blasts them for their pious blasphemy, for "not speaking truthfully about me as my servant Job has done" (42.7). Their very confidence that they alone possessed the truth thus kept them from seeing the truth.

The Job story illustrates two profound implications of what we are calling Christian humanism. On the one hand, it teaches us to recognize what is the deep ambiguity of human existence. That ambiguity is an immensely important truth about us, and to ignore it as Job's three friends did is to cut ourselves off from deeper truth. In this regard it is one of our greatest tasks to disclaim an absolutism we do not deserve and to disabuse our minds of all sorts of prejudices in which we all so confidently rest. That task is not only given to us by Job, it is also the task Socrates exemplified by demonstrating the ignorance of his Athenian compatriots who also had only known by hearsay.

On the other hand, if Job teaches us to avoid dogmatic absolutism, he does not give us any warrant to be relativists. Job may have clearly recognized the ambiguity of his situation, yet he never declared that there is no truth behind it all. Instead he steadfastly maintained that there was a judge before whom he could present his case. He looked for certainty beyond the ambiguity. And because he looked, paid attention, and refused all half-truths, he found the whole truth. This gives us a second task; namely, that in rejecting absolutism we cannot be content with relativism as a new dogma either. It is not enough simply to point out ambiguity; we need to pay attention to wait for the Word that silences all ambiguous words. We may not be able to speak that Word; we can, however, teach that there is something to listen to in the silence when we can say no more.

There is something terribly important in getting clear on the issues surrounding the term *humanism*, especially the one of how we are to use words. What is at stake is less the interpretation of our moral and intellectual experience, and more our individual and cultural moral and intellectual habits. Whether we see ourselves as possessing certainty or as being subject to historical ambiguity, whether or not we see ourselves as being on the way to something involves more than theory. It involves, as Weil saw in the culture of Languedoc, how we are actually related to other beings, including God. If one simply contrasted at the definitional level Catholic dogma and Cathar freedom—at the level of words—one would fail to see the real genius, the motivating spirit of Languedoc. It is not the case that theory and words are unimportant, for, as we saw in the case of Job, they clearly are; however, there is often an underlying spirit, a Word, which directs how the theory will be used. In this sense, there are humane absolutisms, and absolutist relativisms. It is in this sense—the one that indicates that we are motivated by the Word when using ambiguous words, that there can be such a thing as Christian humanism.

It is here that we must pay special attention to education, for it is a crucial area for debate over issues such as humanism. Education shows that what is at stake is not the epistemological issue of whether or not words mirror reality, or whether or not they are relative to culture and history. It is the issue of what we are going to use them for. How and why we educate will determine both whether individual souls can find bridges, and whether the culture itself as a whole can be used as a bridge or not. In this regard, education is more than simply imbuing students with a view, with giving them words; it is also a key practice of a culture toward its participants that will ensure that culture's vitality.

This then leaves us with two problems. The first is to discern what Word it actually is that drives the words of our culture and the education that perpetuates that culture. I have said enough about this above in discussing what is involved in taking absolutism and relativism as alternatives to leave this problem aside by remarking that the spirit in which we use words in education is inadequate to us as transitional beings. The other problem is how to find a true Word behind all our words; in short, how to have an education of real Christian humanism, an education that recognizes the ambiguous nature of our words and which takes them seriously enough to use them to penetrate to the primal silent Word. How we might have that education involves two interrelated key elements, both of which are borrowed from Weil—namely, the development of attention and participation in a tradition that can develop and sustain attention.

To insist that attention be a part of education is in the first place not to make a very astounding observation. At the primary level the ability to pay attention is nothing more than a functional distinction between merely instrumental learning undertaken by rote and learning for insight. Nearly every teacher, indeed almost every person who has ever had an insight, recognizes the difference between the sort of attention that goes hand in hand with fascination with a problem and the dreary concentration of will power that tries "to get a handle" on the problem, that tries "to get on top of it," to manipulate it. The difference results in, on the side of attention, a person who is transformed by what he or she is paying attention to, who sees some hitherto unsuspected value, and, on the side of will power, a person who is doing nothing more than trying to bring the problem into his or her sphere of influence, thus remaining unchanged in his or her vision of what is important.

One way of describing the value of attention is that it allows us to penetrate to the heart of the problem to which we are paying attention. In this sense, attention is that which gives what absolutism really hopes for—namely, entrance into the realm of transcending value and purpose. It gives us access to value and purpose that we are incapable of providing for ourselves. However, describing attention as that which allows us to penetrate truth is both misleading on the nature of attention and may lead to the unfortunate aspects of absolutism. Weil's observation that attention is in fact a sort of negative quality, a type of decreation, is therefore important to keep in mind.

For Weil, we do not penetrate a problem at all by attention; rather "attention consists of suspending our thought, leaving it detached, empty, *and ready to be penetrated by the object.* . . . Above all our thought should be empty, waiting, not seeking anything, but ready to receive in its naked truth the object that is to penetrate" (WG 111; our emphasis). Attention receives; it does not seek to dominate.

The distinction is crucial. An education that deliberately seeks to train attention as Weil understands it is indeed oriented toward a silent eternal Word that speaks in a voice quite different than that which we use to speak words. It gives a transcendent assurance. That assurance, however, is different than the certainty that absolutism seeks. On the one hand, it can only be achieved by humility, since it takes a recognition on our part that we do not penetrate anything at all, but simply receive it. On the other hand, as Weil also notes, it makes us see the value of other people as well, to see beyond the limits of our words and to see that there is something to our relations with others that cannot be put into mere words. As she points out in the essay "Human Personality," often we do not hear what the afflicted are really saying, because we do not pay attention to what is being said behind the words. Attention allows us to hear their distress. To the one who can pay true attention, words such as "master" and "slave" have no absolute meaning.

Thus attention, although it gives us access to what absolutism seeks, is paradoxically not absolutist itself. It is, in fact, in its effect, more pluralist than most relativisms and humanisms, for it allows us to recognize that we need to balance our limited positions against other positions in order to find the real center, which none of us can possess. In the words of T.S. Eliot;

> "Except for the point,
> the still point,
> There would be no dance, and there is only the dance."[5]

While attention therefore ought to be the heart and soul of education, what is involved in being able to pay attention is more than simple spiritual gazing. Simply to claim that education ought to consist of attention, without giving a student anything to pay attention to, to not worry about content, is cultural Montanism.[6] Despite the fact that Weil could say that it did not make any difference whether or not a student "got" a particular mathematical problem, she did think it was important to study mathematics. There is no substitute. We thus come to our second point, the importance of participating in a tradition that can develop and sustain attention.

There are undoubtedly a thousand points of darkness surrounding the issue of what exactly a tradition or culture is. We will confine ourselves to two.

A tradition or culture is at least the preservation of a shared past which gives a common, more or less broadly understood, basis of understanding to a present social grouping. This tradition can be preserved in numerous ways, but for literate traditions it is especially preserved in its books—literary, philosophical and scientific (at least for the West). The importance of this past can be seen by noting a point that Weil makes in an essay on the French colonial problem.

While arguing against French colonial policy, especially of the sort that required Algerian school children to recite the words "Our fathers, the Gauls," Weil raises the crucial point of why it is important for any group to maintain its past. The question that needs to be raised is whether or not we are self-sufficient—that is, if we can by reason alone overcome every moral and technical difficulty and obstacle with which we are faced—we have no need for a past and can throw off its often crushing weight as the Enlightenment and liberalism tried to do to gain a universal, rational morality, a "heritage" with which we are still living. On the other hand, if we are not sufficient, as much of the twentieth century suggests we are not, if we need help from something outside ourselves, then maintaining a past that preserves spiritual treasures is crucial to our flourishing. Admittedly, Weil notes, grace can cut through any obstacle; yet "it is only the radiance from the spiritual treasures of the past which is the necessary condition for receiving grace"(SE 207).

Why these treasures are a necessary condition can be seen in a comment Weil makes in a fragment where she calls culture "the formation of attention" (EL 160). A culture forms attention because we do not experience the world as a *tabula rasa*; we experience it through the lens of our culture, and that teaches us what we are to pay attention to, and how to pay attention. Consider that archcultural product, language. Language at its simplest levels causes us to make fundamental distinctions—say, between men and women, and their anticipated roles in the culture. At its deeper levels, however, especially in the greatest books of the culture, it focuses questions such as what human beings are, what it means to act justly toward them, and what the world is. It takes the received world of words and questions it—with words. Words both give us a world, sometimes for better or for worse, and an ability to see beyond the merely given. We would neither have this world nor the ability to see behind it, however, without a tradition. Thus Weil, who was herself often suspicious of institutional religion, can say: "there is no religion without a religious tradition" (SE 207). There is no penetration of the Word without words, however limited they may be. We need the tradition to penetrate beyond the tradition.

A tradition is therefore necessary for forming attention. However, its value is not simply that of a propaedeutic to attention. Its relation to attention proper is not analogous to the worst-case educational scenario of lecturing a child on how to ride a bicycle and then giving her a bicycle to ride. Instead the ability of a tradition to form attention depends upon its ability to receive the fruits of attention and to use them to increase attention. That is its educational importance.

This can be explained by reference to another of Weil's idiosyncratic historical views. In Weil's eyes nearly all cultures began in an original revelation and are a specific outworking of that revelation. Far from seeing this revelation as some sort of literal verbal message, however, she saw it as the fruit of grace penetrating attention. For example, in another of the London fragments, she claims that "inert matter, by its submission to necessity, gives man the example of obedience to God" (EL 159).

Obedience to God is an idea, Weil thinks, that naturally suggests itself as the meaning of physical labor, for humans in labor, just as matter, find themselves subject to necessity, yet find in matter an inexpressible beauty, a witness to something beyond matter. It is out of this idea that science grew as it sought to contemplate and express this relation, Weil claimed. To say that science grew out of such a revelation, though, does not put science in a position of a mere guardian of the idea. That science grew at all is the result of further attention to the inspiration. Hardly outgrowing the revelation, it preserves it in its own tradition. It is for this reason that Weil, for example, could claim that we might recover the real genius of Western science by paying more attention to physical labor.

The point here, quite aside from the historical speculation, is this: that a tradition preserves the treasures of the past by inspiring and calling forth new treasures, which in their turn are also to be preserved, not as museum pieces, but as something that is inspiring and living. A tradition preserves these treasures by forming itself around them. This is seen in how we educate. Educationally there is a crucial distinction here between the preservation of the works of some minor leader of the Academy for research purposes, and preserving Plato's *Republic* by teaching it to students. The difference lies in the students' being able to make something significant out of their life because they read Plato, even if that something is occasionally unplatonic.

To put it another way, a humanistic reading of tradition is a good one, since what is contained in any tradition is, prima facie, a matter of "man-made truth." We do preserve and reform the original inspiration; we are the history of these acts of preserving. This reading is simply an incomplete one if it fails to recognize why we ever "made" those truths in the past and continue to do so.[7] Although that "why" is only given and preserved in ambiguous words, in those words is preserved a hint and a promise, something to pay attention to. Attention allows that hint to penetrate us so that we may continue to make that truth.

On the other hand, this means that any reading of a tradition or education in a tradition is also incomplete if it merely provides us with stock examples of virtue or rhetorical elegance to "better adorn the Lord's temple with literary richness," which was Erasmus' justification of his humanistic studies.[8] In these cases, there is a far too ready assumption that we already have access to the fruits of attention without having gone through the ambiguity of living within a tradition to find them.

In the end, to have a true and relevant Christian humanism we need to find an education in culture that sees culture itself as an education that forms attention. This would be an education that takes seriously the task of using ambiguous words to find the Word, knowing that they are human words but ones that can incarnate the Word. For it is indeed a humanistic education of which we stand in need, but one that is Christian in the best sense, for the words that are taught are words that spring from the Word and lead back to it by incarnating the Word in us who read and speak them.

That sort of educational tension has been captured nicely by E. M. Forster in his novel, *Howard's End*:

> The business man who assumes that this life is everything, and the mystic who asserts that it is nothing, fail, on this side and on that, to hit the truth. "Yes, I see dear; it's about halfways between," Aunt Juley had hazarded in earlier years. "No; truth, being alive, was not halfway between anything. It was only to be found by continuous excursions into either realm, and though proportion is the final secret, to espouse it at the outset is to insure sterility."[9]

NOTES

PREFACE

1. George Steiner, "Bad Friday", *New Yorker*, (March 2, 1992), 86.

2. Ibid.

CHAPTER 1

1. Chapel Hill, 1991: University of North Carolina Press.

2. *Simone Weil à New York et à Londres* (Paris, 1967: Plon), 76.

3. "Simone Weil (1909 1943) ou l'itinéraire d'une âme: Les derniers jours—Le baptême 'in extremis'" (Autumn 1971).

4. The chief exception is David McClellan's *Simone Weil: Utopian Pessimist* (London: 1989, Macmillan). McClellan correctly identifies Deitz. He adds this comment, quoting a footnote of Pétrement: "Weil merely remarked [when Deitz attempted the baptism]: 'You can do it; it can't do any harm.' Her attitude to her own baptism seems to have remained unchanged" (p.263). This remark Pétrement quotes from her notes, which are not reproduced elsewhere (including Rabi's article). Pétrement's own comment on these words of Weil is that they seem to express a certain indifference, a milder claim than McClellan's. It also ought to be noted, though, that "her attitude to her own baptism" is precisely what is in question here.

5. Since the story is also told in substance by Rabi, I cite his article here where appropriate.

6. Rabi, "Simone Weil," 57–58.

7. Ibid., 59.

8. *The Coherence of Theism* (Oxford, 1977: Oxford University Press), chapters 2 and 3.

9. Simone Pétrement, *Simone Weil: A Life* (New York, 1976: Pantheon Books), 523.

10. Rabi, "Simone Weil'" 59–60.

11. Pétrement, *Simone Weil*, 524.

12. Rabi, "Simone Weil," 59.

13. Ibid.

14. "L'eau du baptême" interview with J.M. Perrin in *Entretiens en marge du colloque du Séte (1979): sur les refus de Simone Weil* (Association pour l'étude de la pensée de Simone Weil), 1982, 44.

15. Ibid.

16. Pétrement, *Simone Weil*, 481.

17. *Les Nouveaux Cahiers* (Spring 1972), 59.

18. Ibid., 58.

19. Nevin, *Simone Weil*, xi.

20. Ibid., 389.

21. Ibid., xi.

22. I note an odd feature of Nevin's research. He does mention the baptism, only to say "but Pétrement makes a good case for the invalidity of this gratuitous act: there is no evidence that Weil requested it" (p. 35). Yet, despite having supposedly researched various Jewish reactions to Weil, including Rabi's (see pp. 252–53), he is curiously unaware of Rabi's own articles on the story and his reaction to them. This may simply be one of many failures to have actually delved into the extensive secondary sources he lists. For a book that advertises itself as using many unpublished and untranslated sources, Nevin rarely uses later material, largely contenting himself with sensational secondary literature that was published before the majority of Weil's works became available, and certainly before there had been the time for scholarship actually to ponder what was said.

23. *Entretiens*, 44.

24. Paul Giniewski, *Simone Weil ou la haine de soi* (Paris, 1978: Berg International).

CHAPTER 2

1. Cambridge, 1989: Harvard University Press.

2. Taylor, *Sources*, 3.

3. See I. Murdoch, *The Sovereignty of the Good* (New York, 1971: Shocken Books) 50, for her generous acknowledgment.

4. Taylor, *Sources*, 4.

5. Ibid., 5.

6. Ibid., 6.

7. Ibid., 7.

8. Ibid., 8.

9. Ibid., 11.

10. In a pamphlet entitled "A Memorial Service for Gregory Vlastos," Dec. 8, 1991. The service was held at Princeton University.

11. *Modernity on Endless Trial* (Chicago, 1990: University of Chicago Press), 73.

CHAPTER 3

1. A-A. Devaux, "Liberté et Nécessité," in *Simone Weil: Philosophe, historienne et mystique* (Paris, 1978: Aubier Montaigne), 303.

2. In his introduction to LP, Winch notes that "she tended, rather like Spinoza, to confuse the senses of 'necessity' which apply to the natural laws established within science, with the fundamentally different sense of 'necessity' connected with ideas like 'fate.'" In our argument here we show that she, in fact, distinguishes these senses, and others, very carefully.

3. In the interests of objectivity all *Timaeus* quotes are from the translation of Benjamin Jowett.

4. The role of reason is active and intelligent, while that of necessity is not: the works of reason are therefore quite different sorts of things than that which is born of necessity.

5. This is demonstrated in the "obstinacy" that it shows to being harmonized. Plato says: "And the rations of their numbers, motions, and other properties, everywhere God *as far as necessity allowed or gave consent*, has exactly perfected and harmonized in due proportion" (56c).

6. See NB 515: "In conditional necessity , no limit is inscribed. The sequence of conditions is without limit. Limit is only inscribed in a relationship between several conditions which compensate each other, in an order." It is important not to confuse the "conditional necessity" in "The Pythagorean Doctrine" with the "conditional necessity" which is spoken of here, for the two are, as we shall see, diametrically opposed.

7. See footnote no. 6.

CHAPTER 4

1. Kallistos Ware, "Ways of Prayer and Contemplation," in *Christian Spirituality*, eds. Bernard McGinn and John Meyendorff (New York, 1985: Crossroad), 398.

2. The translation of this essay that is used here was done by Martin Andic, and is unpublished. The citations allow the reader to refer to a published translation, namely "Essay on the Notion of Reading," trans. Rebecca Fine Rose and Timothy Tessin, *Philosophical Investigations*, vol. 13.4 (October 1990).

3. We are reminded here of Plato's *Republic* in which all things have a degree of reality. The visible things of the universe are an adumbration of those that are invisible.

4. According to the allegory of the cave, a conversion from visible things is needed to begin the ascent. According to the divided line, the progression is from reflection of sensible things to generalizations concerning sensible things, to the foundation of sensible things in intelligible ones, especially mathematical ratios, and finally to the form of the good which, is the source of the ratios that act as limits and so render sensible things into an ordered, harmonious, beautiful whole. Weil seems to offer an updated version of this Platonic vision by stressing the role of the body and in particular the role of manual work in the ascent.

The passage in *First and Last Notebooks* on page 131 is particularly instructive for understanding the role of contradiction in leading one to ascend to the supernatural. Springsted's *Christus Mediator: Platonic Mediation in the Thought of Simone Weil*, pp. 85–89, gives account of this, as does his "Contradiction, Mystery and the Use of Words in Simone Weil," *Religion and Literature*, vol. 17.2 (Summer 1985).

5. "The World as Text—the Hermeneutical Perspective of Simone Weil," *Revue des Sciences Philosophiques et Théologiques*, (Oct. 1980), 509–30.

6. Kuehn, "World," 510.

7. See IC, especially the essay "The Pythagorean Doctrine." One is here reminded of Newman's famous distinction between notional and real

apprehension, the manipulation of terms without an actual apprehension of the reality they concern.

8. For a fuller discussion of "decreation," see J.P. Little's "Simone Weil's Concept of Decreation," in *Simone Weil's Philosophy of Culture,* ed. Richard H. Bell, Cambridge, 1993: Cambridge University Press.

9. The issue of perspective or point of view is discussed in Martin Andic's "Discernment and the Imagination," in Bell, *Simone Weil's Philosophy of Culture.*

CHAPTER 5

1. Peter Winch, *Simone Weil: The Just Balance,* Cambridge, 1989: Cambridge University Press, 13.

2. Ibid., 166.

3. Ibid., 179.

4. Ibid., 184–85.

5. First published as "Metaphysique de la transcendance et théorie des "Metaxu" chez Simone Weil" (CSW v.4 [Dec. 1982]) and later reprinted in *Christus Mediator: Platonic Mediation in the Thought of Simone Weil* (pp. 197–219).

6. Springsted, *Christus Mediator,* 199.

7. For a general discussion of issues raised by Winch's presentation of the idea of the supernatural in Weil, see David Cockburn, "The Supernatural," *Religious Studies,* 28.3, (September 1992) 285–302.

8. Winch, *Simone Weil,* 211.

9. Richard Bell, review of Winch, *Religious Studies,* 26.1 (March 1990), 174.

10. Winch, *Simone Weil,* 200.

11. FLN 147, quoted in Winch, *Simone Weil,* 199.

12. Winch, *Simone Weil,* 204.

13. For a helpful discussion of this issue specifically in Weil see Heinz Robert Schlette, "Langage de la place publique—Langage de la chambre nuptiale: Quelques remarques sur le sens théologique d'une distinction philosophique chez Simone Weil" in *Recherches sur la philosophie et le langage,* no. 13 ("Simone Weil et les langues") Université des Sciences Sociales de Grenoble, 1991.

14. Ludwig Wittgenstein, *Philosophical Investigations*, third edition (New York: Macmillan, 1968), 172e.

15. On this point, see David Burrell, *Aquinas, God and Action*, Notre Dame, 1979: University of Notre Dame Press.

16. Ludwig Wittgenstein, *Culture and Value*, trans. Peter Winch (Chicago: University of Chicago Press, 1980), 32e.

17. *Sources of the Self* (Cambridge: Harvard University Press, 1989) 73.

18. Ibid., 70.

CHAPTER 6

1. *Arrian's Discourses of Epictetus*, 2 vols., trans. W.A. Oldfather, Loeb Classical Library (Cambridge, 1961: Harvard University Press), Book I, chap 6.

2. Epictetus, *Discourses*, I.VI.4–8.

3. Ibid., I.VI.40–41.

4. Ibid., I.VI.37–38.

5. Epictetus, like other Greek Stoics, is following Plato's lead. In Book X of the *Republic*, Plato argued that the just person is immune to external circumstances. Unless we give our consent, external circumstances cannot harm the soul by making it unjust. Likewise Kant claimed that we always are able to act morally regardless of our circumstances and our desire for our personal well-being. Sartre has a Kantian variation. No external circumstance nor previous decisions in our past can determine our actions at any particular juncture. For all of this, there is a final refuge of dignity.

6. Epictetus, *Discourses*, I.VI. 1.

7. "When the inward nature of man, cut off from all carnal influences and deprived of all supernatural light, performs actions which are in conformity with those which supernatural light would impose if it were present, there is utter purity. This is the central point of the Passion" (GG 44).

8. The second point is examined at length by Allen in his book, *Christian Belief in a Postmodern World* (Louisville, 1989: Westminster John Knox Press), chap. 10 and 11.

CHAPTER 7

1. Rowan Williams, "The Necessary Non-Existence of God," in *Simone Weil's Philosophy of Culture*, ed. R. Bell (Cambridge: Cambridge University Press,

1993), 52–76. Peter Winch, *Simone Weil: "The Just Balance"* (Cambridge: Cambridge University Press, 1989), 201–204.

2. See Williams, "Necessary" 60, 63–64.

3. Ibid., 64.

4. Winch, *Simone Weil*, 201.

5. Ibid.

6. Ibid., 204.

7. Ibid.

8. See *Love* (Cambridge, 1987: Cowley Publications).

9. See Winch, *Simone Weil*, 202.

10. Williams, "Necessary", 66–67.

11. Winch, *Simone Weil*, 203.

12. Allen treats many of these in *Love*, cited above.

13. Winch, *Simone Weil*, 202.

14. Williams, "Necessary", 74.

15. Winch, *Simone Weil*, 200.

CHAPTER 8

1. This is the third of three poems in *The Temple* entitled "Love." References in this chapter are to this one only. All quotations from Herbert's poems are taken from the volume in the series, Classics of Western Spirituality, *George Herbert*, ed. John N. Wall, Jr. (New York, 1981: Paulist Press).—George Herbert (1593–1633) was a priest of the Church of England and served the rural parish of Bemerton, Wiltshire, England. Izaak Walton's biography of 1670 gives a misleading picture of a dear, saintly, innocent man living in a peaceful corner of the world. In fact, Herbert was born into one of the most powerful and well-connected noble families of the kingdom. He was a highly polished courtier with the extensive learning of a Renaissance gentleman, and was the Public Orator for Cambridge University, and twice a member of Parliament, during turbulent times. He was a friend of Francis Bacon, the great proponent of the physical sciences, and translated part of Bacon's *The Advancement of Learning* into Latin. The new knowledge did not pose a threat to him.

2. *Selected Essays* (London, 1972; Routledge & Kegan Paul), 28.

CHAPTER 9

1. The cryptic "nurses" refers to Weil's proposal to Allied authorities to parachute a number of unarmed female nurses onto the front lines to tend the wounded and dying, an act she thought would show the world that the Allies were about something quite different than the sort of heroism extolled by the Nazis. It would be difficult to overstate exactly how much the realization of this project meant to Weil, and how disappointed she was that it was never taken seriously by DeGaulle and others.

2. Plato, *Seventh Letter*, 343a.

3. Andrew Louth, *Discerning the Mystery* (Cambridge, 1983: Cambridge University Press), 37.

4. Hobbes, *Leviathan*, Part II, chap. 20.

5. Ibid.

6. While it is Weil's view that we are exploring here there are certainly striking similarities to certain understandings of the relation of social theory and practice as put forth by Charles Taylor. See, for example, his "Social Theory as Practice" and "Understanding and Ethnocentricity" in *Philosophy and the Human Sciences: Philosophical Papers 2* (Cambridge, 1985: Cambridge University Press).

7. In an entry that deserves much fuller commentary than we can provide here, Weil observes: "Truth is what I think—what I read in appearances—when desiring the purely true" (NB 38).

8. C.B. MacPherson, editor, *John Locke: Second Treatise of Government* (Indianapolis, 1980: Hackett), x.

9. C.B. MacPherson, *The Political Theory of Possessive Individualism* (Oxford, 1962: Oxford University Press).

10. Robert Bellah et al., *The Good Society* (New York, 1991: Knopf).

11. Charles Taylor, *The Sources of the Self: The Making of The Modern Identity* (Cambridge, 1989: Harvard University Press), 159.

12. Ibid., 159–60.

13. Weil understands the term *metaxu* meaning "intermediary" as a sort of spiritual bridge from a lower state to a higher. Far more than an undeveloped metaphor in Weil's writings, it appears to have real theoretical content for her. For further discussion, see above, chap. 5, Part I, esp. pp. 80–81.

14. Peter Winch, *Simone Weil: The Just Balance*, (Cambridge, 1989: Cambridge University Press), 85.

15. On this point, see chap. 10, Part III, which also expands points being made here. For further evidence that it is Maritain that is the object of Weil's criticism, see Simone Fraisse, "Simone Weil, la personne et les droits de l'homme," *Cahiers Simone Weil*, Juin, 1984 (VII.2) 120–132.

16. Raymond Plant (*Modern Political Thought* [Oxford, 1991: Basil Blackwell]) disputes Weil's contention that "needs create obligations." Besides misquoting Weil (she says, "obligations stem from needs"), Plant misses the point of obligations that is being made here.

CHAPTER 10

1. Bernard Williams, *Ethics and the Limits of Philosophy* (Cambridge, 1985: Harvard University Press); Martha Nussbaum, *The Fragility of Goodness* (Cambridge, 1986: Cambridge University Press).

2. Charles Larmore, *Patterns of Moral Complexity* (Cambridge, 1987: Cambridge University Press).

3. *New York Times Review of Books*, July 23, 1989.

4. Nicholas Lash, *A Matter of Hope* (Notre Dame, 1982: University of Notre Dame Press), 59.

5. As Richard Rorty has argued (*Philosophy and the Mirror of Nature* [Princeton, 1979: Princeton University Press]), a full-blooded relativism is the alternative to absolutism, and to find absolutism meaningless similarly empties relativism of meaning.

6. Alasdair MacIntyre, *After Virtue* (Notre Dame, 1981: University of Notre Dame Press), chap. 2 and 3.

7. Michael Sandel, *Liberalism and the Limits of Justice* (Cambridge, 1982: Cambridge University Press), 179.

8. See C.B. MacPherson, *The Political Theory of Possessive Individualism: Hobbes to Locke* (Oxford, 1962: Oxford University Press).

9. Stanley Hauerwas, *A Community of Character* (Notre Dame, 1981: University of Notre Dame Press), 79.

10. Richard Rorty, *Contingency, Irony, and Solidarity* (Cambridge, 1989: Cambridge University Press), 86.

11. Ibid., 87.

12. Ibid., 88.

13. We take this to refer particularly to what she was writing in London.

14. See chap. 9, footnote 15.

15. Jacques Maritain, *Scholasticism and Politics* (New York, 1941: MacMillan), 62, 63.

16. See also Springsted's *Simone Weil and the Suffering of Love* (Cambridge, 1986: Cowley Publications) on this issue.

17. On this issue of affliction constituting a destruction of the person, see chapter 6. See also L. Blum and V. Seidler: " . . . she learned to question Kant's confidence that dignity and self-respect are "inner values" that can be sustained in the face of relations of power and subordination; she learned, on the contrary, how *vulnerable* are our dignity and self-respect. Not only does dignity depend on "external reasons" but it can also be 'radically destroyed' with the 'daily experience of brutal constraint' (SL 21)" (*A Truer Liberty: Simone Weil and Marxism* [New York, 1989: Routledge], 178.

18. *Philebus*, 22b.

19. See R.A. Markus, *Saeculum: History and Society in the Theology of St. Augustine* (Cambridge, 1970: Cambridge University Press) on this recognition of Augustine.

20. Simone Pétrement, *Simone Weil* (New York, 1976: Pantheon), 493. It is quite clear that this profession of faith was important to Weil. Her manuscripts include at least three drafts of it, with the one now printed being the second. She further condensed it in the last, apparently so that it could be used as a sort of creed. It is also clearly later than the opening sections of *The Need for Roots* since all three versions contain truth as a need of the soul, whereas truth appears in the *Roots* manuscript as a later insertion. In this respect, *Roots* contains the discovery to the problems discussed in "Human Personality" and the "Draft" is a formulaic creed based on this discovery.

21. The notion of "illocutionary force" brought out by J.L. Austin obviously was not a concept Weil possessed. What we are suggesting is that she is aiming at a phenomenon that Austin described so well.

22. See the essay, "Luttons-nous pour la justice?" in EL, but also "Is There a Marxist Doctrine?" in OL.

23. See esp. "A War of Religions" in *Selected Essays* as well as *The Need for Roots*. See also E. Springsted, "The Religious Basis of Culture: T.S. Eliot and Simone Weil," in *Religious Studies*, 25.1, March 1989, 105 116.

24. See Mary Deitz, *Between the Human and the Divine: The Political Thought of Simone Weil* (Totowa, 1988: Rowman & Littlefield), chap. 8.

25. Weil lists as the "needs of the soul": order, liberty, obedience, responsibility, equality, hierarchism, honor, punishment, freedom of opinion,

security, risk, private property, collective property, truth, and the need for roots. Except for order and the last two, these needs are listed as pairs to be *balanced*.

26. Deitz, *Between*, 124.

27. Michael Ignatieff, "The Limits of Sainthood," *The New Republic*, (June 18, 1990), 44.

28. Larmore, *Patterns*, 138, our emphasis.

29. See chapter 7; also Springsted's *Christus Mediator*, 205–7.

30. John Dewey, *Individualism: Old and New* (New York, 1962: Capricorn Books), 52.

31. This idea of a culture being a balanced reaction to revelation may have been part of Weil's inspiration for her project for a front-line nursing corps. It was just that sort of act of selfless heroism that could reorient and rebalance a culture's values. The point to be kept in mind is that this sort of act is precisely what she had in mind when she talked about culture being a reaction to an original inspiration.

32. The prime example of what this notion of balance might mean within a culture can be seen in two earlier essays Weil wrote on the culture of Languedoc in the twelfth century, which flourished as a balance between the neo-Manichaean sect known as the Cathars and the Catholics. Weil suggests that neither possessed the truth, but by virtue of balancing their otherwise incompatible viewpoints, they achieved a great culture where human beings were truly respected. See chapter 11 for additional discussion of Weil's understanding and use of Occitanian culture.

33. Deitz, *Between*, 185.

34. Martin Andic, "Spiritual Mechanics," unpublished essay delivered to the American Weil Society, 1989.

35. Peter Winch, *Simone Weil: The Just Balance* (Cambridge, 1989: Cambridge University Press), 197.

36. Ibid., 211.

37. Rorty, *Contingency*, 178.

38. See Springsted's *Simone Weil and the Suffering of Love* on this point.

CHAPTER 11

1. *Pragmatism* (Cambridge, 1978: Harvard University Press), 117.

2. "Existentialism Is a Humanism" in *Existentialism from Dostoyevsky to Sartre*, ed. W. Kaufman (Cleveland, 1956: Meridian Books), 291.

3. *Education's Great Amnesia: Reconsidering the Humanities from Petrarch to Freud* (Bloomington, 1988: Indiana University Press), 19.

4. As done by R.W. Franklin and J.M. Shaw in their *The Case for Christian Humanism* (Grand Rapids, 1991: Eerdmans). They argue: "Long neglected and often misunderstood, Christian humanism is nothing other than the traditional message of Christianity with the accent on how the coming of Christ into the world implies God's loving care for human creatures and all that affects our well-being" (p. ix).

5. *Four Quartets*, "Burnt Norton," II.

6. Montanus was an early Christian heretic who refused to accept the received scriptures as normative because, he claimed, he and his followers received new direction from the Holy Spirit. The problem was, as Hippolytus of Rome rightly saw, the divisiveness this caused. Every congregation could have its own truth, which simply meant that there was no unity to Christ's body. There is also, of course, the problem of distinguishing true from false prophecy. If there is no norm, there can be no distinction.

7. Consider the point made by Leszek Kolakowski who argues: "Everywhere we find the same doubly self-destructive process. The Enlightenment emerges from a reconsidered Christian heritage; in order to take root, it must defeat the crystallized and ossified forms of that heritage. When it does begin to take root, in an ideological humanist or reactionary shape . . . it gradually drifts away from its origins to become non-Christian or anti-Christian. In its final form the Enlightenment turns against itself: humanism becomes a moral nihilism, doubt leads to epistemological nihilism, and the affirmation of the person undergoes a metamorphosis that transforms it into a totalitarian idea. . . .

"It is only today that a spiritual movement on both sides is taking shape: Christianity and the Enlightenment, both gripped by a sentiment of helplessness and confusion, are beginning to question their history and their own significance. From this doubt a vague and uncertain vision is emerging, a vision of new arrangements of which, as yet, we know nothing. But this double principle of self-questioning is itself a continuation of the very principle upon which Europe was founded; in this sense, therefore, Europe has remained true to herself in her state of uncertainty and disarray. If she survives the pressure of the barbarians, it will not be because of any ultimate solution she might one day discover, but rather thanks to a clear consciousness that such solutions do not exist anywhere; and *that* is a Christian consciousness" (*Modernity on Endless Trial* [Chicago, 1990: University of Chicago Press], 30).

8. "The Handbook of the Militant Christian" in *The Essential Erasmus*, ed. J. Dolan (New York, 1964: Meridian Books), 96.

9. E. M. Forster, *Howard's End* (New York, 19—: Vintage Books), 195.

SELECTED BIBLIOGRAPHY

Allen, Diogenes, *Three Outsiders*. Cambridge,1983: Cowley Publications.

————. *Christian Belief in a Postmodern World; The Full Wealth of Conviction*. Louisville, 1989: Westminster/John Knox Press.

————. *Love*. Cambridge, 1987: Cowley Publications.

Andic, Martin. "Spiritual Mechanics." Unpublished paper delivered to the American Weil Society, 1989.

Armstrong, A.H. *Plotinian and Christian Studies*. London, 1979: Variorum Reprints.

Auden, W.H. *Protestant Mystics* ed. Anne Freemantle, New York, 1965: American Library.

Augustine. *Confessions*, translated by Henry Chadwick. Oxford, 1991: Oxford University Press.

Bell, Richard, (ed.). *Simone Weil's Philosophy of Culture: Readings toward a Divine Humanity*. Cambridge, 1993: Cambridge University Press.

————. Review of Winch's *Simone Weil: The Just Balance*, in *Religious Studies*. 26.1 (March 1990).

Bellah, Robert (et al.). *Habits of the Heart: Individualism and Commitment in American Life*. New York, 1986: Harper & Row.

————. *The Good Society*. New York, 1991: Alfred Knopf.

Berlin, Isaiah. *The Crooked Timber of Humanity*. New York, 1992: Vintage.

Blum, Lawrence, and Seidler, Victor. *A Truer Liberty: Simone Weil and Marxism*. New York, 1989: Routledge.

Burnaby, John. *Amor Dei: A Study of the Religion of St. Augustine*, Hulsean Lectures of 1938. Norwich, 1991: Canterbury Press.

Burrell, David. *Aquinas God and Action*. Notre Dame, 1979: University of Notre Dame Press.

Cabaud, Jacques. *Simone Weil: A Fellowship in Love*. New York, 1964: Channel Press.

———. *Simone Weil à New York et à Londres*. Paris, 1967: Plon.

Cockburn, David. "The Supernatural." *Religious Studies*, 28.3 (September 1992), 285–302.

D'Arcy, Martin C. *The Mind and Heart of Love*. New York, 1959: Meridian Books.

Deitz, Mary. *Between the Human and the Divine: The Political Thought of Simone Weil*. Totowa, 1988: Rowman and Littlefield.

Dewey, John. *Individualism: Old and New*. New York, 1962: Capricorn Books.

Devaux, André-A. "Liberté et necessité," in *Simone Weil: Philosophe, historienne et mystique*. Paris, 1978: Aubier Montaigne.

Eliot, T.S. *Selected Essays*. London, 1972: Routledge & Kegan Paul.

———. *Four Quartets*. San Diego, 1943,1971: Harcourt Brace Jovanovich.

Epictetus. *Arrian's Discourses of Epictetus*, 2 vols., trans. W.A. Oldfather, the Loeb Classical Library. Cambrdige, 1961: Harvard University Press.

Erasmus. *The Essential Erasmus*, ed. J. Dolan. New York, 1964: Meridian Books.

Fiori, Gabriella. *Simone Weil: An Intellectual Biography*. Athens, Ga., 1989; University of Georgia Press.

———. *Simone Weil: Une femme absolue*. Paris, 1987: éditions du Félin.

Fraisse, Simone. "Simone Weil, la personne et les droits de l'homme," *Cahiers Simone Weil*, Juin 1984 (VII.2), 120–132.

Franklin, R.W., and Shaw, J.M. *The Case for Christian Humanism*. Grand Rapids, 1991: Eerdmans.

Giniewski, Paul. *Simone Weil ou la haine de soi*. Paris, 1978: Berg International.

Goodman, Nelson. *Ways of Worldmaking*. Indianapolis, 1978: Hackett.

Hauerwas, Stanley. *A Community of Character*. Notre Dame, 1981: University of Notre Dame Press.

Hazo, R.G. *The Idea of Love*. New York, 1967: Frederick Praeger.

Herbert, George. *George Herbert*, ed. John N. Wall, Classics of Western Spirituality. New York, 1981: Paulist Press.

Hobbes, Thomas. *Leviathan, Parts I and II*, The Library of Liberal Arts. Indianapolis, 1958: Bobbs-Merrill.

Ignatieff, Michael. "The Limits of Sainthood." *The New Republic*, June 18, 1990.

James, William. *Pragmatism*. Cambridge, 1978: Harvard University Press.

Kierkegaard, Soren. *Works of Love* trans. H. and E. Hong. New York, 1962: Harper & Row.

Kolakowski, Leszek. *Modernity on Endless Trial*. Chicago, 1990: University of Chicago Press.

Kuehn, Rolf. "The World as Text—The Hermeneutical Perspective of Simone Weil," *Revue des Sciences Philosophiques et Théologiques* Oct. 1980, 509–530.

Larmore, Charles. *Patterns of Moral Complexity*. Cambridge, 1987: Cambridge University Press.

Lash, Nicholas. *A Matter of Hope*. Notre Dame, 1982: University of Notre Dame Press.

Little, J.P. *Simone Weil: Waiting on Truth*. Oxford, 1988: Berg.

Locke, John. *Second Treatise of Government*, edited and introduced by C.B. MacPherson. Indianapolis, 1980: Hackett.

Louth, Andrew. *Discerning the Mystery*. Cambridge, 1983: Cambridge University Press.

McClellan, David. *Simone Weil: Utopian Pessimist*. London, 1989: Macmillan.

MacIntyre, Alasdair. *After Virtue: A Study in Moral Theory*. Notre Dame, 1981: University of Notre Dame Press.

MacPherson, C.B. *The Political Theory of Possessive Individualism*. Oxford, 1962: Oxford University Press.

Maritain, Jacques. *Scholasticism and Politics*. New York, 1941: Macmillan.

———. *The Rights of Man and Natural Law*. London, 1944: Geoffrey Bles.

Markus, R.A. *Saeculum: History and Society in the Theology of St. Augustine*. Cambridge, 1970: Cambridge University Press.

———. "The Dialectic of Eros in Plato's *Symposium*," in *Plato*, vol. 1, ed. Gregory Vlastos. New York, 1971: Anchor Books.

Milbank, John. *Theology and Social Theory: Beyond Secular Reason*. Oxford, 1990: Blackwells.

Mitchell, Basil. *Morality: Religious and Secular.* Oxford, 1980: Oxford University Press.

Murdoch, Iris. *The Sovereignty of the Good.* New York, 1971: Schocken Books.

———. *Sartre: Romantic Rationalist.* New York, 1980: Barnes and Noble.

Nevin, Thomas. *Simone Weil: Portrait of a Self-Exiled Jew.* Chapel Hill, 1991: University of North Carolina Press.

Nussbaum, Martha. *The Fragility of Goodness.* Cambridge, 1986: Cambridge University Press.

Nygren, Anders. *Agape and Eros,* trans. P. Watson. New York, 1969: Harper Torchbooks.

Perrin, J.M. *Mon dialogue avec Simone Weil.* Paris, 1984: Nouvelle Cité.

———. "L'eau du baptême," in *Entretiens en marge du colloque de Sete (1979): sur les refus de Simone Weil.* Association pour l'étude de la pensée de Simone Weil.

Pétrement, Simone. *Simone Weil: A Life.* New York, 1976: Pantheon Books.

Plant, Raymond. *Modern Political Thought.* Oxford, 1991: Basil Blackwell.

Plato. *Plato: The Collected Dialogues* ed. Edith Hamilton and Huntington Cairns. Princeton, 1963: Princeton University Press.

Proctor, Robert. *Education's Great Amnesia: Reconsidering the Humanities from Petrarach to Freud.* Bloomington, 1988: Indiana University Press.

Putnam, Hilary. *Reason, Truth and History.* Cambridge, 1981: Cambridge University Press.

Rabi, Wladimir. "Simone Weil (1909–1943) ou l'itineraire d'une âme: Les derniers jours—Le baptême 'in extremis'", *Les Nouveaux Cahiers,* Autumn 1971.

Rawls, John. *A Theory of Justice.* Cambridge, 1971: Harvard University Press.

Rorty, Richard. *Philosophy and the Mirror of Nature.* Princeton, 1979: Princeton University Press.

———. *Contingency, Irony, and Solidarity.* Cambridge, 1989: Cambridge University Press.

Saint-Sernin, Bertrand. *L'Action politique selon Simone Weil.* Paris, 1988: Les éditions du Cerf.

Sandel, Michael, *Liberalism and the Limits of Justice* [Cambridge, 1982: Cambridge University Press]

Sartre, Jean Paul. "Existentialism Is a Humanism," in *Existentialism from Dostoyevsky to Sartre*, ed. W. Kaufman. Cleveland, 1956: Meridian Books.

Schlette, Heinz R. "Langage de la place publique—Langage de la chambre nuptiale: Quelques remarques sur le sens théologique d'une distinction philosophique chez Simone Weil," in *Recherches sur la philosophie et le langage*, no. 13 (Université des Sciences Sociales de Grenoble, 1991).

Singer, Irving. *The Nature of Love: Plato to Luther*. New York, 1966: Harper.

Springsted, Eric O. *Christus Mediator: Platonic Mediation in the Thought of Simone Weil*. Chico, CA, 1983: Scholars Press.

———. *Simone Weil and the Suffering of Love*. Cambidge, 1986: Cowley Publications.

———. "Contradiction, Mystery and the Use of Words in Simone Weil," *Religion and Literature*, vol. 17.2 (Summer 1985).

———. "The Religious Basis of Culture: T.S. Eliot and Simone Weil," *Religious Studies*, 25.1 (March 1989) 105–116.

Steiner, George. *Real Presences*. Chicago, 1989: University of Chicago Press.

———. "Bad Friday," *The New Yorker*, March 2, 1992.

Swinburne, Richard. *The Coherence of Theism*. Oxford, 1977: Oxford University Press.

Taylor, Charles *Sources of the Self: The Making of the Modern Identity*. Cambridge, 1989: Harvard University Press.

———. "Social Theory as Practice," and "Understanding and Ethnocentricity" in *Philosophy and the Human Sciences: Philosophical Papers 2*. Cambridge, 1985: Cambridge University Press.

Tinder, Glenn. *The Political Meaning of Christianity: The Prophetic Stance*. San Francisco, 1991: Harper.

Walzer, Michael. *Spheres of Justice: A Defense of Pluralism and Equality*. New York, 1983: Basic Books.

Ware, Kallistos. "Ways of Prayer and Contemplation," in *Christian Spirituality*, eds. Bernard McGinn and John Meyendorff. New York, 1985: Crossroad.

Williams, Bernard. *Ethics and the Limits of Philosophy*. Cambridge, 1985: Harvard University Press.

Winch, Peter. *Simone Weil: The Just Balance*. Cambridge, 1988: Cambridge University Press.

Wittgenstein, Ludwig. *Philosophical Investigations*, Third Edition. New York, 1968: Macmillan.

————. *Culture and Value*, trans. Peter Winch. Chicago, 1980: University of Chicago Press.

Vetö, Miklos. *La metaphysique religieuse de Simone Weil*. Paris, 1970: J. Vrin; English translation by Joan Dargan, Albany, 1994: SUNY Press.

INDEX